Education, Privatisation and Social Justice:
case studies from Africa, South Asia and South East Asia

Education, Privatisation and Social Justice:
case studies from Africa, South Asia and South East Asia

Edited by
Ian Macpherson,
Susan Robertson & Geoffrey Walford

SYMPOSIUM
BOOKS

Symposium Books Ltd
PO Box 204, Didcot, Oxford OX11 9ZQ, United Kingdom
www.symposium-books.co.uk

Published in the United Kingdom, 2014

ISBN 978-1-873927-37-3

Printed and bound in the United Kingdom by Hobbs the Printers, Southampton
www.hobbs.uk.com

Contents

Privatisation in Education
RESEARCH INITIATIVE

The Privatisation in Education Research Initiative (PERI) is a global research and networking initiative seeking to animate an accessible and informed public debate on alternative education provision. In particular, it examines the social justice implications of changes in the coordination, financing and governance of education services.

Since 2011 PERI has convened numerous regional conferences, roundtables and civil society workshops on privatisation in education; it has further held two summer schools at the Central European University in Budapest, Hungary. The initiative has supported 32 pieces of research in Africa, South Asia, South-East Asia, Latin America and the Middle East and North Africa region. Many are available on the initiative website – www.periglobal.org – as are seven short documentaries on privatisation in education and relevant resources from a range of sources. The initiative engages challenging questions regarding privatised education services and governance and promotes a fundamental commitment to evidence-based policy making with a range of stakeholders.

CHAPTER 1

An Introduction to Privatisation, Education and Social Justice

IAN MACPHERSON, SUSAN ROBERTSON & GEOFFREY WALFORD

Why the Fuss?

Over this past decade, researchers have been documenting the growing and diverse range of privatisation initiatives and private interests in the education sector, arguing something new is afoot which demands closer attention (Ball, 2007; Robertson et al, 2012; Lubienski, 2013; Robertson & Dale, 2013). The involvement of private actors in education is, of course, not new. Most accounts of the privatisation of education rightly point out there is a long history of private education around the world, whether as key sites for the reproduction of social elites, or as places where the student's learning is underpinned by religious values.

Why the fuss, and why now? In this volume, we will be exploring the emerging forms of the private in education and making three related observations. First, that what is new about these manifestations is their *scale*, *scope* and *penetration* into almost all aspects of the education endeavour – from the administrative apparatus to policymaking, and from formal provision in education settings, to out-of-school activities, such as private tutoring. Second, that what is particularly controversial about these current developments is how education itself is being recast; as a sector it is increasingly being opened up to profit-making and trade, and to agenda-setting by private, commercial interests. Third, that the learner is increasingly conceptualised as a consumer, and education a consumer good. These developments raise the very important question around what these developments mean for our conceptualisations of education, learning and teaching, on the one hand, and for education as a site and means for emancipation, on the other.

In her highly influential book – *Not for Profit* – reflecting on these issues Martha Nussbaum (2010) asks: how has this 'silent crisis' been allowed to happen? Understanding this is important for it involves us as players in this unfolding drama. For as David Harvey (2005, p. 5) notes, 'for any system of thought to become dominant' – such as the systematic privileging of private interests, logics and forms of provision over and above that of a more societally oriented set of values, it must appeal to our intuitions, instincts, values and desires in some way. What is the appeal of the idea of the private and individual over more social, collective and relational understandings of individuals and their societies? How might the insights we generate around such questions inform our concerns in terms of strategies for building more equitable opportunities for both teaching and learning? Taken together, these developments raise important questions about the nature of education as a service, and the consequences for society through time (Connell, 2012). These are profound social-justice concerns, and ones that make this volume distinctive. This book sets out to address these hard, but urgent questions.

Complex Logics: education, privatisation, globalisation

Any exploration of education, privatisation and social justice, and the relationship between these three, immediately takes us to a maze of complex meanings, claims and practices. This is because each of these concepts is highly contested – in turn generating heated debates around ideological positions, what might count as evidence and what the alternatives might be. It was precisely because of this state of affairs that we were determined to stand back, to be reflexive about our own ideological positions, and to let the research evidence speak for itself. And though we ourselves have strong views about social justice and the right to quality education, we did not want to start from the premise that *a priori*, the idea of the private – as in private providers, private provision, private-sector logics and so on, in the education sector – were always and forever bad. This is not the case. This might sound a controversial statement to make, but our view has been, and continues to be, that any research with claims to it being 'critical inquiry' does not begin with its conclusion already in place. Instead we need to be open to what the evidence might tell us, and that this evidence must be contextualised. But we were also clear that any assessment of the outcomes of different manifestations of the private would need to be judged against a robust theory of social justice. This would then enable us to see more clearly what was at stake, for whom, with what outcomes, and the consequences for individuals and societies. After all, if justice is a social and thus societal concern, then socially just educational outcomes must also be those that benefit societies in the round, rather than some individuals at the expense of others.

To appreciate the scale of the complexities confronting researchers, policymakers and advocacy groups when working on the privatising of education globally, it is useful to remind ourselves that 'education' itself is viewed in rather different ways by different disciplinary groups. Sociologists, for instance, will tend to view education as a societal good that has both transformational and also regulatory elements. In terms of transformation, access to quality formally organised learning experiences generates reflexivity and understanding about our worlds. However, education systems promote official knowledges, and education credentials – particularly those acquired in more exclusive institutions – are what Fred Hirsch (1977) calls a 'positional good' which enables some individuals to gain a greater return economically, as well as in terms of social status. They are therefore likely to ask questions about how education opportunities are organised and distributed, and to argue for forms of governance that might ameliorate the injustices that such governance frameworks generate.

Economists of education, including those in key policymaking positions in the World Bank promoting the privatisation of education, tend to view education as forming human capital, where investments in the education sector can be conceptualised as investments in the stock of human capital available to the economy. This is a rather narrow understanding of education in that it does not address questions to do with the social or indeed the political and ethical dimensions of education. Philosophers, such as Martha Nussbaum (2010), make the point that education must be about creating the conditions for both the flourishing of the individual and the good of society. She is thus very critical of the dominance of economists of education in shaping education policies and practices, and their view that the goal for any nation ought to be economic growth, with follow-on benefits for sectors like education and health. As she points out, achievements in education and health are very poorly correlated with economic growth. Furthermore, those paradigms that emphasise the relationship between education and economic growth above all else are not necessarily contributing to the conditions for democracy in a society, understood broadly as producing a healthy, engaged, educated population in which opportunities for the good life are available to all social classes.

And it is this latter sentiment – of education being one of the conditions for individual and societal flourishing – that *Article 26: Universal Declaration of Human Rights* (United Nations, 1948) sought to capture in the aftermath of a devastating war and holocaust, and which has continued to inform rights-based arguments for access to quality education for all children as a basis for both individual and societal development. It states: 'Everyone has the right to education. Education should be free, at least in the elementary and fundamental stages. Elementary education should be compulsory ... . Education should be directed to the full development of the human personality and to the strengthening of respect for human rights and fundamental freedoms. It shall promote understanding, tolerance and friendship among all nations' (UN website).

Much of the post-World War II (WWII) period until the 1980s was given over to strengthening education systems around the world, broadly committed to the view that education was central to creating citizens, and nation-building. Yet many of these countries were also new nations, now with formal responsibility for their own education policy. This was seen by the former colonial powers, but also by the United States and Russia, as an opportunity to maintain and increase their spheres of interest internationally. They did this through conceptualising the problem for the newly emergent states as one of 'modernisation' to be addressed by 'new' countries pursuing those same stages of development that had been followed by their former European masters. Of crucial and lasting significance here was the identification of what came to be known as Human Capital Theory (see Schultz, 1971). This theory suggested that the key variable that distinguished more successful economies – such as (the then West) Germany and Japan – from those that weren't, was their investment in education.

Education as development thus essentially followed the same dual objectives –making citizens and making economies – as had informed the growth of Europe in the nineteenth and twentieth centuries. These two very different understandings of 'education' in education policy, the one broadly humanitarian, the other deeply economic, were to become the basis of a division that has persisted across the decades since, but where since the 1990s, a strong reframing of education by economists has become hegemonic, in part a result of processes broadly conceived of as 'globalisation' (Dale & Robertson, 2014).

Globalisation has indeed set in train a number of developments that have been crucial for understanding the kinds of transformations many of the chapters are concerned with. We take the view that globalisation is not a process without a subject. Rather, it involves a range of actors – multilateral agencies, firms, international organisations, national governments and so on – whose projects extend out over national territorial boundaries. The globalisation of neoliberalism as a political project has been advanced by some of these actors with the explicit intention of erasing those boundaries that created frictions for the easier movement of finance, goods, services, people and ideas. Education has been deeply implicated in this, not only because it has become the sector through which the new entrepreneurial self is created and has learnt the techniques of self-regulation, but because the sector itself has come to be viewed as one that can be opened to profit-making activity and trade as well as being mobilised in efforts to build globally competitive economies. These developments have not simply occurred by themselves. Rather, they have been the outcome of projects, processes and practices – such as New Public Management (Hood, 1991) – that has weakened states' ability to direct and develop policy at national level. The special status of state activities as 'public services' was increasingly questioned, so that in countries where public sectors and services had been built, they have been radically rethought. And whilst the outcomes of neo-liberalism as a political project have differed from country to country, their broad form and the basis of how these interventions were legitimated did not. Markets and competition, and the role of the private sector in new and old areas of service delivery (Ball, 2007), were all promoted by key international governmental organisations, such as the World Bank Group, the Organization for Economic Cooperation and Development and the World Trade Organization.

Related to, but a distinct dynamic within, these policies is the idea that education can best be delivered by the private sector, that education systems should operate like private-sector organisations, that private-sector organisations are best placed to shape policy and practices for the sector, and that education is itself a consumer good – much like any other item we might shop for in the supermarket. These assumptions, of course, not only alter the composition of which actors might operate in the sector to deliver education, or indeed which logics and associated metrics might be deployed, but what education actually means. Taken together, this new way of thinking about education and its relation to the economy and society, and most particularly how education is to be governed, has not only radically reworked the shape of education systems in those parts of the world where such policies have been dominant, but the nature of the social relations that education systems produce. Sahlberg (2011) describes this as a global education reform movement, provocatively labelled GERM. The key tenets of this reform movement have broadly been shaped by neo-liberal theory, which argues that education systems will be more efficient and effective if they are reorganised using the principles of the free market: those of choice and competition, and publicly available performance information on quality and standards.

These changes have been further shaped by a commitment by the global community that education is a human right, but that by 2015 the Millennium Development Goal would have been realised where all children around the world would have access to school. As a result, governments, international agencies and non-governmental organisations have sought to support initiatives that expand opportunities for access, including involving a range of new actors – from small local education entrepreneurs to large transnational providers, in turn diversifying the range of establishments offering education (Ball, 2012).

To leave our account here, however, would be to offer too simple a reading of the past two decades. Instead, it is important to point to the intense pressures placed on the education system globally because of its 'positional good' status we highlighted earlier. With a stalling labour market in some countries (see Brown et al, 2011), and with more and more credentialed students seeking well-enough paid jobs, being in the right school, with the right connections, and in some cases the promise of English as the medium of instruction, has led to parents jockeying for places with the result that new patterns of exclusion are created. Private schools, for instance, to the extent they offer the promise of a competitive edge, have become favoured by those families who can afford them, including relatively poor families who sacrifice a great deal for the hope that this is an investment with a return in the future. So great has the pressure been for learners to perform well on examinations in some countries – particularly many in South and East Asia, but now also in Europe – that this has been paralleled by a rapidly growing industry of out-of-school provision that Mark Bray (2009) has called 'shadow schooling': that is, a form of provision that mimics the curricular and learning activities of the main system in the hope that it can boost student performance.

Diverse Manifestations of Privatisation *in* and *of* Education

It is immediately obvious from contributions in this volume that there are diverse manifestations of the private in education in different parts of the world – from the individualising of the aspirations of families for a good-quality education, to accessing personal tutoring services out of school time, the idea that a 'private' education is always better than one that is public-provided, or that public services should be run like private entities by mimicking markets and competition to realise efficiency gains and greater educational effectiveness. This is by no means an exhaustive list. But it does help to make the point that this level of diversity makes the business of understanding the privatising of education a particularly complicated one.

One distinction developed by Stephen Ball (2007, 2012) is the difference between privatisation *in*, and the privatisation *of*, education. By 'in', Ball means the many and complex ways in which the mentality of the business world has been injected into education, such that it operates like a competitive market, with choice, marketing managers, branding, data on student performance as proxies of quality and so on. It also refers to the ways in which education departments and ministries have similarly operated in more corporate-like ways, with competitive units, performance targets, outputs and forms of performance management. One way of viewing this is that it represents the colonisation of the idea of education as a public service by more an economic logic that is aligned with the idea of a free market.

By privatisation 'of', Ball is talking about a range of ways in which what was once public-sector activity – whether funding, forms of provision, the ownership of buildings, the making of policy, forms of regulation and so on, have now been outsourced to the private sector through tendering, consultancies, joint ventures or new forms of financing. Included in the privatisation of education services are a popular and more recent phenomenon – Public Private Partnerships – which are contractual relationships between the public and the private sector to deliver a range of different kinds of education services (Robertson et al, 2012). These services might be the development of infrastructures that are then rented back to the state, or state-funded vouchers for students to attend privately provided education. It is this latter arrangement that is preferred by the education-policy entrepreneurs within the World Bank, as well as by national governments – such as in the United Kingdom, Chile, the United States, New Zealand and Sweden.

The increased numbers of Charter Schools in the United States over this past decade (with nearly 5700 schools in 41 states – Lubienski, 2013, p. 2), for instance, exemplifies the myriad and complex ways in which the private sector has become involved in education provision – with in some cases chains of for-profit firms delivering teaching and learning. These initiatives have been flanked by both philanthropists and policymakers in the United States who seem to have 'elevated individual preferences through privately and publicly funded vouchers in a growing number of cities and states, expanded the use of tax credits to subsidise family choice of private schools, and loosened restrictions on home schooling' (Lubienski, 2013, p. 2). Again, arguments as to why these developments should be levered into place are bolstered by the claim that Charter Schools are more effective and equitable, though as Lubienski points out, in many cases their practice can be distinctly inequitable in that Charter School operators tend to avoid areas of highest need, or relocate geographically as soon as possible to service the 'better' students.

In countries like India, Pakistan, Malawi, Kenya, Ghana, Nigeria and South Africa, a different kind of market-oriented approach has emerged called Low Fee Private Schools – which are given momentum by the view that the poor should be allowed to be consumers, like the middle and ruling classes. Low Fee Private Schools (LFPS) are particularly controversial on a number of fronts: first, because to some observers, they exploit the aspirations of the poor to do well for their child; second, because they are relatively expensive for the poor, the result is that households on meagre incomes will be faced with choosing which child the family invests in, making it particularly divisive; and third, these schools may not be any better than the government school – but the promise of a (not particularly good) private education and in some cases an English-medium private education, is regarded as highly desirable by families.

There is little doubt that one of its leading spokespeople, United Kingdom-based Professor James Tooley, has added to the controversy in this area. His work strongly advocates pro-market for-profit provision of education, particularly in low-income countries, and, as Ball (2012) describes, Tooley has set up his own charity, businesses and schools; he is also part of a complex transnational network of think tanks, entrepreneurs, foundations and funds, including the global education giant Pearson Education Foundation, the Bill and Melinda Gates Foundation, McKinsey & Company and others. The point to be made here is that there has been a shift in the centre of gravity around where decisions are made and agendas set – which is away from the state and civil society, toward the corporate sector and its related foundations. All these, of course, raise important social-justice questions.

The discussion of issues raised in this volume is very timely given the fever of activities setting the post-2015 development goals. Following on from the EFA (Education for All) targets and Millennium Development Goals, the post-2015 goals will frame the global education agenda for the next 20 years. Narrow targets focused on learning outcomes risk not only limiting the role of education for societal development, but also risk opening up national spaces to testing and, consequently, testing services and forms of provision that support corporate interests. Neither is a foregone conclusion and civil-society organisations such as Education International and the Global Campaign for Education are collaborating with national governments to mobilise a broader agenda for education and guard against an impoverished vision of education being ossified in the global goals that risks paving a way for the deeper penetration of private-sector logics, models and actors in national education systems.

Unpacking the 'Private-School Promise'

A key question we ask in the volume is what 'the private-school promise' is, and how might the studies reported here help us determine the veracity or not of that promise? Further, how might the chapters here speak to the wider research evidence, and what does this mean for social justice? In a final synthetic chapter to this volume, Ian Macpherson draws these insights together around three promises that dominate current debates: (1) private schools provide real choice; (2) private education provision is more effective and more efficient that state education; and (3) competition by private providers increases quality in both the private and the public sectors. These are powerful claims, but what of the evidence?

Answering this question is all the more important as these promises are typically mobilised by global agencies, such as the World Bank, to support its preference for privatisation as a policy setting for education systems around the world. For example, in their various publications on rethinking the governance of education systems, they argue that '[i]ncreasing the private sector's role in education may have several potential advantages over traditional public delivery of education. Whether these benefits are realised depends greatly on the design of the partnership between the public and the private sector in the regulatory framework of the country, and the capacity of the government to oversee and enforce its contracts and partnerships with the private sector' (Barrera-Osorio et al, 2012, p. 201).

The Bank is right to qualify its claims here: that the benefits that might emerge would be dependent upon the nature of the regulatory environment in place. Indeed, the Organisation for Economic Cooperation and Development (OECD) has argued that not only is education a complex activity and therefore difficult to specify in contracts, but it requires robust governance structures for proper regulation. Yet it is precisely this aspect of governance that is missing in many of the environments in which private provision for the poor in low-income settings has flourished, causing the 2009 EFA Global Monitoring Report (GMR) to point out that in many countries, private providers such as those involved in low-fee schooling operate in a 'governance free zone' (GMR, 2009, p. 168). This leaves already marginalised communities prey to commercial opportunities and potential exploitation, even if willingly signing up to these schools. This raises the question of how one might collect evidence if their existence is even somewhat ephemeral. Or, how might we detect shadow schooling practices when many of these operate quite literally 'in the shadows'? We pick up some of these concerns in our discussion on social justice and privatisation in the following section, and address the question of evidence and conclusions in the final chapter of this book. But the private-school promise does raise the thorny question of which societal norms we might foster through our education systems and their modes of governance which bring us closer to the humanitarian values that underpinned the role and outcomes for education in the Universal Declaration of Human Rights.

A (Not So) Silent Crisis:
education, privatisation and social justice

We now want to address the social-justice issues that are both implicit and emerging outcomes of the privatising education. To do this, we need to make explicit our normative framework so as to make visible our assumptions, including the role of education in shaping the conditions for both individual as well as societal flourishing. This means a view of social justice that sees the relations between individuals as important and that benefits or gains for one are not at the expense of another. Clearly this is a major challenge for education systems as they are also an institution that tends to reproduce social inequalities over time. However, to simply abandon *any notion* that things could be made better – or more socially just – through how we govern our education systems, would be to walk away from a major responsibility to those whose lives are shaped through injustices in education as a consequence.

As Dewey (1950, p. 147) proposed, the purpose of education should be the development of critical democratic citizens and all institutions (including the state and the market) should facilitate personal growth and be judged on the 'contribution they make to the all-round growth of every member of society' as well as on their contribution to human development. In this sense, Dewey believed that education was essential for the development of deliberative democracy, wherein members of society engage in the task of improving themselves and society through engaging with each other and practising the habits of open-mindedness, tolerance of diversity, rational understanding, respect for truth and critical judgment (Hursh, 2009). These are also aligned with the underpinning values of the Universal Declaration of Human Rights referred to earlier.

This means bringing social-justice theories more centrally into our assessment of education-governance frameworks more generally, and those that privilege privatisation, in particular. Social-justice theorists, such as Fraser (1995, 2008), Gerwirtz (1998, 2006) and Young (2000, 2006a, 2006b), are all concerned with the dynamics of how different institutions (including the state and the market), as well as socio-cultural and politico-economic processes, structure the (re)distribution of resources, rights and values across, between and within societies with reference to democratic societal development. Fraser defines justice as 'parity of participation' and contends that according to the radical-democratic principle of equal moral worth, 'justice requires social arrangements that permit all to participate as peers in social life' (2008, p. 16) . We believe this is not only important for society – but also important for education. This is because education and social justice are intrinsically connected in the development of open, democratic societies: the extent and manner in which the institution of education (as a system and as discrete forms of provision) affect justice (as parity of participation) has consequences for deliberative democracy; equally the extent and manner in which social injustice (economic mal-distribution and cultural misrecognition) affect education access and quality has implications for deliberative democracy.

In her seminal 1995 work, Fraser posits a spectrum of pervasive disadvantage in contemporary societies that is rooted in processes that systematically disadvantage some groups *vis à vis* others. At one end lie socioeconomic injustices rooted in the political-economic structure of society and committed through processes of mal-distribution. At the other end lie cultural injustices rooted in patterns of representation, interpretation and communication that lead to practices of misrecognition. Yet she argues that the two poles are heuristic and in practice both are intertwined:

> Even the most material economic institutions have a
> constitutive, irreducible cultural dimension that is shot
> through with significations and norms. Conversely, even the
> most discursive cultural practices have a constitutive,
> irreducible political-economic dimension; they are
> underpinned by material supports ... Cultural norms that are
> unfairly biased against some are institutionalized in the state
> and the economy, meanwhile, economic disadvantage
> impedes equal participation in the making of culture, in the
> public spheres and in everyday life. The result is often a
> vicious cycle of cultural and economic subordination.
> (pp. 71-72)

Hence, in reality, injustice tends to affect groups of people who exist between these two poles, in what Fraser calls 'bivalent collectivities' that are differentiated as collectivities 'by virtue of *both* the political-economic structure *and* the cultural-valuational structure of society' (1995, p. 78, emphasis original) and they suffer hybrid disadvantage through both political-economy and culture simultaneously. These ideas are particularly important for this volume, for we will see that not only does the nature of the political economy of a household matter in terms of economic resources, but who gets to go to a private school is often mediated culturally by gender dynamics as well.

From a different direction the accelerating dynamics of globalisation outlined earlier are now deepening the influence of a particular set of educational ideas and ideology. While they stop short of dictating or prescribing policy, they have been 'enormously successful in creating a discursive framework within which a particular conception of globalization is now promoted, and within which its implications of education are now debated' (Rizvi & Engel, 2009, p. 531), to the extent that 'education is now increasingly focused on the production of self-capitalizing, flexible neo-liberal subjects' (p. 534).

This hegemony is significant from a social-justice perspective and Fraser (2008) argues that the influence of regional and global agendas on national policy spaces is an injustice of framing that limits participatory justice, one of two forms of misrepresentation whereby a community's boundaries are drawn in such a way so as to exclude some people from the chance to participate in authorised contests over justice. In this instance, the hegemony of neo-liberal globalisation and its attendant education discourse (instrumentalist human-capital formation for servicing the economy) dominate possible alternative visions of education. Fraser's other participatory injustice is what she calls 'ordinary political representation' (2008, p. 19), meaning the rules and processes of political participation that deny some people the chance to participate fully in decision-making. This can be understood as the dynamics of debates on 'good governance' in education and embraces issues of participation, accountability, voice and decision-making at different levels of the education system (Tikly & Barrett, 2009).

Concretely, in many places the very poor, girls and the marginalised are doubly disadvantaged through not only the imposition of global, top-down agendas and ideologies shaping education in the national space, but also through their limited ability to influence the form and content of education for their children and their inability to hold schools and governments accountable for performance. Hence addressing social justice in education requires action at a range of levels from the international to the local, undertaken by an array of actors including those that represent those unable to make justice claims in certain spaces, as well as those who are directly affected by social injustices. Yet what informs this work?

Overcoming injustice for Fraser means 'dismantling institutionalized obstacles that prevent some people from participating on a par with others as full partners in social interaction' (2008, p. 16). 'Institutionalised obstacles' are the economic structures that deny people access to resources that are needed to interact with others as peers; the cultural hierarchical values that may deny people requisite standing for peer interaction and exclusion from the community that is entitled to make justice claims on one another; and the structures that shape public processes of contestation (Tikly & Barrett, 2009). Remedial political action through economic redistribution and cultural recognition can address misdistribution and misrecognition yet *improperly* addressed can serve to entrench a redistribution-recognition dilemma whereby economic redistribution can deepen cultural misrecognition and, reciprocally, cultural recognition may deepen economic mal-distribution. As Fraser states:

> Recognition claims often take the form of calling attention to, if not performatively creating, the putative specificity of some group, and then of affirming the value of that specificity. Thus they tend to promote group differentiation. Redistribution claims, in contrast, often call for abolishing economic arrangements that underpin group specificity. (An example would be feminist demands to abolish the gender division of labour.) Thus they tend to promote group de-differentiation. The upshot is that the politics of recognition and the politics

of redistribution appear to have mutually contradictory aims. Whereas the first tends to promote group differentiation, the second tends to undermine it. The two kinds of claim thus stand in tension with each other; they can interfere with, or even work against, one another. (1995, p. 74)

Vouchers that provide economically disadvantaged parents the means to select a private school of their choice are a prime example of this dynamic in the education sphere, as while vouchers promote group de-differentiation in economic terms they equally promote cultural differentiation by affirming the specificity of those parents that are economically disadvantaged, thus undermining de-differentiation. Similarly, section 12(1) of the Right to Education Act (2009) in India that compels private schools (whether low-fee or otherwise) to allocate 25% of their places in Class 1 for free to 'children belonging to weaker section(s) and disadvantaged groups' [1] (Government of India, 2009) both promotes economic de-differentiation while at the same time affirming the cultural specificity of EWS pupils, thus undermining de-differentiation.

Affirmative action of this nature cannot therefore address the redistribution-recognition dilemma, which is only viable through transformative remedies that redress unjust distribution by changing the underlying political-economic structure and changing the social division of labour, hence the conditions of existence for all citizens.

This again raises the question about how research might also be mobilised to address the poverty of imagination that neo-liberal projects bring with them around our societal obligations to each other, and how education experiences can be so much richer when they take the full view of what it means to be human into account.

A feature of Young's (2006b) work is to engage with the question of social justice in a more globally connected world. For Young, processes of globalisation challenge fundamental justice questions around notions of obligation and responsibility. Obligations have historically presupposed a single political community – that of the Westphalian national state. Yet as education becomes more globalised – whether as a result of transformations in the field of symbolic control over education policies (such as global rankings), of the growth of global education firms, or of the increased power of international and multilateral agencies, this results in education activity extending over national territorial boundaries, posing new questions around how and where obligations and responsibilities are to be negotiated.

As a way forward, Young proposes a 'social connection model' of responsibility, arguing: 'All agents who contribute by their actions to the structural processes that produce injustice have responsibilities to work to remedy these injustices' (2006b, p. 103). She goes on to suggest that there is a need for political institutions that are 'wide enough in scope

21

and sufficiently strong to regulate these relations to insure their fairness *follows from* the global scope of obligations of justice, rather than *grounding* those obligations' (p. 106, emphasis in original). Moreover, those who are institutionally and materially situated in ways that enable them to have a greater effect on the poor and vulnerable have greater obligations and responsibilities. Global education firms that provide education services and multi-lateral and bi-lateral donors that provide global education aid and work closely with national governments therefore have greater obligations and responsibilities to ensure fairness, accountability and democracy precisely because of their global power, corporate interests and influence in world forums.

This Volume

The three editors of this volume have been engaged with the Privatisation in Education Research Initiative (PERI) since its inception in 2010. PERI is funded by the Education Support Programme of Open Society Foundations and is a multi-annual global initiative that seeks to contribute to a better understanding of the nature and effects of privatisation in and of education. One of the key PERI objectives was to fund research in developing countries that would describe aspects of the nature of privatisation and assess the effects of such changes in terms of social justice and how they influence the development and maintenance of open, democratic societies. An open call for proposals relating to Africa, South Asia and South East Asia was made in 2010 and subsequently funded, with most projects concluding in 2012 and some in 2013. Full academic reports on these projects are available on the PERI website (www.periglobal.org) yet it was felt useful to bring together key findings in a concise book form such that that the evidence and arguments presented in this volume may be more readily taken into account by academics, researchers, civil-society, organisations and policymakers.

Notes

[1] Those children are understood as coming from Economically Weaker Sections (EWS) of society.

References

Ball, S. (2007) *Education plc*. London: Routledge.

Ball, S. (2012) *Global Education Inc*. London: Routledge.

Barrera-Osorio, F., Guaneueta, J. & Patrinos, A. (2012) The Role and Impact of Public Private Partnerships in Education, in S. Robertson, K. Mundy,

A. Verger & F. Menashy (Eds) *Public Private Partnerships in Education: new actors and new modes of governance*. Cheltenham: Edward Elgar.

Bray, M. (2009) *Confronting the Shadow Education System: what government policies for what private tutoring?* Paris: UNESCO-IIEP.

Brown. P., Lauder, H. & Ashton, D. (2011) *The Global Auction: the broken promises of education, jobs and incomes*. New York: Oxford University Press.

Connell, R. (2012) Just Education, *Journal of Education Policy*, 27(5), 681-683.

Dale, R. & Robertson, S. (2014) Global Education Policy, in N. Yeates (Ed.) *Global Social Policy*. Bristol: Policy Press.

Dewey, J. (1950) *Reconstruction in Philosophy*. New York: The New American Library/Mentor Books.

Fraser, N. (1995) From Redistribution to Recognition? Dilemmas of Justice in a 'Post-Socialist' Age, *New Left Review,* 212 (July–August), 68–93.

Fraser, N. (2008) *Scales of Justice: reimagining political space in a globalizing world*. Cambridge: Polity Press.

Gewirtz, S. (1998) Conceptualising Social Justice in Education: mapping the territory, *Journal of Education Policy*, 13(4), 469-484.

Gewirtz, S. (2006) Toward a Contextualised Analysis of Social Justice in Education, *Educational Philosophy and Theory*, 38(1), 69-81.

Global Monitoring Report (2009) *Overcoming Inequality: why governance matters*. Paris: UNESCO.

Government of India (2009) *The Right of Children to Free and Compulsory Education Act, 2009*. No. 35 of 2009, 26th August 2009. New Delhi.

Harvey, D. (2005) *A Brief History of Neoliberalism*. Oxford: Oxford University Press.

Hirsch, F. (1977) *The Social Limits to Growth*. London: Routledge & Kegan Paul.

Hursh, D. (2009) Beyond the Justice of the Market: combating neoliberal educational discourse and promoting deliberative democracy and economic equality, in W. Ayers, T. Quinn & D. Stovall (Eds) *Handbook of Social Justice in Education*. London: Routledge.

Hood, C. (1991) A Public Management for All Seasons? *Public Administration*, 69 (Spring), 3-19.

Lubienski, C. (2013) Privatising Form or Function? Equity, Outcomes and Influence on American Charter Schools, *Oxford Review of Education*, 39(4), 498-513.

Nussbaum, M. (2010) *Not For Profit: why democracy needs the humanities*. Princeton and Oxford: Princeton University Press.

Rizvi F. & Engel L. (2009) Neoliberal Globalisation, Educational Policy and the Struggle for Social Justice, in W. Ayers, T. Quinn & D. Stovall (Eds) *Handbook of Social Justice in Education*. London: Routledge.

Robertson, S. & Dale, R. (2013) The Social Justice Implications of Privatisation in Educational Governance Frameworks: a relational account, *Oxford Review of Education,* 39(4), 426-445.

Robertson, S., Mundy, K., Verger, A. & Menashy, F. (Eds) (2012) *Public Private Partnerships in Education: new actors and new modes of governance.* Cheltenham: Edward Elgar.

Sahlberg, P. (2011) *Finnish Lessons: what the world can learn from educational change in Finland.* New York: Teachers' College Press.

Schultz, T.W. (1971) *Investment in Human Capital: the role of education and of research.* New York: Free Press.

Tikly, L. & Barrett, A. (2009) *Social Justice, Capabilities and the Quality of Education in Low Income Countries.* EdQual Working Paper No. 18. Bristol: University of Bristol.

Young, I.M. (2000) *Inclusion and Democracy.* Oxford: Oxford University Press.

Young, I.M. (2006a) Taking the Basic Structure Seriously, *Perspectives in Politics*, 4(1), 91-97.

Young, I.M. (2006b) Responsibility and Global Justice: a social connection model, *Social Philosophy and Policy Foundation*, 23(1), 102-130.

United Nations (1948) *Article 26: Universal Declaration of Human Rights.* http://www.un.org/en/documents/udhr/ (accessed November 3, 2013)

CHAPTER 2

De facto Privatisation of Basic Education in Africa: a market response to government failure? A Comparative Study of the Cases of Ghana and Nigeria

CAINE ROLLESTON & MODUPE ADEFESO-OLATEJU

Introduction

In spite of improvements in access to public-school provision, families in Ghana and Nigeria are opting increasingly for private education when they have a choice. In Nigeria, conservative estimates suggest that private schools currently account for more than 15% of all enrolments, while in Ghana the figure is higher than 20%. Ghana and Nigeria have both undergone significant economic and regulatory liberalisation since the 1980s and are environments in which private schooling has flourished in the presence of modest economic growth, despite the implementation of fee-free policies in public education since the 1990s. These trends reflect a broader pattern of *de facto* privatisation of basic education found in many developing countries, including among the poor.

Important recent studies have attested to the role of quality education and of cognitive development rather than school attendance *per se* as key to economic wellbeing of both individual and nation (see Hanushek & Woessmann, 2007). However, basic education in many parts of the sub-Saharan Africa region is of poor quality in comparative terms, while its costs to the national budget remains relatively high. Limited and controversial evidence suggests that in some contexts, low-cost private schools are of higher quality, in terms of their production of learning outcomes, than their public counterparts (Tooley & Dixon, 2006; Aslam, 2009; French & Kingdon, 2010). Such schools often operate at a fraction of the unit costs of public schools, drawing attention to issues of efficiency and cost-effectiveness in the public-school sector.

Nonetheless, since access to even low-cost private schooling is linked to ability to pay fees, *de facto* privatisation, a 'bottom-up' process of parents 'voting with their feet', raises questions of equity and social justice. Moreover, part of the conventional economic justification for state provision of basic schooling consists of the extensive social benefits that arise from public education and the consequent failure of markets to make socially optimal provision, while it is clear that the shift towards private basic schooling in both Ghana and Nigeria is in part a response to perceptions of poor quality in public provision. Accordingly, 'government failure' in public-education delivery further complicates the issues of equity and efficiency, since universal access to free provision is not a marker of equity in education where that provision is of inadequate quality. Accordingly, the implications of expanding private provision for social justice are unclear. Where access to private schooling brings wider access to higher levels of learning at affordable cost, it may be argued that the trend is indeed pro-equity overall by comparison with a low-quality exclusively public system.

This paper explores the reasons behind the increase in private-school enrolments in Ghana and Nigeria through analysis of purposively collected qualitative data from two communities in which de facto privatisation is found. Secondary data analysis is employed to shed light on the more general trends in private-school enrolment. Focus is on 'non-elite' or 'low-fee' private schooling (LFPS) since, despite considerable heterogeneity in the private-schooling sector, it is the relatively low-fee sector, often led by individual entrepreneurs which has seen most significant expansion (see Härmä, 2011).

Data and Methodology

The paper adopts a mixed-methods approach, combining analysis of purposively collected qualitative data and of secondary data from both household and school surveys. The qualitative study explores issues surrounding households' decisions to send their children to LFPSs in two communities in which LFPSs have recently grown in number, but where public-school alternatives exist. The communities were selected purposively as low-income peri-urban sites with relatively low education levels among the adult population. In the Ghanaian site, all basic schools (public and LFPS) were included in the study, whereas in Nigeria, the community is larger, so a random selection of schools was included. LFPSs were defined as those charging a maximum of an equivalent US$20 per month [1], although in practice fees were usually much lower. Semi-structured interviews were conducted with three groups of participants selected in consultation with head teachers to represent a range of perspectives – teachers, head teachers and proprietors in low-fee private schools, parents of children enrolled in these schools, and parents of children enrolled in public schools (included for a comparative perspective).

The case-study site in Ghana is the Dominase community in Mfantesman District of the Central Region. The site includes two public schools and two LFPSs. The main economic activities in the community are farming and fishing (GSS, 2005); around 60% of the inhabitants of Mfantesman district live below the poverty line (GSS, 2000), while around a third of the adult population has never enrolled in school. The case-study site in Nigeria is Pedro: a densely populated community in Bariga Local Government Area (LGA) of Lagos State. The site has 30 public primary schools and the LGA as a whole contains an estimated 422 private schools, mostly LFPS (Härmä & Adefisayo, 2013). Pedro is an economically deprived community comprised mostly of petty traders, artisans and blue-collar workers.

Table I reports the number of interviewees and schools included in the study, by country and school type.

	Teachers	Parents	Schools	Proprietors/ head teachers	Total
Nigeria					
Private	15	15	3	5	38
Public	0	6	2	0	8
Ghana					
Private	10	10	2	3	25
Public	0	6	2	0	8
Total	25	37	9	8	79

Table I. Sample of interview respondents.

The interviews explored the perceptions which surround school 'choice' and the growth of LFPS, including regarding the quality of education and care in both school types, the affordability of private schooling, perceptions of value for money and of the reasons behind differences in school quality, including those relating to school infrastructure, teacher quality, pupils' opportunities to learn, and issues of school management and accountability. Secondary data analysis employs data from the Ghana Living Standards Surveys (GLSS), Nigeria Living Standards Surveys (NLSS), the Ghana Education Management Information System (EMIS) and a recent census of private schools conducted in Lagos State, Nigeria.

Background and Literature Review

In some sub-Saharan African contexts, the absence of public schools has driven the establishment of low-fee private schools, while in many others, private and public provision coexist, leading to a possibility of choice, for those families whose budgets permit. A range of providers inhabit the private and non-government sectors in Ghana and Nigeria, including private entrepreneurs and companies, social entrepreneurs and charitable organisations, both local and international (see Walford, 2011). While private schooling for social elites has endured since the colonial era, the substantial rise in the number of low-fee private schools run primarily for profit is a relatively new phenomenon. As the sector has grown, it may be argued increasingly persuasively that:

> The notion that private schools are servicing the needs of a
> small minority of parents is misplaced ... a low cost private
> sector has emerged to meet the demands of poor
> households.(Watkins, 2000 cited in Tooley et al, 2009)

Such low-fee private schools are frequently rudimentary where infrastructure and facilities are concerned and many are not officially recognised, often because it is expensive and complex to meet required registration criteria, which in Nigeria for example, include meeting demanding land-area and classroom-size standards (see Härmä, 2011).

The growth of enrolments in the low-fee private-school sector in Ghana and Nigeria is linked to rising incomes following steady economic growth in recent years, as well as to increased levels of education among parents – associated with shifting educational preferences – and in some cases to apparent perceptions of low or declining quality in the public sector – including that government schools 'do not actually teach children well', that 'teachers fail to attend school regularly' and that 'when they do, [they are] not actually teaching' (see Walford, 2011, pp. 408-409). Moreover, it may also be argued that the increases in enrolment in public schools which have followed the implementation of free universal basic-education policies in many developing countries are linked to a decline in quality, and thus somewhat paradoxically, to the demand for private schooling, despite these policies having the effect of increasing the cost differential between the public and private sectors.

In Nigeria, federal-government financing of primary education was progressively withdrawn during the 1980s, linked to overcrowding and poor learning environments, especially in urban public schools (Olaniyan & Obadara, 2008). Thereafter, provision in the public sector has failed to keep up with growing demand, providing part of the explanation for rising private provision and enrolment (Tooley, 2005) as well as for the high number of out-of-school children. Private enrolment has increased across all levels of schooling, accounting, at the primary level, for as much as 70% of enrolment in Lagos (Härmä, 2011).

Inadequate investment in the public-education system in Nigeria remains a pervasive criticism (Olaniyan & Obadara, 2008; Adebayo, 2009) and learning achievement levels at primary level are found to be low (see Johnson et al, 2008). The issue of inadequate public-school supply is less of a driver of private-sector growth in Ghana, where pupil–teacher ratios remain relatively low. Growth in private enrolments is nonetheless rapid, especially in urban areas, arguably being associated with 'choice' more often than 'necessity'. In a survey conducted in 2004 in the three urban districts, it was found that although a majority of households were living below or close to the poverty line, almost two-thirds of children (64%) were attending private schools (Tooley et al, 2007). Critics also emphasise continuing deficiencies of quality in Ghanaian basic education (see Kandingi, 2004, p. 15) and indeed per pupil expenditure has seen little improvement despite large total increases in education spending (see Rolleston, 2009; Penrose, 1998).

Both Ghana and Nigeria implemented free basic-education policies in the 1990s. In Ghana, 'Free Compulsory and Universal Basic Education' (FCUBE) was implemented from 1996, eliminating all basic school fees. Nigeria adopted its policy of free and compulsory basic education in 1999 (Olaniyan & Obadara, 2008, p. 12). Eliminating fees may be expected to reduce the cost burden of basic education, although other educational expenses also constitute an important barrier to access (see Patrinos, 2000). Notable other costs include those of uniforms, books, transport and food. Policies intended to address indirect cost barriers have included the Capitation Grant Scheme (CGS) implemented in 2005 in Ghana, which provides a small annual grant per pupil enrolled (around US$6) used to purchase textbooks and other requirements previously the responsibility of households. When fees are relatively low in comparison to other costs, the difference in costs between public and LFPS can be small (see Colclough et al, 2003), in which case the balance of costs and benefits may be rather more in favour of private schooling, if it is perceived to be of higher quality. Nonetheless, the literature also suggests that, given the option, many would ideally prefer to send their children to high-quality government schools (Akyeampong, 2009; Walford, 2011). Perceptions of poor quality in the public sector are thus arguably as important as those of higher quality in the private sector.

Where 'choice' exists, schooling decisions may be understood, in economic terms, as part of a household's long-term welfare-maximisation strategy and may be analysed within the cost–benefit analysis framework of Becker's (1964) household production function. This framework conceptualises household schooling decisions in terms of an attempt to compare the direct and opportunity costs of schooling options with the future economic benefits to the household. On the economic model, in addition to depending on income, household demand for education reflects the perceived net benefits of education which in turn depend on features of the particular child, including gender (UNESCO, 2005; Kingdon & Theopold, 2006) and birth order (Glewwe & Jacoby, 1994), as well as on characteristics of its parents, especially their own educational backgrounds and preferences (UNESCO, 2005; Sackey, 2007; Kazeem et al, 2010).

While school quality is often difficult to measure, some studies show a link with school participation (e.g. Lloyd et al, 2000), including studies in Ghana (Lavy, 1996; Fentiman et al, 1999). Moreover, the availability of opportunities for progression to higher levels of education has been found to affect enrolment earlier on in a child's school career (Glewwe & Jacoby, 1994; Lavy, 1996) and there is evidence that negative effects on participation associated with child and household disadvantage rise with a child's age, including because direct (school fees) and opportunity costs (foregone earnings from labour) are often much greater at higher levels of education (Checchi, 2001). Further, distances to school are found to be negatively associated with school participation (World Bank, 2004; Filmer, 2007). The supply of public education is of course largely determined by local and national education policy, while the supply of private schooling, at least of the profit-making variety, is linked to the local 'market' conditions, including the prevailing costs of 'inputs', the regulatory environment, the quality of public provision (competition), and the availability of 'entrepreneurship'. Costs in large measure determine the fees private schools are able to charge, while incomes determine the fees households are able to pay, so that the establishment of affordable LFPS in low-income contexts is heavily dependent on a ready supply of relatively low-paid teaching staff.

Beyond economic considerations, a range of other values also influences parents' educational choices. These include educational, social, religious and moral values (Dreze & Kingdon, 2001). Noddings (2005) emphasises the importance of an 'ethic of care' in an increasingly achievement-oriented educational environment, and proposes that education decisions do and should follow a 'calculus of care' in place of a purely economic rationale. Considerations in such a calculus include evaluations of the relationships between teachers and parents, the responsibility and accountability of schools to parents and pupils, the use of corporal punishment, and the availability of extra-curricular and enrichment activities.

Where a narrow definition of school quality in terms of the production of achievement outcomes is employed, robust evidence for a quality premium in LFPS is very limited in the context of sub-Saharan Africa. Studies are often very small in scale and national datasets do not usually contain all the necessary data for thorough analysis of the issue. Walford (2011), among others, calls into question the adequacy of the data typically employed. Nonetheless, some evidence is emerging in certain selected contexts for higher levels of performance, or at least perceptions thereof among caregivers, in private schools in Ghana and Nigeria (Tooley et al, 2005; Tooley et al, 2007; Akyeampong, 2009; Härmä, 2011). Some of the explanations offered include higher levels of teacher commitment, lower levels of absenteeism (Rose, 2009), higher levels of teacher accountability and supervision (Adefeso-Olateju, 2012) and a perception that private schools tend to be more goal-oriented and learning-focused (Akaguri, 2011). The evidence on the issues of cost-effectiveness and 'value for money' is not comprehensive or conclusive, but is arguably somewhat stronger than on achievement production because per pupil costs in LFPS are notably lower than costs in public schools (Tooley & Dixon, 2006). Undoubtedly, LFPS operate with somewhat different incentives from public schools, and, in low-income communities, are required to make efforts to recruit pupils from poor households, often using innovative strategies. For example, some adopt flexible fee strategies to induce demand, offering discounts for early payment or for the enrolment of multiple children, as well as flexible payment plans and concessionary fees (Tooley & Dixon, 2006; Akaguri, 2011).

Enrolment Trends in Private Schooling

The tables in this chapter show the percentages of children in Ghana and Nigeria enrolled in private schools using the most recent comparable nationally representative household-survey data. The figures for Ghana (Table II) are for all children in the 6-17 age group, presented by household-poverty status. Among the non-poor group, close to a third of all enrolled children were in private schools in 2005/6, rising from 8% among the 'extremely poor' group. In 1991/2 the proportion in private school of all those enrolled was 15.4% among the non-poor, a figure which doubled in the 14-year period to 2005/6. As shown in Figure 1, the proportion of children enrolled in private primary schools in Ghana continued to grow after 2005, rising to around a quarter of all pupils enrolled overall. For Nigeria in the 5-19 age group (Table III), figures are shown by household economic quintile, for those enrolled in school only. The pattern by economic status is similar to that in Ghana. Just over 8% of children in the poorest households were attending private school in 2004, rising to almost 23% in the richest households.

Enrolments in private primary schools in Ghana (Figure 1) increased steadily until 2004/5 when they dropped back. Since this coincided with the introduction of the Capitation Grant, it appears that some families decided to opt for public schooling in place of private in that year, owing to reductions in cost. In 2005/6, private primary-school enrolments again began to increase steadily, recovering to their 2004/5 levels by 2007/8. The elimination of public-school fees may have caused a 'supply-side shock' which altered the calculus of relative costs and benefits facing households so that public schooling became relatively better value for money, persuading households at the margin to select public schools for new enrolments and/or to transfer their children from private to public schools between 2004/5 and 2005/6, but this was not sustained, arguably due to concerns about quality in an expanding public system.

Poverty status	Schooling type			% enrolled in private school
	No school	Public	Private	
Extremely poor	36.4	58.5	5.09	8.00
Poor	20.1	69.0	10.9	13.6
Non-poor	13.2	60.1	26.7	30.8
Total	22.6	60.5	16.9	21.8

Table II. Type of school attended by household poverty status, Ghana 2005/6 (aged 6-17). *Source*: Computed from GLSS 5 (the fifth round of the GLSS survey, conducted in 2005/6).

Economic quintile	Schooling type		
	Government	Other	Private
1 (poorest)	85.98	5.71	8.31
2	84.60	5.59	9.81
3	85.54	3.84	10.63
4	81.09	4.62	14.28
5 (richest)	73.05	4.29	22.66

Table III. Type of school attended by economic quintile, Nigeria 2004 (aged 5-19). *Source*: Computed from NLSS

Data from a census of private schools in Lagos state (Lagos State Ministry of Education, 2010) show rapidly increasing numbers of private schools in the country's most urbanised state. Figure 2 shows enrolments in 2010. By far the largest share of private enrolments is at the primary level, where they are one and a half times as high as public enrolments. This pattern reverses at the junior and senior secondary levels.

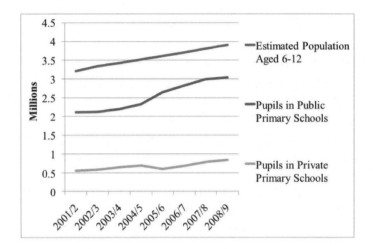

Figure 1. Enrolment in public and private primary schools 2001-9. *Source*: Authors' calculations from EMIS.

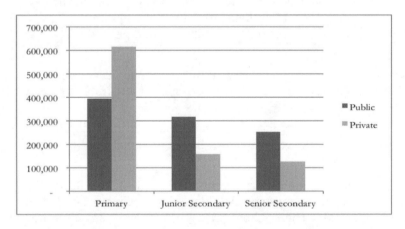

Figure 2. Total pupil enrolment in primary and secondary schools in Lagos State (2010). *Source*: Lagos State Annual Schools Census Report 2010 (Lagos State Ministry of Education, 2010)

Perceptions Driving the Growth in LFPS

The Quality of Education and Care

While a range of more nuanced views was expressed, respondents including parents of children in public schools most often considered education quality to be higher in LFPS than in the public system in both countries. When asked which schools they would patronise if choice were unrestricted, most favoured LFPS, explaining that the primary barrier to private schooling consisted of the level of fees. When asked about how they chose schools for different children, a common response was that private schools would be selected for more able pupils, who might be expected to benefit most:

> If I had more children I would see which ones did well and send those to private school and the ones who are not good to the public school. (Parent, public school, Ghana)

The benefits of LFPS at the basic level in both countries were often explained in terms of improving the chances of access to public senior secondary schools:

> At the secondary schools level the public school is usually preferable ... it would be ... more appropriate to have school certificate exam in public school than private school. (Parent public school, Nigeria)

Parents, especially in Ghana, expressed serious concerns about public-school quality:

> Realizing how the teachers in the school are behaving towards the children, not teaching them, allowing them to loiter around; I moved them to a private one. (Parent, private school, Ghana)

Respondents' views diverged somewhat in Nigeria, however, where some parents expressed support for the government's attempts to improve quality:

> As far Lagos state is concerned ... public schools are becoming reputable due to the government influence. (Parent public school, Nigeria)

In Ghana, parents frequently mentioned the high-stakes BECE (Basic Education Certificate Examination). This public examination serves to ration places at Senior High School (SHS), in turn the gateway to higher levels of education and training. One private parent explained:

> I am keeping my child in private school because I want him to go to a good high school so I know he will perform well. So when the results are released, the computer will select my child to go to a good senior high school. (Parent, private school, Ghana)

In fact, the link between private-school choice and hopes for better performance on the BECE was made by almost every respondent in the Ghana case study. Moreover, dissatisfaction with public schools among parents whose children attended them was frequently expressed in terms of poor examination performance:

> In the government school, the examination results are not
> good. This public school almost scored zero in their last
> examinations. (Parent, public school, Ghana)

Parents in Ghana commented favourably on private schools' organisation of sporting competitions, drama productions and school trips as well as on children's standards of dress. Parents in Nigeria concentrated less directly on examination results per se, but emphasised academic achievement more generally as an incentive to choose LFPS, while parents in both countries frequently spoke enthusiastically about the level of individual care and attention provided at private schools. For example:

> The teachers in a private school are more concerned for the
> children so if a child has been absent for more than a day or
> two they will come to you and ask why the child is in the
> house. (Parent, private school, Ghana)

One parent in Nigeria explained that better care may be linked to better pupil–teacher ratios in LFPS:

> We have fewer people there compared to the public school, so
> I believe in private school the children would have close
> relationship with their teachers. (Parent with children in both
> public and private schools, Nigeria)

However, in Ghana class sizes are in fact often larger in LFPS than in public schools, yet parents also noted better care in these schools, by comparison with public schools:

> I do visit but that place ... when I complain the teachers tell
> me it is a government school and free, and if I want I can take
> my son out of the school. (Parent, public school, Ghana)

In Ghana, it was explained that the higher status of teachers in public schools, and hence the greater 'social distance' between them and poor parents, may in part explain the difference in responsiveness to parents:

> Instead of welcoming you ... you'll be standing there for
> minutes and they will not mind you; but for the private
> school, even though the teachers are younger, they give you so
> much respect. (Parent, public school, Ghana)

Parents in Nigeria expressed a similar view of the approachability of teachers in LFPS. While it is clear that perceptions of better care and of more cordial relationships with schools and teachers are a strong draw of the LFPS, these advantages may be valued especially by poorer groups whose social or cultural 'capital' may be limited and who may consequently have limited influence in the public-school system. The fact that these parents are paying fees arguably empowers them to hold the school accountable in a way that the public school is not.

Reasons for Differences in Quality

The key feature of public schooling about which parents in Ghana were positive was the comparatively low cost:

> What I like best is just the capitation budget they give to the children which makes the costs of schooling a bit lower ... anything regarding the curriculum, teachers, exam results, it is not good. (Parent, public school, Ghana)

They also reported that school infrastructure is generally better in public schools, but emphasised nonetheless that differences in learning favour private schools:

> In a public school, the buildings are nice, they have good infrastructure. They are trained and good teachers but the kind of learning there is not good. (Parent, private school, Ghana)

In Nigeria, parents' views on the advantages of public schooling in terms of infrastructure diverged somewhat more, and some drew attention to better facilities in private schools:

> We have teachers that are very careful in private schools; there is laboratory, good libraries, computer facilities and so many other things. (Parent, public school, Nigeria)

Regarding pupils' 'opportunities to learn', in both Ghana and Nigeria, teachers and parents explained that there is little difference in the core curriculum between public and private schools. Nonetheless, private schools were found to prioritise the teaching of English and parents typically valued an early start in teaching English, but also commented on the apparently more successful teaching styles in private schools:

> The teachers in private schools force children to speak English ... but in public schools they learn English but they don't speak it and they don't know why. (Parent, private school, Ghana)

In Nigeria, some LFPS were found to be offering an 'enhanced curriculum' as well as employing pedagogies more squarely focused on children's individual understanding, including through the use of 'reading clubs' and specialist teachers:

> When we started this programme we were having teachers for different subjects like music, French and other subjects, and when the parents see that they were impressed and happy. (Proprietor, private school, Nigeria)

Private-school teachers in Ghana were considered to adopt pedagogical strategies aimed more specifically at ensuring that pupils have mastered the intended curriculum:

> The teachers force them to understand what they teach by giving them a lot of exercises and organizing quizzes. For instance, if it is science, it will be taught differently in a private school so that when the children go to BECE they will pass and pass well. (Parent, private school, Ghana)

Parents believed the extra classes provided in private schools to be particularly important in consolidating learning:

> Whatever is taught in the daytime is retaught after school ... In public schools, they teach what they are supposed to teach and don't care whether the children have understood or not. (Parent, private school, Ghana)

Private-school teachers also emphasised differences between public and private schools in relation to marking and student monitoring:

> In our school we make sure that children read, do the assignment, we mark and make sure they do the corrections and that is what the public schools do not do. (Teacher, private school, Ghana)

Teacher Quality and Professionalism

Respondents in both countries agreed that public-school teachers are usually better qualified and more experienced than private-school parents. However, parents of children in LFPS argued that attitudes and behaviours adopted by teachers in LFPS counteract the effects of qualification and experience. Public-school parents in Nigeria, on the other hand, indicated the better qualification and experience of teachers as reasons for choosing public schools, for example:

> Teachers in public school are full of knowledge ... unlike the private school they employ people that are not knowledgeable about teaching ... all in the name of making money. (Parent, public school, Nigeria)

Conversely, it was suggested in Ghana that the relative youth of less-experienced private-school teachers might be advantageous to pupil learning:

> Some of the [public school] teachers are old and lack some of the modern language that they do have in the private schools especially ICT ... the training they had was a long time ago. (Parent, private school, Ghana)

The lack of professional qualifications and limited experience of LFPS teachers was also linked to better supervision of teachers in LFPS, a feature parents valued highly:

> Because most of the teachers are senior school graduates, they are very serious with the teaching and if they don't teach the owners of the school would ask them to leave. (Parent, private school, Ghana)

While at the same time, one parent of a pupil in public school expressed some scepticism in relation to the competence of private-school teachers, linked to the lack of regulation and to commercial incentives:

> The private schools are just a business so that they get some money in their pocket. So they recruit all kinds of teachers to teach in those schools. (Parent, public school, Ghana)

Particular attention was given by respondents to differences in teacher behaviour between school types. Firstly, they emphasised the higher levels of attendance and punctuality of private-school teachers:

> The private school teachers are very punctual, if it is 8am, you will find them at school but for the public school ... teachers can stay at home till 10am. (Parent, private school, Ghana)

In Nigeria, parents referred frequently to the issue of teacher strikes in the public sector:

> In the private school they don't go on strike it's only public school that goes on strike; any little thing like this they will go on strike. (Parent, private school, Nigeria)

School Management and Accountability

The issue of accountability of both teachers and schools was central to many interviewees' responses. In public schools, teacher accountability was considered lacking, including through the absence of incentives or monitoring. Differences in accountability were linked by respondents to ownership and management structures, including the role of the school proprietor in private schools:

> The owner of the school is accountable to parents; teachers are very careful the way they behave during school hours so if you misbehave the owner of the school can quickly expel you or sack you. (Parent, private school, Ghana)

Conversely, in the public school:

> They think they are on their own, not under anyone else's control ... they spend a lot of time making phone calls during teaching time. (Parent, private school, Ghana)

The payment of fees was linked by respondents in both countries to differences in accountability between school types. For example:

> No proprietor would like to see the teachers not working ...
> because they know that it is where they are getting their
> money from. (Parent, private school, Nigeria)

Fees are low in absolute terms, but so are incomes. In the Ghana case study, salaries were reported by teachers to be between 30 GhC (US$17.7) and 80GhC (US$47.2) per month. By comparison, teachers in public schools would usually earn between US$120 and US$350. Difficulties in collecting fees impact upon the school's income and, in turn, on the ability to pay teachers' salaries:

> If we don't get the school fees we don't get a salary. We can't
> buy food so we have no energy to teach. It affects our
> motivation to teach. (Teacher, private school, Ghana)

Extra classes were found to be essential for supplementing private-school teachers' incomes:

> After 1.30pm to 3.30pm they have their extra classes, because
> they know that this is the way to get paid and to increase their
> salary ... They get paid more for extra classes, which goes
> directly to them. (Proprietor, private school, Ghana)

Affordability and Value for Money

While the fees payable at private schools in the study were found to be low by international standards and sometimes by parents, they remain difficult to afford for many. Parents of children in public schools explained that fees presented a serious barrier to enrolling their children in private schools:

> For private school their fee is on the high side, it takes a lot of
> plan and savings to be able to pay. (Parent, public school,
> Nigeria)

Some parents of children in private schools explained that they sometimes take loans to afford school fees. In some cases, affording fees sometimes required considerable sacrifices to be made:

> Sometimes I have to borrow, but my wife is aware that an
> education is important so sometimes we don't eat in order to
> provide an education for our children. (Parent, private school,
> Ghana)

While other parents reported that they found the fees affordable, several also argued that the costs of books, food and extra classes may be an even greater burden, especially given that these payments cannot be deferred.

However, private schools were often found to adopt strategies to aid affordability, including flexible payment terms. Parents most often spoke positively about 'value for money' in terms of the service provided by private schools, citing in particular the school's examination results, success in progression to post-basic education and pupils' learning of English. One teacher cited speaking English as a litmus test in parents' minds for 'value for money':

> If you go home and the boy/girl speaks English the parent will admire it and say, 'ah, the money I am spending is being returned to me so I will pay whatever you ask from me.' (Teacher, private school, Ghana)

One parent in Nigeria dissented notably on the issue of 'value for money', however, while this response was untypical:

> My child in private school is not really better ... we would buy books that they would not read a page in a section and those around me that are going to a public school are performing well. (Parent, public school, Nigeria)

Discussion and Conclusions

While limited to the study of two communities, interview data gathered for this study show considerable consonance among the views of parents and teachers across the communities, including with regard to the reasons for choosing private schooling, to the perceptions of differences in quality between public and private schools, as well as to how these differences might be explained. Parents considered learning progress to be better in LFPS and perceived these schools to provide for better opportunities for progression in the higher levels of the public system. Given the potentially high returns to higher levels of schooling and the high costs of attending private schools at this level, this view may be considered in one sense at least a 'rational' one, provided that LFPS produce better outcomes. The level of state subsidy at higher levels of education is high, so that if enrolment in private basic schools provides better access to progression by 'jumping the queue', it may lead to considerable long-term benefits. Reform of the state education system in Ghana in 1967 shortened the length of the basic education cycle after which secondary schooling was rationed by examination. Following this reform, private primary schools flourished (see Addae-Mensah et al, 1973) and the share of secondary-school pupils from these schools increased. The present situation is somewhat similar, and raises many of the same equity questions, yet on a larger scale.

The commercial incentives of LFPS were a concern to parents in some cases, but many parents and teachers believed these incentives to promote unity among the goals and incentives of schools, teachers and parents, since school enrolments depend upon reputation, which in turn depends on performance. On the other hand, LFPS in the low-income communities in this study paid teachers close to a subsistence wage and teachers were found sometimes to depend on 'extra classes' to earn an adequate income, leaving them open to the charge of exploitation of teaching staff and of an excessive incentive to extend the hours for which children are instructed.

While clearly not all of the practices of LFPS provide for good 'policy learning' in the public system, the critical views of parents in relation to that system suggest considerable dissatisfaction and, a perception at least, of 'government failure' in the sector, especially in Ghana. Failure of the public system to provide for good-quality basic education has negative implications for social justice regardless of the actions of LFPSs, since it denies children an essential opportunity for human development. But the emergence of LFPSs as an alternative may add inequality to inequity, especially if the benefits of enrolment in private basic schools serve to allow some pupils to progress more readily beyond that stage, with the result that initial advantage is compounded through the rest of a child's educational career and beyond. Depending on the affordability of fees, LFPS may also introduce a stronger link between educational quality and ability to pay, potentially worsening the relative outcomes of the poorest for whom such schools are beyond reach. Further, to the extent that parents' resource-constrained decisions concerning whom to send to LFPSs favour more able children, weaker pupils may also be further disadvantaged in relative terms by the expansion of LFPS, while the extent of selection by ability makes it complex to disentangle the real effect on learning of private schools.

The state may reduce inequality in one sense by 'clamping down' on unregistered private schools through the use of regulatory enforcement, as has been observed in several countries (Rose, 2007), including in Nigeria. But dealing squarely with inequity requires addressing the issues of quality within public schools, and in this there may be considerable opportunities for 'policy learning' from LFPS. Perhaps the most important lessons appear to be those less concerned with 'inputs' in the conventional sense of infrastructure, facilities and measured teacher characteristics and more concerned with school and classroom 'processes', including monitoring of pupil progress and welfare, communication with parents, and the motivation and supervision of teachers. While the available evidence is inadequate to support the use of radical measures such as 'vouchers', the satisfaction of parents with LFPSs nonetheless suggests a case for strengthening the mechanisms through which public schools can learn from innovation in the LFPS sector in low-income communities, through collaboration or partnership. Nonetheless, the improvement of learning quality in government basic schools, which continue to serve the majority of children from low-income households, remains paramount among public-policy priorities where social justice in basic education is concerned.

Note

[1] US$20 represents approximately 40% of the minimum wage in Ghana and Nigeria.

References

Addae-Mensah, I., Djangmah, J. & Agbenyega, C. (1973) *Family Background and Educational Opportunities in Ghana.* Accra: Ghana Universities Press.

Adebayo, F. (2009) Parents' Preference for Private Secondary Schools in Nigeria, *International Journal of Educational Sciences*, 1(1), 1-6.

Adefeso-Olateju, M. (2012) A Critical Enquiry into the Effectiveness of Public and Private Schools in Nigeria, and Implications for Public-Private Partnership. PhD thesis, Institute of Education, University of London.

Akaguri, L. (2011) Quality Low-Fee Private Schools for the Rural Poor: perception or reality? Evidence from Southern Ghana. CREATE (Consortium for Research on Educational Access, Transitions and Equity) Pathways to Access Research Monograph 69. Brighton: CREATE, University of Sussex.

Akyeampong, K. (2009) Revisiting Free Compulsory Universal Basic Education (FCUBE) in Ghana, *Comparative Education,* 45(2), 175–195.

Aslam, M. (2009) The Relative Effectiveness of Government and Private Schools in Pakistan: are girls worse off?, *Education Economics*, 17(3), 329-354.

Becker, G. (1964) *Human Capital: a theoretical and empirical analysis, with special reference to education.* New York: National Bureau of Economic Research.

Checchi, D. (2001) *Education, Inequality and Income Inequality. Distributional Analysis Research Programme. The Toyota Centre, Suntory and Toyota International Centres for Economics and Related Disciplines.* London: London School of Economics.

Colclough, C., Al Samarrai, S., Rose, P. & Tembon, M. (2003) *Achieving Schooling for All in Africa.* Aldershot: Ashgate.

Dreze, J. & Kingdon, G. (2001) School Participation in Rural India, *Review of Development Economics*, 5(1), 1-24.

Fentiman, A., Hall, A. & Bundy, D. (1999) School Enrolment Patterns in Rural Ghana: a comparative study of the impact of location, gender, age and health on children's access to basic schooling, *Comparative Education*, 35(3), 331-349.

Filmer, D. (2007) If You Build It, Will They Come? School Availability and School Enrolment in 21 Poor Countries, *Journal of Development Studies,* 43(5), 901-928.

French, R. & Kingdon, G. (2010) *The Relative Effectiveness of Private and Government Schools in Rural India: evidence from ASER data.* Department of Quantitative Social Science (DoQSS) Working Paper 10-03. London: Institute of Education, University of London.

Ghana Statistical Service (GSS) (2000) *Poverty Trends in the 1990s.* Accra: GSS.

Ghana Statistical Service (GSS) (2005) *2000 Population and Housing Census. Central Region: analysis of district data and implications for planning.* Accra: GSS.

Glewwe, P. & Jacoby, H. (1994) Student Achievement and Schooling Choice in Low Income Countries: evidence from Ghana, *Journal of Human Resources,* 29(3), 843-864.

Hanushek, E. & Woessmann, L. (2007) The Role of School Improvement in Economic Development. NBER Working Paper 12832. New York: National Bureau of Economic Research.

Härmä, J. (2011) *Lagos Private School Census 2010-11 Report.* Lagos: ESSPIN.

Härmä, J. & Adefisayo, F. (2013) Scaling Up: the challenges facing low-fee private schools in the slums of Lagos, Nigeria, in P. Srivastava (Ed.) *Low-Fee Private Schooling: aggravating equity or mediating disadvantage?* Oxford: Symposium Books.

Johnson, D., Hsieh, P. & Onibon, F. (2008) *Baseline Evaluation for State Education Sector Projects, Nigeria.* Washington, DC: World Bank

Kadingdi, S. (2004) Policy Initiatives for Change and Innovation in Basic Education Programmes in Ghana, *Educate,* 4(2), 3-18.

Kazeem, A., Jensen, L. & Stokes, C. (2010) School Attendance in Nigeria: understanding the impact and intersection of gender, urban-rural residence and socioeconomic status, *Comparative Education Review,* 54(2), 295-319.

Kingdon, G. & Theopold, N. (2006) Do Returns to Education Matter to Schooling Participation? Global Poverty Research Group Working Paper 52. Oxford: Centre for the Study of African Economies, University of Oxford.

Lagos State Ministry of Education (2010) *Annual Schools Census Report 2009-2010.* Lagos: Lagos State Ministry of Education.

Lavy, V. (1996) School Supply Constraints and Children's Educational Outcomes in Rural Ghana, *Journal of Development Economics,* 51(2), 291-314.

Lloyd, C.B., Mensch, B.S. & Clark, W.H. (2000) The Effects of Primary School Quality on School Dropout among Kenyan Girls and Boys, *Comparative Education Review,* 44(2), 113-147.

Noddings, N. (2005) *The Challenge to Care in Schools: an alternative approach to education,* 2nd edn. New York: Teacher's College Press.

Olaniyan, D.A. & Obadara, O. (2008) A Critical Review of Management of Primary Education in Nigeria, *The Social Sciences,* 3(6), 411-419.

Patrinos, H. (2000) Market Forces in Education, *European Journal of Education,* 35(1), 61-79.

Penrose, P. (1998) Cost Sharing in Education – public finance, school and household perspectives. Education Research Paper 27. London: Department for International Development.

Rolleston, C. (2009) Financing Primary Education for All: trends post-Dakar and the importance of growth. Background Paper for the UNESCO Education for All Global Monitoring Report 2010. Paris: UNESCO.

Rose, P. (2007) Supporting Non-State Providers in Basic Education Service Delivery. CREATE (Consortium for Research on Educational Access, Transitions and Equity) Pathways to Access Research Monograph 4. Brighton: CREATE.

Rose, P. (2009) Non-State Provision of Education: evidence from Africa and Asia, *Compare*, 39(2), 127-134.

Sackey, H. (2007) The Determinants of School Attendance and Attainment in Ghana: a gender perspective. African Economic Research Consortium (AERC) Research Paper 173. Nairobi: AERC.

Tooley, J. (2005) Is Private Education Good for the Poor? Working paper. Centre for Market Solutions in Education. Newcastle: University of Newcastle.

Tooley, J. & Dixon, P. (2006) 'De facto' Privatisation of Education and the Poor: implications of a study from sub-Saharan Africa and India, *Compare,* 36(4), 443-462.

Tooley, J., Dixon, P. & Amuah, I. (2007) Private and Public Schooling in Ghana: a census and comparative survey, *International Review of Education*, 53(4), 389-415.

Tooley, J., Dixon, P. & Gomathi, S. (2009) Private Schools and the Millennium Development Goal of Universal Primary Education: a census and comparative survey in Hyderabad, India, *Oxford Review of Education*, 33(5), 539-560.

Tooley, J., Dixon, P. & Olaniyan, O. (2005) Private and Public Schooling in Low-Income Areas of Lagos State, Nigeria: a census and comparative survey, *International Review of Education*, 43(3), 125-146.

UNESCO (2005) *Children Out of School: measuring exclusion from primary education.* Montreal: UNESCO Institute for Statistics (UIS).

Walford, G. (2011) Low-fee Private Schools in England and in Less Economically Developed Countries: what can we learn from a comparison?, *Compare*, 41(3), 401-413.

Watkins, K. (2000) *Oxfam Education Report.* Oxford: Oxfam Great Britain.

World Bank (2004) *Books, Buildings, and Learning Outcomes: an impact evaluation of World Bank support to basic education in Ghana.* Washington, DC: World Bank.

CHAPTER 3

Private Schooling: determinants and implications for social justice in rural Punjab, Pakistan

HAMNA AHMED, SAHAR AMJAD & MASOOMA HABIB

Introduction

Many developing countries have experienced a surge in low-fee private schooling in response to the inadequate supply and low standard of government schools (Psacharopoulos et al, 1997; Muralidharan, 2006; Srivastava, 2007; Muralidharan & Kremer, 2008). Pakistan is no exception (Andrabi et al, 2007). There has been an increasing demand for private schooling in a country where only 54% of children are enrolled in private, public, community or religious schools amongst the rural poor. Compared to males, a greater percentage of girls are out of school: the gender gap between the male and female enrolment rate is 21% (Table I).

Up to 15% of school-age enrolments in rural Pakistan are in private schools. Private schooling is important not just for the rich: it also plays an important role for the poor. The spread of private schooling has been uneven across the country, catering to almost one fourth and one fifth of all school-going children in Punjab and Khyber Pakhtunkhwa (KP), but its spread has been quite limited in Sindh and Balochistan (Table I). The spread of private schooling has also been uneven within Punjab, being most widespread in the northern and central parts of the province compared to the west and the south (Table II).

The growth of private schooling has meant that many parents have the option of sending their children to private schools. With this backdrop, the main overarching question that this study aims to address is: Why do parents choose low-cost private schools when free public schools are available? The main emphasis in answering this question is on the role of parents' perceptions in school choice while controlling for a range of child-, household- and school-specific characteristics. Andrabi and others (2007) show that in 'low-cost' private schools, 'the overall cost of educating a child in the median rural private school is Rs. 1,000 or $15 a year.'

Area/ gender	Enrolled	Out of school	School type			
			Private	Public	Madrassa	Other
Pakistan	54.4	45.6	14.9	82.5	1.5	1.1
Males	64.1	35.9	14.3	83.1	1.7	1.0
Females	42.8	57.2	16.1	81.3	1.3	1.2
Punjab	61.9	38.1	23.4	73.9	1.5	1.3
Sindh	47.4	52.6	5.51	92.6	0.9	1.0
KP	60.3	39.7	16.9	80.9	1.4	0.7
Balochistan	43.6	56.4	3.7	92.6	2.6	1.2

Table I. Interprovincial (rural) patterns of enrolment and out-of-school children (5-18) (%). *Source*: Pakistan Bureau of Statistics (2010), PSLM Survey 2008/09.

Region	Enrolled	Out of school	School type			
			Private	Public	Madrassa	Other
Northern	80.7	19.3	25.1	73.3	1.3	0.3
Central	67.9	32.1	27.8	69.6	1.2	1.4
Southern	50.7	49.3	20.4	75.4	2.8	1.5
Western	51.9	48.1	10.4	87.0	1.3	1.3

Table II. Patterns of enrolment and out-of-school children (5-18) in rural Punjab by region (%). *Source*: Pakistan Bureau of Statistics, Multiple Indicator Cluster Survey, 2008/09.

The existing literature on the topic argues that school-choice behaviour can be driven by demand-side determinants, supply-side determinants or both. The former entails: (1) child-specific characteristics, such as age, gender and intelligence; (2) parent-specific characteristics, such as education and awareness (Lloyd et al, 2005; Iram et al, 2008); and (3) household-specific characteristics, such as distance to school, income and wealth (Sathar & Lloyd, 1994; Burney & Irfan, 1995; Alderman et al, 2001; Lloyd et al, 2005; Andrabi et al, 2007; Lloyd et al, 2009). Supply-side factors typically include school-specific characteristics, such as schooling quality, lower teacher absenteeism, infrastructure, test scores and whether (or not) the school is English-medium (World Bank, 1996; Harlech-Jones et al, 2005; Lloyd et al, 2005; Das et al, 2006; Muralidharan, 2006; Andrabi et al, 2007; Siddiqui, 2007; Annual Status of Education Report, 2010). Although the education literature discusses demand-side and supply-side factors at length, it does not focus on parents' perceptions of the alternative options available to them in making school choices.

This study departs from the existing literature in that it explores the role of parents' perceptions in shaping school-choice behaviour. Thus, we use perceived indicators of child and school quality rather than actual measures (for instance, parents' assessment of their children's and teachers' competence levels rather than actual IQ or academic measures) since notions of school and teacher quality, children's capabilities and employment opportunities may form an important basis for defining the value of education in parents' eyes and in choosing a school for their children.

The study draws on primary data, specifically the Privatization in Education Research Initiative (PERI) School Choice Survey, which was conducted in April 2011 by the Lahore School of Economics in collaboration with the Punjab Bureau of Statistics.

The scope of this study is limited to Punjab. Punjab has been chosen on two accounts: (1) the spread of private schooling has been most widespread in Punjab compared to the other provinces: almost one fourth of all school-going children in the 5-18 age bracket are enrolled in private schools in Punjab compared to one fifth in Khyber Pakhtunkhwa and one twentieth in Sindh and Balochistan (Table I); and (2) Punjab is the largest province in terms of population and therefore representative of education trends at the national level.

The chapter is organised as follows: Section 2 describes the sampling approach and the PERI dataset; Section 3 discusses the research methodology; Section 4 presents results; Section 5 offers the social-justice implications of our findings and Section 6 concludes.

Sampling and Data

Sampling Methodology

Punjab is geographically divided between northern, western, southern and central Punjab. Since western Punjab was severely affected by floods at the time of the survey, it would not have been representative of normal conditions in the area and was thus excluded from the sample.

The study was focused on rural tehsils only, whereby a rural tehsil was defined as having a rural population of more than 32.5%. Provinces are divided into districts, which are further divided into tehsils. Thus tehsil is an administrative sub-unit of a district.

Southern Punjab is, historically, a deprived region in terms of socioeconomic conditions and access to public services. Private enrolment is relatively low here compared to other parts of the province (Annual Status of Education Report, 2010). Therefore, southern Punjab was further divided into two regions on the basis of private-school availability, using a private-school enrolment threshold of 20% as a proxy for availability of choice. The main objective of this exercise was to avoid surveying a 'no choice' area since this would have defeated the study's objective of examining parents' school-choice behaviour between private and public schools.

Thus, a random sample with a probability proportional to size approach was drawn from a target population in the rural regions of central, northern and southern Punjab with < 20% private enrolment and in southern Punjab with ≥ 20% private enrolment.

Data

The PERI School Choice Survey was conducted in seven rural districts of Punjab (one in northern Punjab, four in central Punjab and two in southern Punjab). A total of 1024 households were surveyed in 64 clusters spanning over eight tehsils across seven districts. These households are a subsample of the households surveyed under the MICS for 2007/8, thus allowing the construction of a panel dataset.

The total sample is made up of 1543 children between 5 and 18 years of age (inclusive), of which 73% consist of children in the 5-14 age bracket, while the rest fall in the 15-18 age bracket. In terms of gender composition, 52% are male and 48% are female.

Gender	In school*	Out of school*	
	Enrolled	Never attended	Dropped out
Overall	66.7	17.9	15.4
Males	70.9	15.1	14.0
Females	62.1	20.8	17.1

Gender	Type of school**			
	Private	Public	Madrassa	Other
Overall	26.8	69.5	0.3	3.4
Males	23.9	72.9	0.2	3.1
Females	30.6	65.2	0.4	3.8

Notes: * = percentage of children, ** = percentage of enrolled children.
The 'Other' category includes foundation-assisted schools, trust-run schools, vocational and technical-training schools.

Table III. Overall enrolment by gender and type of school (%).
Source: PERI School Choice Survey (2011).

As shown in Table III, 33% of all children in the 5-18 age bracket are currently out of school. Of these, 17.9% have never attended school while 15.4% are dropouts. The public sector is the main provider of education services in rural areas. Enrolment in madrassas and other types of schools is relatively low at 0.3% and 3.4%, respectively.

As Table III shows, the private sector plays a significant role in providing education services in the area under study: almost 27% of all enrolled children currently attend private schools. The table also shows that private-school enrolments are higher among females than males even though overall female enrolment is lower and the proportion of females who have never attended school is higher relative to males. Overall male enrolment is nine percentage points higher than female enrolment in our sample. Moreover, compared to males, a much greater percentage of females are out of school (37.9% compared to 29.1% for males), either because they have never attended school or because they have dropped out.

In terms of type and level of schooling, Table IV reveals that private schools cater to all levels of schooling, even in rural Punjab. One fourth of all enrolled children at the primary and middle levels attend private schools. What is interesting to note is that this proportion increases for high school, where one third of all enrolled children attend private schools. Thus, contrary to the commonly held view that private schools cater only for the primary level, the private sector appears to have a much broader outreach even in the rural areas of the province.

Schooling level/ gender	Type of school			
	(1) Private	(2) Public	(3) Madrassa	(4) Other
Primary	24.7	71.2	0.2	4.0
Males	24.1	71.4	0.0	4.6
Females	25.5	70.6	0.4	3.6
Middle	24.1	75.0	0.0	0.9
Males	17.3	82.7	0.0	0.0
Females	32.7	65.4	0.0	1.9
High	34.4	61.2	0.6	3.8
Males	22.3	74.5	1.1	2.1
Females	51.6	41.9	0.0	6.5

Note: The 'Other' category includes foundation-assisted schools, trust-run schools and community schools.

Table IV. Gender-disaggregated enrolment patterns by level of schooling (%).
Source: PERI School Choice Survey (2011).

An examination of the gender-disaggregated data shows that, for girls, private enrolment increases and public enrolment declines with the level of schooling. At the high-school level, more than twice as many females as males attend private schools.

Methodology

This analysis is based on children between 5–18 years of age, who are enrolled in a private or public school, and who have the 'choice' of being sent to a private school. 'Choice' is defined as affirmative if there was at least one child attending a private school in that cluster.

Out of the initial working sample of 1543 children, 254 were excluded because they belonged to a 'no-choice' area. This yielded a sample of 1289 children, of which 889 were enrolled in school and 400 were out of school at the time. Out of the 889 children enrolled in school, 42 attended schools other than public or private schools (e.g. madrassas, trust-run, foundation-assisted or community schools), yielding a working sample of 847 children. Of this working sample of 847 children, 264 children were enrolled in private schools and 583 in public schools – 520 (60%), 204 (24%) and 140 (16%) of these children were enrolled at the primary-, middle- and high-school level, respectively.

In order to answer the research question, we carry out our investigation in two stages. The first stage entails employing an aggregated approach to gain a broad overview of the determinants of school choice for the pooled sample. In the second step, we extend the analysis by undertaking two distinct types of disaggregation: the first at the gender level to capture differences in the private-school enrolment of males and females, and the second at different levels of schooling to gauge how enrolment patterns in private schools change across the primary-, middle- and high-school tiers.

Thus, to understand what determines school choice in a rural setting, our model incorporates a set of child-specific, parent-specific and household-specific characteristics, along with an array of variables capturing the role of parents' perceptions with regard to their child's 'quality', the quality of the school he/she attends and the employment opportunities available to the child. Accordingly, we specify the following probability-choice model:

$$\mathrm{Pr}ob(S_{ik} = 1 | PS, X) = \gamma + \sum_{n=1}^{4} \beta_n (PS_{ikn}^p - PS_{ikn}^g) + \beta X + \varepsilon_{ik} \tag{1}$$

S is a dummy variable that is equal to 1 if child i of parent(s) k is enrolled in a private school and 0 if the child is enrolled in a public school. The variable of interest is the parents' perceptions of the child's school (PS). Since the objective is to study the attractiveness of private schools relative to public schools, the variable of interest takes a differenced form to account for the 'relativity' aspect. Thus, PS_k^g measures parent k's perception of the quality of the private school in which child i is enrolled, while PS_k^g represents the perceived quality of public schools. Since it is a child-level analysis and the sample under study is made up of only private- and public-school-going children, if child i is enrolled in a private school, the counterfactual will refer to a public school and vice versa.

For all children going to school, the counterfactual is constructed using a tehsil-specific mean of the perception of all parents whose children attend the alternative school type. For instance, if child i attends a private (public) school, $PS_k^g(PS_k^p)$ will represent the mean perception of all parents in that tehsil of the quality of the public (private) schools in which their children are enrolled.

The quality of the school in which the child is enrolled is quantified along n in various dimensions. These include the quality of subject teaching, the quality of the child's class teacher and the school's infrastructure. For each of these dimensions, we construct an index (rescaled to lie between 0 and 10) using principal component analysis (PCA) due to the presence of high correlation among the individual elements (see Box 1 for further details on each of these indices).

Box 1. Indices measuring parents' perceptions of school quality

Quality of subject teaching. Measures how parents rate the teaching of mathematics, English and science in their child's school on a scale of 1 to 3, where 1 refers to poor and 3 refers to excellent.

Teacher quality. Measures perceived quality of the class teacher's teaching. It includes: (1) parents' knowledge of the teacher's educational qualifications; (2) their opinion of the teacher's regularity; and (3) their rating of the teacher's teaching skills on a scale of 1 to 4, where 1 refers to poor, 2 to average, 3 to above average and 4 to excellent.

School infrastructure quality. Measures: (1) parents' observations about the condition of the school building and their knowledge of whether the school has (2) a boundary wall, (3) a functional latrine, (4) electricity and (5) water.

X is a vector of child-specific (gender, perceived competence), parent-specific (parents' education and awareness of private schooling) and household-specific controls (size, socioeconomic status, distance from the child's school and regional location). For further details on how these variables were constructed, please refer to the original report entitled 'Determinants of School Choice: Evidence from Rural Punjab, Pakistan' (DSC). The report is available on the Privatization in Education Research Initiative (PERI) website [1] where more details are available.

An additional dimension that is studied is parents' perceptions of the employment opportunities available to their child. The nature and type of employment opportunities that parents perceive for their child are expected to play an instrumental role in the former's choice of school. The types of employment parents perceive are aggregated to define two broad categories: (1) jobs that require specialised education;

and (2) jobs that do not require specialised education and thus might not justify investing in high-cost private education. The first category includes jobs in teaching, medicine, engineering or in the government sector (which is considered very prestigious in rural areas). The second category of employment perceived by parents entails jobs in manual labour, factory work or farm labour, for which they may think less education is needed.

To capture the effect of parents' perceptions of the prevalent employment opportunities on school choice, we estimate specification (2), which includes a binary variable given by Emp_c, equal to 1 if 'low-skill' jobs are available and 0 if parents perceive 'high-skill' jobs to be available for their children in area c. The perceived availability of employment opportunities is likely to have a differential impact on school choice across wealth quintiles. To formally test this, we augment the specification by adding an employment*wealth interaction:

$$Prob(S_{ik} = 1 | PS, Emp, X) = \gamma + \sum_{n=1}^{4} \beta_n (PS_{ikn}^p - PS_{ikn}^g) + \beta_5 Emp_c + \beta X + \varepsilon_{ik} \quad (2)$$

Results and Discussion

Enrolled versus Non-Enrolled Children

Household socioeconomic status appears to be an important determinant of schooling. Table V shows that enrolment rates for children in the 5-18 age bracket is 29 percentage points higher in the richest wealth quintile compared to the poorest quintile. Almost half the children in the poorest households do not attend school. In addition, the percentage of children who have never attended school is more than six times as high in the lowest quintile (37.5%) compared to the highest quintile (6.3%).

Quintile	In school*	Out of school*		Type of school**			
	Enrolled	Never attended	Dropped out	Private	Public	Madrassa	Other
Lowest	50.8	37.5	11.7	9.2	86.5	0.0	4.3
Second	68.5	14.4	17.1	14.9	80.6	0.5	4.0
Third	65.8	18.7	15.5	32.2	66.8	0.0	1.0
Fourth	69.2	9.9	20.9	28.6	65.2	0.0	6.2
Highest	79.4	6.3	14.3	44.1	53.4	1.0	1.6

Note: * = percentage of children, ** = percentage of enrolled children.

Table V. Patterns of enrolment and out-of-school children (5-18) by socioeconomic status (%). *Source*: PERI School Choice Survey (2011).

Our regression analysis of the determinants of enrolment corroborates this finding: as wealth increases, parents are 5% more likely to send their child to school. Even if the tuition fee is zero, parents incur considerable expenditure on uniforms, books, stationery, etc. Also, if the child goes to school, it means that he/she is unavailable for household chores, which is especially relevant for females. All these factors make the socioeconomic status of a household a barrier to a child's schooling.

Males are more likely to attend school than females. The regression results indicate that, when we control for other household factors, males are 10% more likely to be sent to school than females. A possible reason, as posited by Dreze and Kingdon (2001) is that parents are less concerned about females' education given that their daughters leave home when married.

The pro-male gender bias is higher at lower wealth levels. Table VI reports gender-disaggregated numbers for each wealth quintile. Poverty seems to be an important factor in explaining gender differentials in schooling: the male-female gender gap widens from a negative 5% (implying female enrolment is greater than male enrolment) in the richest 20% of the population to 11% in the bottom 20% of the population. When resources are limited, there may be a tendency to invest more in sons in the intra-household allocation of education expenditure.

| Quintile | In school* | Out of school* | | Type of school** | | | |
	Enrolled	Never attended	Dropped out	Private	Public	Madrassa	Other
Lowest = 1							
Males	56.0	34.3	9.6	8.6	88.2	0.0	3.2
Females	44.8	41.2	14.0	9.4	84.4	0.0	5.2
Second							
Males	74.1	13.2	12.6	15.8	78.7	0.0	4.7
Females	61.1	22.1	16.8	21.1	77.6	0.0	1.3
Third							
Males	70.4	16.4	13.2	22.3	75.0	0.0	2.7
Females	61.2	21.0	17.8	26.9	68.8	0.0	4.3
Fourth							
Males	77.3	7.1	15.6	23.9	73.4	0.0	2.7
Females	61.6	12.6	25.8	40.9	54.8	0.0	4.3
Highest = 5							
Males	77.2	4.7	18.1	40.4	57.0	0.9	1.8
Females	81.8	8.0	10.2	47.7	48.6	0.9	2.7

Note: * = percentage of children, ** = percentage of enrolled children.

Table VI. Patterns of enrolment and out-of-school children (5-18) by gender and socioeconomic status (%). *Source*: PERI School Choice Survey (2011).

Intergenerational effects exist in education. The level of parental education increases the likelihood of their child's education. Its impact on the enrolment decision is twice as high for maternal literacy (4%) relative to paternal literacy (2%). Because educated parents are more likely to be aware of the benefits of schooling, parental education emerges as a stronger predictor of school attendance. A possible reason for the higher effect of maternal education on enrolment is that it is strongly related to females' school participation (Dreze & Kingdon, 2001).

District	Tehsil	In school*	Out of school*	
		Enrolled	Never attended	Dropped out
Northern Punjab				
Chakwal	Talagang	86.5	4.7	8.9
Central Punjab				
Jhang	Jhang	67.4	16.8	15.8
Nankana Sahib	Sangla Hill	69.4	15.3	15.3
Faisalabad	Jinnah Town	76.6	15.3	8.1
Hafizabad	Hafizabad	73.0	8.4	18.6
Southern Punjab				
Khanewal	Mian Channu	61.7	17.3	21.0
Bahawalpur	B. Sadar	46.9	35.4	17.7
Bahawalpur	Khairpur Tamewali	36.2	53.6	10.1

District	Tehsil	Type of school**			
		Private	Public	Madrassa	Other
Northern Punjab					
Chakwal	Talagang	30.7	68.1	0.0	1.2
Central Punjab					
Jhang	Jhang	26.5	67.5	0.4	5.6
Nankana Sahib	Sangla Hill	26.0	74.0	0.0	0.0
Faisalabad	Jinnah Town	39.8	54.6	1.1	4.6
Hafizabad	Hafizabad	34.7	61.2	0.6	3.5
Southern Punjab					
Khanewal	Mian Channu	15.8	84.2	0.0	0.0
Bahawalpur	B. Sadar	17.0	74.0	0.0	9.0
Bahawalpur	Khairpur Tamewali	14.3	82.1	0.0	3.6

Table VII. Regional patterns of enrolment and out-of-school children (5-18) (%).
Source: PERI School Choice Survey (2011).

There is considerable regional variation in enrolment in Punjab: enrolment is higher in northern Punjab and lower in southern Punjab relative to the central region. Educational indicators are the most encouraging in the northern part of the province as demonstrated by

Table VII; the enrolment rate in Talagang (Chakwal) is the highest (86.5%), while the ratio of out-of-school children is lowest. This implies that approximately one in every 10 children is not in school in Talagang.

The average enrolment rate in the surveyed tehsils in central Punjab is 71.6%, while the situation in the southern part is very different. Compared to the northern and central parts, the region lags behind in socioeconomic indicators. The average enrolment rate for the three surveyed tehsils in southern Punjab is only 48.3%, implying that every second child is out of school. Thus, along a spectrum ranging from lowest to highest, northern Punjab ranks highest, southern Punjab lowest, and central Punjab falls midway between the two in terms of performance in the education sector.

Our multivariate regression framework also reveals that parents in the northern region are 18% more likely to send their child to school relative to central Punjab; in southern Punjab, parents are 12% less likely to enrol their child in school relative to central Punjab. This may be linked to the socioeconomic conditions of these regions, since the northern part is primarily a non-agricultural area where people rely on wage employment as an income source as opposed to the rural areas in the central and southern parts where farm wages are the main source of income. This is in line with the evidence from Cheema and others (2008), who find that northern Punjab performs better in socioeconomic indicators relative to the other regions.

Paid child labour is a deterrent to a child's schooling. An additional hour of child labour carried out for remuneration reduces the probability of that child attending school by 5%. When a child engages in paid labour, the opportunity cost of school participation is the foregone wage income. There is, therefore, less incentive for parents to send their child to school since not only will it mean losing the income from the child's work but also incurring the costs of his/her schooling.

Private versus Public Schooling

Wealth. Private schools are accessible to poor parents. Enrolment rates by wealth quintile show that 9% of all school-going children in the bottom 20% of the population are enrolled in private schools (Table V). This, in part, reflects the rise of low-fee private schools.

Wealthier parents are more likely to send their children to private schools than poor parents. The share of private-school-going children increases with socioeconomic status, the share in the top 20% being four times as great as that in the bottom quintile (Table V). Our regression results substantiate this finding. With each successive quintile, the probability of enrolling in a private relative to a public school increases by 6%.

55

Parents across all socioeconomic groups favour females in the private versus public schooling decision. While parents discriminate against females in the enrolment decision, they are more likely to choose private schooling for their daughters rather than for their sons. This is evident from the fact that a greater percentage of females are enrolled in private schools than males across all wealth quintiles (Table VI).

This differential persists in our regression results even when we control for other factors. It could point to the limited public-schooling options available for girls since the Punjab Program Monitoring and Implementation Unit's 2009 census of public schools in Punjab shows that there are more public schools for boys than for girls in the tehsils that were surveyed under the PERI survey. Thus, private schools may be filling an important void in the market for education. To fully establish this argument, a more detailed profile of government schools by gender and schooling level in the surveyed areas is needed.

Girls from richer households are more likely to go to private schools than girls from poorer households. Gender-disaggregated regressions show that the impact of wealth on school choice varies by gender: females in the second quintile have a 7% higher chance of being enrolled in a private school relative to their counterparts in the bottom 20% of the wealth distribution. Wealthier households tend to have a greater pool of resources, thus making it easier for parents to bear the expenses associated with private education.

The wealth effect on the choice of private schooling is stronger for high-school children compared to primary-school children across all socioeconomic groups. The results show that the wealth effect is three times greater for high-school children (20%) than for primary-school children (6%). This is not surprising given that private high-school education is more expensive than primary or middle-school education. For the sample under consideration, the average monthly tuition fee reported for private high-school children is more than double (PKR 518) that of private primary- school children (PKR 242). Therefore, as wealth, i.e. the pool of available resources, increases, the impact on private education witnessed at the higher tier of schooling is far greater relative to the primary level.

Parents' perceptions of employment opportunities. Parents are more likely to choose private schools if they think employment opportunities that require a high level of education are available for their children. Such jobs might entail working overseas, government employment, school teaching or a profession such as medicine, engineering or banking. All these jobs require a minimum level of education and have strict eligibility criteria. The availability of lucrative employment opportunities would motivate parents to undertake greater investment in their children (the choice of private over public schooling in some ways reflects that willingness) since the availability of such jobs would promise higher future returns on their children's education.

Parents are less likely to choose private schools for their children if they perceive that the prevailing job opportunities do not require specialised education. The prevalence of jobs that parents perceive as requiring a comparatively low level of education –such as running a family business, working on a farm, in a factory or as a labourer – is associated with a 12% less likelihood of their choosing a private school for their child. Investment in a child's education seems to be linked to weighing the costs of education with the expected returns on that education. If the expected future returns are low (as would be the case in most of the jobs in this category), parents will be less willing to bear the costs of private schooling. Additionally, if parents do not think that the quality of education their child will acquire in school is likely to improve the likelihood of his/her availing of the prevalent job opportunities, they may not consider it worthwhile to invest in private education.

Richer parents are more likely to send their children to private schools even when they perceive that the prevailing job opportunities do not require specialised education. At lower levels of the wealth distribution, households that perceive low-education jobs to be prevalent are less likely to choose private schools for their children. The effect is reversed for households at the upper tail of the wealth distribution. Despite the perceived availability of low-education jobs, these households continue to have a greater likelihood of choosing private schools for their children. Thus, the impact of perceived availability of employment opportunities on school choice varies by household socioeconomic status.

Parents perceive different jobs for their sons and daughters. Figure 1 constructed from our data gives an insight into the employment opportunities that parents perceive for their children. It reveals that the nature of employment varies by the sex of the child: 53% of female children are perceived as likely to gain employment as teachers as opposed to only 5% of the male sample. The percentage of male children perceived as likely to work in the government sector is about twice as high as that of females.

Access to schools. Parents show greater preference for private education as the accessibility of private relative to public schools increases in a cluster. The less time it takes to travel to a private school relative to a public school within a cluster, the higher the probability of enrolling in a private school (7%). Of the sample of school-going children under study, 82% reported walking to school. In a rural context where going to school on foot is the predominant means of travel, distance emerges as a significant determinant of school choice.

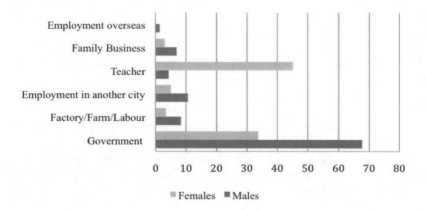

Figure 1. Parents' perception of employment opportunities by gender (percentage of children).

Parents are sensitive to the proximity of private relative to public schools when choosing a school for their daughters. The gender-disaggregated results show that, as the relative distance between private and public schools increases in a cluster, parents are 7.5% less likely to choose a private school for their daughters. Regressions by level of schooling indicate that this effect holds at the primary and middle tiers but not for high-school girls. The impact is, however, stronger for younger females (13% for primary-school-going girls and 8% for middle-school-going girls). Figure 2 shows the modes of transport used by children for going to school. Given that more than 90% of primary- and secondary-school-going females walk to school, it is not surprising that parents consider distance an important determinant of school choice for their daughters.

Parents' choice of private school for their sons is not tied to the proximity of that school relative to a public school in the area. Thus, while distance matters for females, it is insignificant in the case of males. This is evident both from the overall male regression and gender-disaggregated regressions at the primary and middle tiers of schooling. Almost 57% of males at the primary level are reportedly accompanied by their parents, a sibling, friend or relative on their way to school. Thus, even though more than 90% of the male children sampled walk to school, as long as they are accompanied by another person, their parents might not consider distance an important constraint when choosing a school for their sons.

Distance does not influence school choice for either males or females at the high-school level. A much larger percentage of children at this level use some sort of vehicle. Half of all males and one third of all females have access to a motorcycle, school van, rickshaw or public transport. It could be either that high schools are located far away from the main settlement or that parents perceive these modes of transport as safer than walking to school, and do not consider distance a significant determinant of school choice for children at this level. Needless to say, older children are less vulnerable than younger children and parents may be more comfortable sending their older children to schools farther

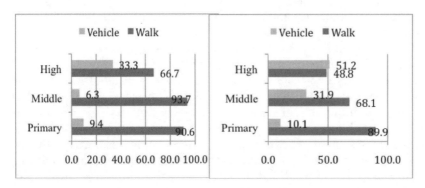

away.

Figure 2. Modes of transport by gender (percentage of children).

Perceived quality of schools. The findings in this section are based on parents' perceptions of school quality rather than on actual measures of quality.

The quality of subjects taught is instrumental in explaining school choice at the middle and high-school level, but not at the primary level. Our results indicate that the subject-teaching quality index is insignificant at the primary level but significant in explaining school choice at higher tiers. In particular, the impact of better teaching at private schools relative to public schools on private-school enrolment is almost twice as strong for high-school children (8%) relative to middle-school children (4%). A possible reason could be that parents, given the greater expenditure they incur at higher levels of schooling, are more concerned about the quality of knowledge their children acquire at school.

The quality of subject teaching matters for males, but not for females. For the male sample, parents with better perceptions of the quality of teaching at private schools (relative to public schools) are 5% more likely to send their sons to private schools. For females, however, this effect is insignificant. This could be because parents perceive that the benefits of educating their children are likely to differ by gender. For example, higher academic quality may be deemed important for sons to

59

enhance their income-earning potential, while for daughters other considerations such as improved marriage prospects may be considered more important.

A study by Halai (2011) on gender awareness in a rural district in Pakistan indicates that both male and female teachers viewed mathematics as a more useful subject for boys than for girls since they felt that mathematical skills would likely be more important for future careers that boys might pursue. For girls, the predominant view was that they would be homemakers and apart from helping in household expenditure calculations, mathematics would be of little value in their future lives.

Teacher quality (measured by a composite index of perceived teaching skills and teacher presence) matters for females but not for males. The quality of a teacher (measured by an aggregated index of the teacher's presence, qualifications and skills) surfaces as an essential factor in explaining school choice for females, but is insignificant for males. The likelihood of parents choosing a private school for females improves by 4% since the perceived difference in teacher quality in private schools relative to public schools increases. Comparing this result to our previous findings on subject teaching quality shows that, while the latter matters for males, teacher quality is important for females. This could be because parents regard the presence of teachers more important for females as a safety concern, whereas for males, better academic quality plays a vital role in improving their job opportunities.

School infrastructure is an important determinant of school choice for high-school children. Parents who perceive the quality of infrastructure at private schools to be better than public schools are 14% more likely to choose a private school for their child. In each individual cluster, the demand for high schooling is low compared to primary and middle schooling, and the need for well-equipped science labs makes it financially more feasible to have larger high schools serving several settlements or clusters. As a result, high schools in rural areas are likely to be, on average, farther away from a particular settlement than the primary or middle schools serving that area.

For parents choosing between private and public high schools, a school's infrastructure signals the overall quality of the school since the infrastructure is easily visible and comparable with that of other schools. Due to the school's distance from the main settlement, parents do not have the chance to interact with their children's teachers frequently or to keep track of their attendance. This may be why the school infrastructure index emerges as a significant determinant of school choice at the high-school level and not at other levels of schooling.

Schooling costs. The expenditure incurred on private education is higher relative to public education. Schooling costs were calculated from expenditure data by adding up the reported primary expenditure on schooling, consisting mainly of admission/registration/examination fees (monthly), school-tuition fees (monthly) and miscellaneous school costs made up of the monthly cost of uniforms/shoes/books, private tuition-centre fees and the cost of transport. We looked at total schooling expenditure across wealth quintiles. The data suggests that there is a significant wedge between per capita expenditure on private and public schools. Parents of a private-school-going child spend far more on their child's schooling than the parents of a public-school-going child (columns 1 & 2 in Table VIII); gender-disaggregated results also support this finding. This shows that some parents in rural Punjab prefer to send their children to private schools despite the relatively high expenditure it incurs relative to public education.

Quintile	(1)	(2)	(3)	(4)	(5)	(6)
	Private schools	Public schools	Private schools		Public schools	
			Boys	Girls	Boys	Girls
1	245	75.6	330	124	71	86
2	289	82.5	284	296	86	79
3	520	105.0	761	381	99	116
4	399	234.0	434	370	238	230
5	592	206.0	756	432	205	208

Table VIII. Total expenditure per capita for public and private schools by quintile and gender (PKR per month). *Source*: PERI School Choice Survey (2011).

School choice for females is elastic to the expenditure incurred on private education relative to public education. For regression results, we used relative expenditure on each child calculated by comparing the cost of his/her private schooling and the average cost of schooling in the alternative public school in the cluster. These results show that the cost of educating a child has a significant impact on the choice of school for females. In particular, a unit increase in expenditure on private schooling relative to public schooling decreases the probability of female enrolment in private schools by 13%. For males, however, this factor is insignificant in explaining school choice. This reveals that the costs of schooling are a key factor when deciding on the type of school for girls, but not for boys.

The impact of relative expenditure on school choice differs by the level of schooling: it is smallest at the primary tier and largest at the highest tier. The effect of expenditure on school choice is twice as large at the highest level (18%) relative to the primary level (9%). A possible reason for this differential impact is that the private-public gap in expenditure increases by the level of schooling, thus having a stronger impact at higher levels.

Findings from the Lens of Social Justice

The 'Enrol versus not Enrol' Decision

The findings from this study reveal disparities along various dimensions such as gender, socioeconomic status and wealth levels. Wealthier parents are more likely to send their children to school compared to parents at the lower end of the wealth ladder. Males are more likely to attend school than females – this bias becomes stronger at low wealth levels. Moreover, there is considerable regional variation in enrolment in Punjab with enrolment rates being higher in northern Punjab but lower in southern Punjab relative to the central region. Theoretical approaches towards social justice show that the conceptualisation of social justice entails concepts like equity and diversity. Hart (2003) defines equity to mean equal opportunity, equal treatment and equal outcome. On the other hand, diversity is concerned with culture and linguistics (Thomas, 1996; Sepheri & Wagner, 2000). Employing these definitions of social justice (equity in particular) one can see that the findings from this study provide insights for identifying the marginalised and disadvantaged groups in Punjab. These entail females, children from poor families and children residing in Southern areas of Punjab, where one in every two children is out of school.

The 'Type of School' Decision

In sum, findings on private-school choice show that private schools are accessible to the poor. However, children from wealthy families are more likely to go to private schools compared to children from poor families. Moreover, the wealth effect is strongest for high-school children compared to primary-school children across all socioeconomic groups. While the accessibility of private schools for the poor reveals that the opportunity of receiving private education is there for the poor, analysing these findings from the lens of social justice reveals that this opportunity is not equal across the rich and the poor: compared to the rich, it is difficult for the poor to afford private education. This inequality of opportunity is likely to perpetuate and reinforce intergenerational differences in income-earning potential across the rich and the poor.

Conclusions

The objective of this study was to explore why Pakistani parents in rural Punjab choose to send their children to low-fee private schools when free public schools are available. Findings reveal five important determinants of private-school choice namely: (1) socioeconomic status; (2) perceived employment opportunities; (3) access; (4) perceived school quality; and (5) costs of schooling.

Private enrolments vary by socioeconomic status, gender and region: wealthier families are more likely to send their children to private schools. Females are more likely to attend private schools compared to males: female private enrolment is seven percentage points higher than male private enrolment. Private enrolments are higher in the northern and central Punjab compared to southern Punjab: private enrolment accounts for about 30% of enrolments in the north and centre, but only 16% in the southern areas of the sample.

These findings have important implications for education policy. In the past, there has been huge emphasis on investing in physical infrastructure facilities within the education sector. While infrastructure matters at the high-school level, our findings suggest that it may not be a very important factor in explaining why children are out of school. This calls for revisiting the debate on whether lagging education indicators in Pakistan are a consequence of supply- or demand-side characteristics.

Our findings also show that a significant number of children from the bottom quintiles of the population are also benefitting from private schools. Given that private schools *are* catering to the rural poor, they can serve as an important tool for reducing inequality in the future. Thus, if the government wants to improve schooling quality and improve participation rates, it should make use of existing private schools. This will require a shift in the government's focus from 'providing' education to 'facilitating' education.

Acknowledgements

This chapter is a modified version of a report titled 'Determinants of School Choice: Evidence from Rural Punjab, Pakistan' that was submitted to the Privatization in Education Research Initiative (PERI) in February 2012.

We gratefully acknowledge the research grant awarded by the Open Society Institute to undertake this study.

We would also like to thank the Lahore School of Economics and the rector, Dr Shahid Amjad Chaudhry, for providing additional funding for the survey. Last but not the least, we are especially grateful to Dr Naved Hamid, for providing guidance and support throughout the course of the research study.

Note

[1] The web address for the original report is as follows:
    http://www.periglobal.org/low-fee schooling/document/document-
    determinants-school-choice-evidence-rural-punjab

References

Alderman, H., Orazem, P.F. & Paterno, E.M. (2001) School Quality, School Cost, and the Public/Private School Choices of Low-Income Households in Pakistan, *Journal of Human Resources*, 36(2), 304-326.

Andrabi, T., Das, J., Khwaja, A.I., Vishwanath, T. & Zajonc, T. (2007) *Learning and Education Achievements in Punjab Schools (LEAPS): insights to inform the education policy debate.* Washington, DC: World Bank.

Annual Status of Education Report (2010) *Annual Status of Education Report (rural): Pakistan (2010).* Lahore: South Asian Forum for Education Development.

Burney, N.A. & Irfan, M. (1995) Determinants of Child School Enrolment: evidence from LDCs using choice-theoretic approach, *International Journal of Social Economics*, 22(1), 24-40.

Cheema, A., Khalid, L. & Patnam, M. (2008) The Geography of Poverty: evidence from the Punjab, *Lahore Journal of Economics,* September, 163-188.

Das, J., Pandey, P. & Zajonc, T. (2006) Learning Levels and Gaps in Pakistan. Policy Research Working Paper No. 4067. Washington, DC: World Bank.

Dreze, J. & Kingdon, G.G. (2001) School Participation in Rural India, *Review of Development Economics*, 5(1), 1-24.

Halai, A. (2011) Equality or Equity: gender awareness issues in secondary schools in Pakistan, *International Journal of Educational Development*, 31(1), 44-49.

Harlech-Jones, B., Baig, M., Sajid, S. & Rahman, S. (2005) Private Schooling in the Northern Areas of Pakistan: a decade of rapid expansion, *International Journal of Educational Development*, 25(5), 557-568.

Hart, L. (2003) Some Directions for Research on Equity and Justice in Mathematics Education, in L. Burton (Ed.) *Which Way Social Justice in Mathematics Education?*, pp. 25-49. London: Praeger.

Iram, N., Hussain, Z., Anwar, S., Hussain, I. & Akram, W. (2008) Determinants of Child School Choice in Punjab: policy implications, *European Journal of Scientific Research*, 23(2), 285-293.

Lloyd, C.B., Mete, C. & Grant, M.J. (2009) The Implications of Changing Educational and Family Circumstances for Children's Grade Progression in Rural Pakistan: 1997-2004, *Economics of Education Review*, 28(1), 152-160.

Lloyd, C.B., Mete, C. & Sathar, Z.A. (2005) The Effect of Gender Differences in Primary School Access, Type, and Quality on the Decision to Enroll in Rural Pakistan, *Economic Development and Cultural Change*, 53(3), 685-710.

Muralidharan, K. (2006) Public–Private Partnerships for Quality Education in India. *Seminar*, 565 (September). http://www.india-seminar.com/2006/565/565_karthik_muralidharan.htm

Muralidharan, K. & Kremer, M. (2008) Public and Private Schools in Rural India, in P. Peterson & R. Chakrabarti (Eds) *School Choice International: exploring public-private partnerships.* Cambridge, MA: MIT Press.

Pakistan Bureau of Statistics (2010) *Pakistan Social and Living Standards Measurement Survey 2008-09.* Islamabad: Pakistan Bureau of Statistics.

Psacharopoulos, G., Arieira, C.R. & Mattson, R. (1997) Private Education in a Poor Country: the case of urban Bolivia, *Economics of Education Review*, 16(4), 395-406.

Sathar, Z.A. & Lloyd, C.B. (1994) Who gets Primary Schooling in Pakistan: inequalities among and within families, *Pakistan Development Review*, 33(2), 103-134.

Sepheri, P. & Wagner, D. (2000) Managing Diversity – Wahrnehmung und Verständnis im Internationalen Management. *Personal – Zeitschrift für Human Resource Management*, 52(9), 456-462.

Siddiqui, S. (2007) *Rethinking Education in Pakistan: perceptions, practices, and possibilities*. Karachi: Paramount Publishing Enterprise.

Srivastava, P. (2007) For Philanthropy or Profit? The Management and Operation of Low-Fee Private Schools, in P. Srivastava & G. Walford (Eds) *Private Schooling in Less Economically Developed Countries: Asian and African perspectives*. Oxford: Symposium Books.

Thomas, R.R. (1996) Redefining Diversity. New York: Amacom.

World Bank (1996) Improving Basic Education in Pakistan. Report No. 14960-PAK. Washington, DC: World Bank. http://www.periglobal.org/low-fee-schooling/document/document-determinants-school-choice-evidence-rural-punjab

CHAPTER 4

Public Desire for Private Schooling in Nepal

PRAMOD BHATTA

Introduction

In April 2013, while I was visiting some public schools in Kailali district of Far Western Nepal, the head teacher of the first school I stepped into stated that student numbers in his school were gradually decreasing, particularly in the primary grades. The reason for this, he quickly pointed out, was the establishment of private schools in the vicinity. When asked what plans he had to check this decline, he replied – 'we are opening a "boarding" section from the current academic year.' In the few hours that I spent at the school, I counted a number of parents who came to admit their ward in the boarding.

Such incidences have become increasingly commonplace in Nepal, reflecting the growing parental desire for schooling in private or boarding [1] institutions. As a result, various types of private schools have sprung up (Bhatta & Budathoki, 2013), accounting for an increasing share of students. According to the administrative data of the Ministry of Education (MoE), enrolments in private schools have nearly doubled at all levels: from 6% to 13% at primary; 7.6% to 15% at lower secondary; and 9.7% to 17% at secondary level between 2005 and 2010 (MoE, 2005, 2010).[2]

Concomitant with this growing participation in private education institutions, however, is the continuing ideological–political debate on education privatisation, particularly from the standpoints of equity and social justice. This debate has its global dimensions (Tooley, 2001; Walford & Srivastava, 2007; Nambissan, 2010; Sarangapani & Winch, 2010; Tooley, 2010), and Nepal remains no exception. At present, one can observe at least three responses to education privatisation in Nepal: a (vociferous) radical leftist view that calls for a blatant nationalisation of

Pramod Bhatta

all private schools; a (not so prominent) rightist view that calls for an unhindered and unregulated proliferation of private schools based on a democratic 'right to choose'; and a more centrist view that advocates for a respectable yet better regulated place for private schools, which is also the approach adopted by successive governments (Bhatta, 2009a; Poudel & Chhetri, 2009). Some political groups have often used violent means to shut down private schools and demanded an end to all forms of privatisation and commercialisation in education (Caddell, 2007; Neupane, 2007). However, they have had relatively little success in curtailing the expansion of private schools, especially in a context where public school's credibility as the provider of quality education is under increasing scrutiny (Mathema, 2007).

As private schools have gradually become part of everyday life for a significant number of people, my aim in this chapter is to examine the private 'educationscape(s)' and their various effects on public-school education. I believe that the debate on whether private schools should exist in Nepal has become obsolete, given that the very political bastions that have vehemently opposed such institutions are themselves participating in private schools, either through sending their children to such institutions or informally investing in them.[3] At the same time, my aim here is not to assess whether or to what extent private schools are providing better-quality education as measured in terms of student learning outcomes, but rather to understand why the faith and confidence of the general public has shifted in favour of the private schools.

The rest of this chapter is structured as follows. I start with a brief discussion of the methodology. I then discuss the major research findings, including the reasons for increased participation in private schools, strategies used by private schools to enhance their enrolments, and the responses of public schools to the challenges posed by private schools, as well as the contrasting nature of parental involvement in private and public schools. I also explore the effects of participation in different types of schools on the everyday relationships of peers. Finally, I draw out some implications for the future of both private and public education institutions in Nepal, particularly in the context of increasing preference for private schooling. In particular, I highlight two aspects: the relative success of private schools in the greater formalisation of schooling and linking this with quality education; and the response of public schools that centre on becoming 'boarding-like' institutions.

Method

This chapter builds on research that was conducted in 2011-12 (Bhatta & Budathoki, 2013). We conducted the research in four peri-urban communities with functioning public schools, but which have also seen the establishment of one or more private schools in the past three to five years. We selected the sites purposively through widespread consultations with various people and organisations, including officials from the Department of Education and District Education Offices. From each site we selected two schools – one private and one public – except in Makawanpur, where we selected two private and one public school. This was because the two private schools in Makawanpur had been established simultaneously in the same locality. Thus, in sum, we selected nine schools from four districts: Baglung (in the central hills); Bardiya (western Tarai); Makawanpur (central Tarai); and Morang (eastern Tarai). The distance between the selected private and public schools ranged from about 20 to 100 metres. Among the selected schools, all public schools operated classes up to secondary level (grade 10, with the schools in Baglung and Bardiya running up to grade 12 or higher-secondary level). However, in the case of private schools, one was operating up to grade 5 (primary), two up to grade 8 (lower secondary), and two up to grade 10 (secondary).

In each school community, we spent on average 20 days collecting data and information using various tools. We collected data on annual student enrolments from the school records/attendance registers for analysing enrolment trends based on social category and gender. Likewise, information on the establishment history of the schools was collected from the school-improvement plans and other documents, as well as through interviews with the founders/owners and head teachers. Moreover, information on the physical infrastructure was collected through a structured questionnaire. We used separate open-ended questionnaires for interviews with parents, teachers, students, school management committee (SMC) and parent-teacher association (PTA) members, as well as owners of private schools. In total we conducted interviews with more than 300 respondents, including: 28 teachers from public and 23 from private schools; 51 students from public and 50 from private schools; 44 parents from public and 39 from private schools; 19 SMC and PTA members from public and 12 from private schools; and 11 private school owners. In addition, we conducted detailed interviews with 14 students who had transferred from public to private school and vice versa, to understand the motives and consequences of the shift from one system to another.

Private Schools as Universal Preference

The desire for private schooling was quite well reflected in the communities we visited. In all four sites, we observed a strong desire among parents to send their children to private schools. For instance, during an interview we asked a daily-wage labourer what his perception of the private school was. He answered:

> I send my children to public school but do not see them
> studying or learning anything at all. If I had money, I would
> send them to private school because there you can see
> children studying.

Another parent who had recently switched his ward from a public to private school said:

> My son studied up to grade four in the public school. But he
> could not even recognize and write fundamental *devanagari*
> letters taught in grade one. So I took him to the boarding
> school where after an entrance examination, teachers admitted
> him in grade one. He is now in grade three and studies well.
> He can read and speak in English. He knows much more than
> in the previous school.

And yet another parent with her son in private and daughter in public school said:

> When I have more money, I will also send my daughter to
> boarding because there is no teaching-learning in public
> school. My son is always studying and doing homework but
> my daughter barely concentrates on studies. (Interview,
> 2068/9/24)

Such opinions were not isolated remarks but commonplace among the parents, students and other education stakeholders we interviewed. And, they were well capitalised by private-school proprietors – many of whom were existing or retired public-school teachers (although most schools had multiple partners) – who stated that it was this demand from parents for a locally available good-quality education that prompted them to establish the boarding school to fill the quality vacuum.

The respondents considered private schools as sites where high-quality education is provided in an orderly and disciplined environment. They regarded private-school teachers as regular, available, caring and inspiring whereas public-school teachers were irregular, apathetic and dishonest towards their duty. Likewise, the respondents regarded private-school students as disciplined, studious and enthusiastic, whereas public-school students were considered undisciplined, vulgar and out of control. Similarly, they considered private-school management efficient and smooth, whereas public-school management was deemed chaotic, disorderly and marred by political interference (Table I).

The desire for private schooling primarily stemmed from the fact that private schools use English as the medium of instruction. During interviews, parents and students gave education in English as the most important motive for their participation in private schooling because 'mastery in English is essential in modern times as it is used globally,' 'children need to learn English in this era of English language,' 'English is needed even to use computer' and 'English education will provide good job as doctor, engineer or pilot and in NGOs.' Even when nearby public school(s) also offered education in English medium, many respondents replied that the quality of teaching in the private school was better, supplementing this conviction with statements such as 'boarding students are required to speak in English at all times in the school premises' and 'boarding students speak English fluently without stammering.'

Component	Private	Public
Teachers	Caring, encouraging, inspiring, supportive, regular, supervise children closely, provide individual care, friendly, available, poorly paid, high turnover, strict	Qualified, experienced, liberal, apathetic, irregular, reluctant, irresponsive, not committed, involved in recrimination if parents complain, involved in politics and strikes, thagne (not sincere to one's duty)
Students	Studious, hard-working, sincere, enthusiastic, well-dressed, neat and tidy, disciplined, do homework regularly, perform well in English and computer studies, inquisitive, busy, happy	Household workers, from poor families, unhappy, neglected, better off in Nepali, play more, out of control, undisciplined, use foul language, smoke and chew tobacco
Parents	Responsive, actively participate, show extra care for children, sometimes complain to school staff, consult about children's education, satisfied	Non-responsive, unwilling or reluctant to participate, little involvement in children's education progress
Homework	Regular assignment and checking of homework, vyaunanasaknegari (overloaded)	Infrequent assignments and checking, little or no homework set or checked
Teaching–learning	Slight progress, quality education, achieve 100% results, practical teaching, more teaching, teachers ask	Regress in teaching–learning, poor-quality teaching, no teaching, only textbook-based, rote

71

	students if they understand or not, more experimental materials, rote learning	learning, no revision, course not completed on time, many free periods due to teacher absenteeism
Discipline and Punishment	Strict rules and regulations, good discipline, tight controls, strict Physical punishment, beating with stick	Ineffectual or no discipline, out of control No punishment, loose control
Language of instruction	English language, students forced to speak in English, English is good	Nepali language, some schools started to instruct in English medium
Extra-curricular activities (ECA)	More and regular ECA, more opportunities to participate in ECA, all students are encouraged to participate, more sport materials	ECA absent or irregular, boys participate more, fewer sport materials, students proactive in conducting ECA
Student enrolment	Conduct door-to-door enrolment campaigns, increasing student enrolment	Enrolment campaigns conducted infrequently, declining enrolment
Parental participation	Regular interactions with parents, parents invited regularly to discuss student progress, invited to participate in ECAs	Participate in SMC and PTA formation, no mechanism for inquiring about children' education, infrequent interactions between teachers and parents, not invited
Administration	Chusta (efficient), strict, smooth operation	lathalinga (chaos/disorder), negligence, high level of political interference, not operating smoothly on a regular basis
Overall infrastructure	Poor but continuously improving, clean and well maintained	Good but not well maintained, dirty

Table I. Differing community perceptions of private and public schools. *Source*: Field interviews, 2011.

Coupled with instruction in English medium was the 'regular', 'disciplined', 'competitive' and 'more' teaching–learning happening within private schools. Parents stated that private schools were strict, which obliged the students to attend the school regularly, do homework promptly, study hard, be disciplined and develop good moral character. Parents often contrasted the private from the public as follows:

> There is no regular teaching in public school. If students are absent, the classes are called off by the teacher. If teachers are absent, students go home early. On the contrary, boarding is tight and there is regular teaching. (Interview, 03/11/2011)

Parents stated that private-school students had more knowledge than those from the public school. As evidence of this, they stated that 'a five grade student of boarding is equivalent to eight or nine grade student of government school,' 'son in class five teaches English to his sister in grade 10,' 'there was visible improvements in learning and behavior after switching to boarding,' and 'boarding has better SLC [4] results.' Parents reasoned that this was so because students in private schools used multiple books but public schools used only one set of textbooks provided by the government.

The majority of students who had shifted from public to private school stated that there were considerable differences between the public-school and private-school environments, and that they have made significant progress after transferring to the private school. A student from Bardiya said: 'Teaching used to be "loose" in the public school. Teachers were not good and did not teach well; students too were not committed' (Interview, 02/03/2012). Likewise, another student from the same school said: 'In the government school, they did not check our homework, monitor students' attendance and regularity, and there were no extra-curricular activities. There would also be no revision of lessons taught' (Interview, 03/03/2012). Similarly, another student said: 'Teaching in the government school was based only on textbooks. We used to do practical by ourselves' (Interview, 02/11/2011). For these students the environment in the private school was quite the opposite, with readily available, caring and attentive teachers, a variety of textbooks, and a choice of many extra-curricular activities.

Parents and students alike gave credit to private-school teachers for their intensive and individualised supervision and care of the students. They stated that teachers regularly checked their work, inquired about their problems, encouraged them to communicate without fear and behaved like a friend, which enhanced their confidence and also enabled them to be more inquisitive. The comparatively much lower student–teacher ratio in private schools (Figure 1) would also point towards the existence of such tailored supervision and care. In contrast, public-school classrooms (particularly in the higher grades) were described as crowded and noisy, with the teacher finding it difficult to control the class, check class work and homework and attend to all students. A student from Makwanpur said:

> My behavior has changed now. I did not study and do my homework when I was in public school. This was because there were many students and no one would care. But now I do my homework every day because the teachers ask for it as soon as I enter the class. (Interview, 08/01/2012)

Despite the frequent teacher turnover in private schools, parents and students lauded the teachers for being concerned not only about their studies but also their health and hygiene, sports and overall personality development. This can be summed up in the following quote from a private-school student in Baglung:

> Teachers have taught us to respect elders and to love and help others. They do not let us become undisciplined. They also teach us to play various games by following the rules. (Interview, 06/08/2011)

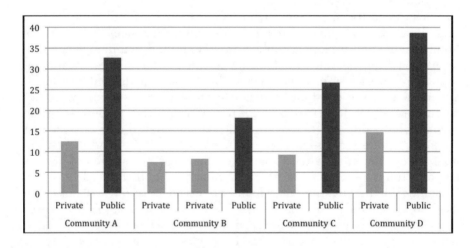

Figure 1. Student–teacher ratios in private and public schools.
Source: Records of various schools, 2011.

Finally, many respondents also stated that private-school students were not only good in studies but also in sports and other extra-curricular activities. This was because private schools have made extra-curricular activities a part of the daily routine of the students, requiring all students to participate in sports, music and dance, quizzes and public debates. According to a public-school parent from Makwanpur: 'Boarding students are good in sports because there are regular extra-curricular activities. But in the public school, such activities are very irregular' (Interview, 2068/09/19). Likewise, a private school student from Baglung stated that his school held 'relay race, dance, volleyball, basketball, quiz, etc on a regular basis, which we find enjoyable and refreshing' (Interview, 01/11/2011).

Strategies Used by Private Schools to Enhance Enrolments

In a national context where more than 95% of the five-to-nine-year-old children are reported to be enrolled in primary education (MoE, 2012), and poverty cited as a major barrier for those children not attending school (CBS, 2011), it is not surprising to note that private schools thrive by attracting students from public schools that provide 'free' education.[5] Private schools have used various strategies to increase their enrolments, especially as they have to compete with the free public school as well as other existing private schools in the vicinity. In particular, we were informed of the proactive roles played by private-school management in disseminating the image of the private school as a centre of academic excellence and overall growth and development of the child. In Baglung, a parent stated that 'boarding schools conduct door-to-door campaigns, often using microphones and loud speakers, urging parents to send children to that particular school and not anywhere else.' Another parent from the same community stated that private-school teachers visit every prospective household and also post pamphlets about the school in public places. He added that he was not aware of the public school conducting such campaigns in the last four to five years. Similarly, a parent from Bardiya reported that private-school owners and teachers also relay significant messages during such campaigns, such as: 'boarding school provides regular teaching and uses English as the medium of instruction;' 'there is high competition in boarding;' and 'children will have a good foundation.' Such enrolment campaigns were also reported in the other school communities where teachers went from door to door to advertise, encouraging parents to send their children to the boarding school. During such campaigns, teachers were reported to emphasise that the private school had good teaching and provided various facilities not available in other schools in the locality.

At the same time, we came across instances of private schools trying to woo the best-performing students from public schools. For the private schools, this was particularly important to demonstrate good results in the board examinations. We found that private-school operators were in constant contact with public-school teachers, students and parents in order to attract brilliant students from the public schools. In this regard, a parent said:

> When my daughter was studying in grade 5 in the government school, the school teachers asked me to send my daughter to boarding school. Boarding teachers had come to the school and talked with the teachers and my daughter. The principal also visited us and told us that the boarding school has good education and suggested that we send her to boarding school. He even said that he would reduce the monthly fee if we admitted her to boarding school. (Interview, 10/03/2012)

In another instance, a parent recalled how private-school proprietors resorted to persuading his wife when he refused to send his daughter to a boarding school. He said:

> Some of the shareholders of the boarding school were our neighbors. They would come to my house while I was away and tell my wife that the boarding school has good quality education and that my daughter would do much better in the boarding school. Soon my wife started telling me that the boarding school has a good education and that many children from the neighborhood are studying there. Finally, I decided to send my daughter to the boarding school. (Interview, 10/03/2012)

Contrary to popular belief that all private schools use English exclusively as the medium of instruction, we found that some schools also resorted to instruction in Nepali medium, particularly in the higher grades, to attract students from nearby public schools. For instance, a school in Baglung started secondary education in Nepali medium as it planned to upgrade to higher secondary level in the near future. We also came across similar phenomenon in Bardiya. However, we were told by the principals that this was a temporary measure that would be reversed once they had enough students graduating from their own schools.

These various strategies used by private schools paid off in the form of increased student enrolments (Figure 2). In terms of gender, boys significantly outnumbered girls across all social groups. And, in terms of social groups, the 'other' category comprised mainly of Brahmins and Chhetris was the largest, followed by the Janajatis. However, as shown in Figure 2, there has been a gradual increase in private-school enrolments from all social groups over the years, indicating that economic status may be the most important determinant of participation (or lack thereof) in private schooling.

Effects on Public-School Enrolments

On the contrary, we recorded a noticeable decline in public-school enrolments as private schools were established in their vicinity (Figure 3). This decline was especially pronounced at the primary level.

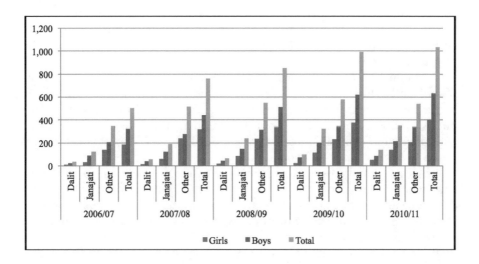

Figure 2. Enrolments in private schools by social groups, 2011.
Source: Records of various schools, 2011.

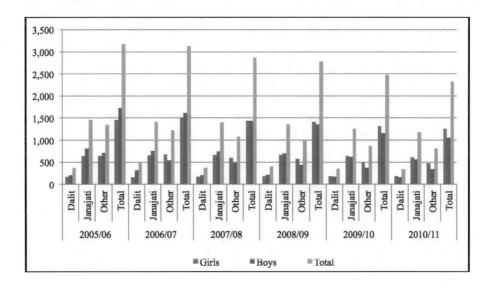

Figure 3. Enrolments in public schools by social groups, 2011.
Source: Records of various schools, 2011.

This was mainly because many parents wanted to send their children to private schools at least in the early grades so as to provide them with a strong foundation even if the children later switched to public schools in higher grades. Another reason cited by the parents for increased early-grade enrolments in private schools was the provision of pre-school facilities starting from the age of two.[6] For many parents, sending children to school at an early age was important for developing the habit of studying well.

Gender was an important determinant of who went to private school and who remained in public school. As can be seen clearly in Figure 3 (and also Figure 2), with a decline in total enrolments in the public schools, both the absolute number and proportion of girls attending such schools outnumbered that of boys.[7] Moreover, this was found to be true across all social groups.

As the newly established private schools have led to declining enrolments in public schools, we noted that public schools have also devised various strategies to retain their students. The most common strategy in all four communities was to become 'boarding-like' by establishing English-medium sections. This meant, in essence, using English as the medium of instruction particularly in the early grades, including adopting textbooks used by private schools, providing computer education from grade 1, and enforcing a dress code for the students that includes specifically coloured shirts, trousers, skirts, shoes, belts and ties. Many parents and teachers reported that such strategy was becoming successful in retaining students. In this regard, the public-school head teacher in Bardiya stated:

> This year, all the head teachers from neighboring public schools had a meeting at our resource centre where we discussed that public schools would not get any students if we did not follow English medium. We then consulted with SMC and parents for approval to which they immediately agreed. We also made tie and belt compulsory as this is a kind of fashion in boarding and it is also attracting students. (Interview, 09/03/2012)

Similarly, an SMC member from Makwanpur noted that 'instruction in English language has pleased all parents' (Interview, 02/01/2012). In this community, many parents stated that public-school teachers have adopted the teaching style of boarding teachers after this switch from Nepali to English medium, which can be summed up in the following quote from a parent:

> There have been visible differences in the public school in the past three years, after the school became boarding. It was very loose before but now students are more disciplined. English has improved. Our children are doing like boarding school students now. (Interview, 31/12/2011)

However, this switch to English medium has also led to the imposition of monthly tuition fees as the schools have to generate resources to pay salaries to the additional teachers or existing teachers opting to instruct in English medium. In addition, students have to pay for additional textbooks, ties and belts. Many teachers who have long been working in public schools admitted having difficulties in using English, largely because they themselves did not come from an English-education background, and acknowledged that they were compelled to switch to English medium to ensure that the public school continues to exist. We also observed other dimensions of becoming boarding-like. The public school in Makwanpur started conducting monthly examinations from 2011, the results of which are instantly shared with the students. Another school in Bardiya constructed a compound wall with gate to ensure that all students remained on the school premises during school hours. All schools also stated that the SMCs and PTAs were becoming more active in monitoring teacher attendance, urging teachers to teach well and focus on improving student learning, interacting with parents and urging them to be more concerned about children's education, as well as liaising with various non-governmental organisations to improve the schools' pedagogical environment and processes. According to an SMC member from Morang:

> Teachers had monopoly before. But now we have become strict about their attendance. For the past one year we have monitored their attendance regularly, and kept record of those who do not come on time. As a result, teachers have corrected themselves and their attendance has improved. Our vigilance has been fruitful so far. (Interview, 10/09/2011)

Parental Participation in Public Schools

The Education Act envisages a primary role for locally elected SMCs in the governance of the public school. The core members of the SMC are elected from among the parents and are entrusted with functions such as school management and development, teacher recruitment, financial management and transparency and accountability in the use of funds. In the research sites, parents stated that they participated in SMC formation, social audits, school-construction activities and mobilisation of resources for the schools. However, we found little evidence of parental engagement in teaching–learning processes. According to a member of the public school's SMC: 'Parents think that their responsibility is to send the children to school and it is the teachers' responsibility to provide good education to the children.'

In all four public schools, teachers complained about parents not coming to school, even when invited. According to the teachers, parents are invited to the school during the formation of the SMC and PTA, social auditing, the annual results day and other annual functions but most of them do not come to these events. Public-school teachers also blamed the parents for having no interest in their children's learning and for failing to provide an enriching environment at home, including providing the children with the required education materials. A teacher from public school in Makwanpur stated that:

> They come on parents' day and results day. They come to pay school fees from time to time. But there are very few parents who come to inquire about their child's learning. (Interview, 03/01/2012)

Parents stated that they had no time to come to school regularly, and even when they came, they did not get proper respect or response from the teachers. According to a public-school parent: 'I don't go to school because I don't know what to say and to whom there.' This view was echoed by a parent from Baglung who lamented that he had not gone to the school because he did not know who to approach and was unable to check the attendance register or question the teachers on their regularity. Many parents felt that public-school teachers did not care about quality education because their children were not studying in public schools. Teacher involvement in party politics was also cited as a reason for their apathy towards the public school. Other parents reported going to the school 'on the day of Saraswoti Pooja [the day for worshipping *Saraswoti*, the goddess of learning] to eat the *prasad* [token food received in lieu of a blessing]', 'to watch dance and cultural programs' and to 'see football games'. Few parents stated that they discussed their children's education informally when they met teachers 'on the way'.

Parental Participation in Private Schools

According to the legal provision, private schools are also expected to form SMC with representation from parents. However, private schools did not expect much input from the parents on matters related to the overall management of the school. The parent members of such committees we interviewed stated that these SMCs 'existed in name only, formed to fulfill the legal requirements' and it was the principal who decided all matters related to the functioning of the school. On the contrary, private-school parents were expected to be more actively involved in their children's educational progress. Private schools invited parents more often to discuss their children's progress; this usually happened at least four times a year at the time of quarterly, half-yearly and annual examination results. Private schools expected all parents to show up for these meetings and discuss their children's progress with the concerned teacher(s) in person. In this regard, a private-school parent from Morang said:

> The school invites parents for a meeting at least once a month
> to discuss about teaching-learning processes in the school. If
> students do not have regular attendance, the school sends a
> letter to the concerned parents asking them to come to the
> school for a talk. (Interview, 08/09/2011)

Likewise, according to a private-school teacher in Makwanpur: 'Parents have good participation. They inquire about their child with the principal; then the subject teacher, principal and parent sit together to discuss about the child's progress' (Interview, 30/12/2011). Another teacher from the same school added:

> Parents regularly come to ask us about their child's studies.
> We discuss how to deal with children who are weak in
> studies. We also interact with parents who are concerned
> about their children not studying at home and provide them
> with suggestions on what to do. (Interview, 07/01/2012)

In addition, parents were also invited to attend various functions organised by the school, such as the annual day, sports day, cultural and other extra-curricular functions. It was stated that almost all parents participated in such functions mainly to 'watch their children's performance'. In several cases of poor performance, the private school sent letters to individual parents to discuss the child's studies. Parents are also called if a child remains absent from the school. Further, because the private schools have strict codes of dress and personal hygiene, parents are also called if children are untidy, come in dirty clothes or improper uniform, or if they have not trimmed their nails or cut their hair.

Moreover, it is interesting to note is that there is a change in the level of involvement of parents as they transfer their children from public to private school. According to a student who had recently moved from public to private school: 'The attitude of my parents changed when I moved from the government to boarding school. Before, they did not care about how I was doing in my studies, but now they frequently tell me to study well and work hard' (Interview, 31/08/2011). Similarly, another student said:

> Parents did not care about my studies when I was in the
> government school and I also did not obey. But as I started
> studying here [boarding school], they have started to show
> care and have bought educational materials. My parents did
> not know about how I was doing in my studies while in the
> government school but now they show more concern and are
> regularly inquiring about my progress. They have even started
> sending me to coaching [tutoring] classes. (Interview,
> 30/11/2011)

According to the parents, their increased involvement with their children's education in private schools is only natural because of the avenues the private schools have created for interactions with parents. A mother who has a son in private school and a daughter in public school said: 'No one from the school has so far inquired with me regarding my daughter's education. However, the boarding regularly invites me to discuss my son's education' (Interview, 31/11/2011). She added that the private school calls parents if children do not do their homework, but in the government school, teachers do not check homework and do not care even if the students do not bring their books and copies.

The Pauperisation of Public Schools

It is often argued that the growing participation in private schooling, especially from the higher income groups, is gradually leading to an institutionalisation of class inequalities in Nepali society (e.g. Khadka, 1998; Sharma, 2012). Data from the three consecutive Nepal Living Standards Surveys (1995/96, 2003/04 and 2010/11) also suggests that both the number of children attending private schools and the gap in participation in private schools by income and consumption quintiles is increasing.[8] Coupled with this is the argument that such a dual education system (consisting of private schools for the rich and public schools for the poor) is leading to a gradual pauperisation [9] of public schools (Bhatta, 2009b).

In the research sites, we did not carry out a socioeconomic profiling of the students in private and public schools to ascertain the type of schools attended by socioeconomic status. However, we were interested in understanding the local perceptions regarding the enrolment of different socioeconomic strata in private and public schooling. The responses we received suggested the strong presence of opinion that public schools are for the poor and the private are for those who can afford them. An SMC member of a public school observed:

> People who work in the factory and farms send their children to this school. Those who have more than five *bigha* of land do not send their children to this school. Only the poor send children to this school. (Interview, 09/09/2011)

Such views were also echoed by both public-school and private-school teachers. According to a public-school teacher in Bardiya:

> There are very few students from upper and middle classes in public schools. Middle-class families send children to boarding school when they have money and they send children to public school when they do not have money. However, the poor always remain in the public school. (Interview, 03/03/2012)

Another public-school teacher stated:

> Most of the students are from lower-class families who depend
> on daily wage labor. But the children of better-off families go
> to boarding school. The number of poor students has increased
> in this school because they do not have to pay fees and cannot
> go elsewhere either. (Interview, 06/09/2011)

Private-school teachers also agreed with the views of their public-school
counterparts. According to a private-school teacher:

> The students from middle-class families who can pay fees
> attend private school. The rich families send children to other
> better private schools though some of them also enroll here.
> Children from the poorest category do not attend this school.
> (Interview, 05/09/2011)

We also noted that even in these peri-urban communities, households
belonging to different economic strata were sending their children to
different types of private schools. For example, the comparatively richer
were found to be sending their children to 'better' private schools in
bigger cities – i.e. to Pokhara (in the case of Baglung), Hetauda (in the
case of Makwanpur), Biratnagar (in the case of Morang) and Nepalgunj
(in the case of Bardiya), while those who could afford less sent their
children to the local private schools. As expressed by a public-school
SMC member from Morang: 'The children of the rich go to Biratnagar
because teaching is good there and parents are also more concerned
about their children's progress as they pay more fees' (Interview,
06/09/2011). In many cases, this was also facilitated by the provision of
pick-up and drop-off facilities provided by the private schools.

Everyday Relationships between Private- and Public-School Students

Together with worries about the institutionalisation of class inequalities
through education institutions, there are also concerns that the
participation of different income groups in different types of educational
institutions will lead to decreasing everyday interactions among the
children from different socioeconomic strata and will further polarise
society. In this research, we were thus interested in finding out the
effects of participation in different types of schooling on the everyday
interactions of the children who are otherwise neighbours and peers. In
particular, we explored the changes in extant relationships between
friends/peers when one or more members switched schools while others
remained in the same school.[10]

Interestingly, the students we interviewed did not report any
significant changes in their everyday relationships brought about by

changes in the type of school attended. Even if attending private and public schools, children reported doing household chores, playing, doing homework and studying together after school. It was generally reported that students from private schools would help their friends in public schools with English and Science whereas students from public schools would help their friends in private schools with Nepali. Children also reported attending after-school paid tutorial classes and the annual functions of both private and public schools together. Nonetheless, we did encounter subtle changes in these relationships. For instance, students from public schools stated that their friends in private schools were 'overloaded' with homework and had less time to play together on weekdays. They also stated that private-school parents did not want their children to play a lot and were constantly asking them to study. On a more personal level, some students from public schools expressed that they wished they could also go to a private school like their friends who had transferred, and lamented at their being unable to do so due to economic hardships.

We believe that this general lack of change in relationships is partly so because of the predominantly rural or peri-urban setting in which we carried out this research, in which the everyday lives of the people still revolve around subsistence farming. The scenario might have been different had we conducted this research in a more urban locale.

Conclusion

In this chapter, I have highlighted the growing parental desire to send their children to fee-paying private schools in spite of the state rhetoric of free and universal public education built around the global education-for-all movement. Such widespread preference for private schooling is premised on the perception that private schools are inherently better than public and can enhance the life chances of those who participate in them. Private schools have been successful in consolidating their credibility through a greater formalisation of the curricula and co-curricula that are delivered in an orderly, efficient and strict environment, through which their claim of better teaching and all-round development of the child can be easily discerned by the parents. This superiority of the private over public is further aided as public schools also emulate them and become 'boarding-like'. Such parental preference for securing better education and comparative advantages for their children, together with the response from public schools to become like private schools, is likely to exert additional pressures on private schools to be more competitive and innovative, thereby leading to a further differentiation of the existing private educationscapes.

I also seek to challenge the prevalent notion that public-school parents participate less because of their ignorance, lack of awareness, or lack of desire to do so. Evidence shows that the indifferent parents of the public school become more involved in their children's education when they switch from public to private schools. While this renewed interest may stem in part from the fact that parents have 'invested' in their children's education, it nonetheless indicates the possibility of formalising parent–teacher/parent–school interactions in public schools more around the educational performance of children, rather than merely in the 'management' of the school.[11]

Notes

[1] Private schools are variously known in Nepal. The government nomenclature uses the term 'institutional school' for all types of private schools, and 'community school' for all types of public schools. The term 'boarding' is commonly used to denote private schools. However, such boarding schools are not necessarily places with boarding facilities, although some may have limited hostel facilities to accommodate parental demand. In this chapter, I have used 'private' and 'public' schools throughout, except when referring specifically to the government nomenclature. I have also used 'private' and 'boarding' interchangeably to reflect colloquial usage.

[2] It should be noted that these figures are self-reported by the private schools to the MoE. Not all private schools report their data. Moreover, there are a number of private schools that are not registered, and some further operate classes beyond the official permit. As a result, actual enrolments in private schools are likely to be much higher.

[3] In early May 2011, various national daily newspapers covered stories of warnings issued by All Nepal National Free Student Union (Revolutionary) and All Nepal Teachers' Organization to the leaders of their mother party (the United Communist Party of Nepal-Maoist) asking the Maoist leaders to withdraw both their investment and children from private schools.

[4] SLC refers to the annual School Leaving Certificate examinations conducted at the end of grade 10. A school's performance in the SLC is widely seen as an important indicator of the quality of education provided therein. In these examinations, private schools have consistently out-performed their public counterparts, both in terms of the average pass rates and the average marks achieved in individual subjects (Bhatta, 2004). In our research too, the only private school that had appeared in SLC (in Bardiya) had a 100% SLC pass rate compared to only 25% in the nearby public school.

[5] The Interim Constitution of Nepal, 2007 has mandated the government to provide free education up to secondary level. Under free education, all public-school students up to grade 8 are provided with free textbooks, and schools are not allowed to charge any kinds of annual and monthly tuition fees. However, it is not uncommon for public schools to impose

various fees mainly to generate resources for additional teachers hired by the school.

[6] It should be noted that the provision of pre-school education is not available in all public schools (where it is also known as early-childhood education and development or ECED), and even where available is of a one-year duration, requiring students to be admitted at the age of four.

[7] This finding is consistent with the national data, which shows that girls constitute less than 45% of total enrolments in private schools compared to 50% or more in public schools (MoE, 2012).

[8] According to the Nepal Living Standards Survey data, participation in private school/college has increased from 7.5% (1995/96) to 16.7% (2003/04) to 26.8% (2010/11). Similarly, 60.1% from the richest-consumption quintile attended private school/college compared to only 6.4 from the poorest quintile. Moreover, of those currently in school/college, 56.1% in urban areas attend private schools/colleges as compared to 19.6% in rural areas (CBS, 2011).

[9] I use the term pauperisation not in the sense that public schools are actually getting poorer but rather that they are becoming places where the poor are being concentrated as the rich flock to private schools.

[10] For this purpose, in our interviews with students of both public and private schools, we asked them about their relationships with each other, the type of activities they participated in in groups, and any changes they have felt in their relationships due to participation in different types of schools.

[11] This observation is consistent with a previous study that states: 'Whilst a lack of educational consciousness among parents must be viewed as being partially responsible for parental indifference towards their children's progress, schools' neglect to keep parents informed about their children appeared to be a significant cause of poor relations between the school and the parents' (Bista & Carney, 2004).

References

Bhatta, S.D. (2004) Disparities in School Performance in the SLC Exams: an exploratory analysis, *Studies in Nepali History and Society,* 9(2), 293-343.

Bhatta, P. (2009a) Federalism and Private Schooling: issues and implications for Nepal. Paper presented at the National Symposium on Federalism and Education, organised by the Federalism and Education Support Group and facilitated by UNESCO, Kathmandu Office, 18 November.

Bhatta, P. (2009b) Improving Schools through Decentralization: observations from Nepal's primary education, in P. Bhatta (Ed.) *Education in Nepal: problems, reforms and social change,* pp. 151-186. Kathmandu: Martin Chautari.

Bhatta, P. & Budathoki, S.B. (2013) *Understanding Private Educationscape(s) in Nepal.* Sponsored Research Report for the Open Society Institute/Soros Foundation Education Support Programme. London: OSF.

Bista, M. & Carney, S. (2004) *Reforming the Ministry to Improve Education: an institutional analysis of the Ministry of Education and Sports (MOES) of Nepal.* Paris: UNESCO, IIEP.

Caddell, M. (2007) Private Schools and Political Conflict in Nepal, in P. Srivastava & G. Walford (Eds) *Private Schooling in Less Economically Developed Countries: Asian and African Perspectives*, pp. 187-207. Oxford: Symposium Books.

CBS (Central Bureau of Statistics) (2011) *Nepal Living Standards Survey 2010/11: statistical report volume 1.* Kathmandu: CBS Secretariat, National Planning Commission.

Khadka, R. (1998) *Bargiya ShikshakoUdaya* [Rise of class education]. Kathmandu: Education Network and ActionAid Nepal.

Mathema, K.B. (2007) Crisis in Education and Future Challenges for Nepal, *European Bulletin of Himalayan Research,* 31, 46-66.

MoE (Ministry of Education) (2005) *Flash Report I 2005-2006.* Kathmandu: MoE, Department of Education.

MoE (2010) *Flash Report I 2010-2011.* Kathmandu: MoE, Department of Education.

MoE (2012) *Flash Report I 2012-2013.* Kathmandu: MoE, Department of Education.

Nambissan, G.B. (2010) The Indian Middle Class and Educational Advantage: family strategies and practices, in M.W. Apple, S.J. Ball & L.A. Gandin (Eds) *The Routledge International Handbook of the Sociology of Education,* pp. 285-295. Oxford: Routledge.

Neupane, L. (2007) *Shiksha ra Rajniti* [Education and politics]. Kathmandu: Vision Publication.

Poudel, S. & Chhetri, A. (2009) Niji vidhyalaya ra rajnitik dal [Private schools and political parties], in J. Subedi (Ed.) *Kasima Niji Vidhyalaya* [Private schools under scrutiny], pp. 197-222. Kathmandu: Education Journalists Group and ActionAid Nepal.

Sarangapani, P.M. & Winch, C. (2010) Tooley, Dixon and Gomathi on Private Education in Hyderabad: a reply, *Oxford Review of Education,* 36(4), 499-515.

Sharma, R. (2012) Shikshama bargiya bivedh [Class discrimination in education], *Mulyankan,* July–Aug., 26-29.

Tooley, J. (2001) *The Global Education Industry.* Washington, DC: Institute of Economic Affairs.

Tooley, J. (2010) *The Beautiful Tree: a personal journey into how the world's poorest people are educating themselves.* New Delhi: Penguin.

Walford, G. & Srivastava, P. (2007). Examining Private Schooling in Less Economically Developed Countries: key issues and new evidence, in P. Srivastava & G. Walford (Eds) *Private Schooling in Less Economically Developed Countries: Asian and African Perspectives*, pp. 7-14. Oxford: Symposium Books.

CHAPTER 5

Primary Education in Rural Bangladesh: degrees of access, choice and participation of the poorest

CHRISTINE SOMMERS

Introduction

Since 1990, Bangladesh's primary education priorities have centred on expanding enrolment to achieve the Education for All (EFA) targets and Millennium Development Goals (MDGs), as well as upholding legislation mandating free primary education for all children aged 6 to 10. To date, Bangladesh has reached over 90% net enrolment for primary-school-age children and its schools have achieved gender parity. However, these impressive achievements have not been paired with a corresponding increase in education quality and barely half of children complete the primary cycle.

Bangladesh's primary education providers include those funded by the government to various degrees; private, fee-charging schools; non-formal schools; and religious schools for Islamic education. Within this diverse system of multiple providers and funding sources the government provides little regulation of non-state institutions. The government's hands-off approach leads to a system that offers 'different qualities of education, regardless of equity consequences' (Ahmed et al, 2007, p. 72).

This article aims to articulate elements of quality and access at each of these providers to better understand how social justice is affected in one poor sub-district. Social justice here is defined as 'parity of participation' and the idea that social structures allow all individuals to participate in decision-making on equal footing (Fraser, 2008). Melanie Walker (2006, p. 164) stresses that 'education is a matter of social justice, and that schooling is a site for state intervention and public policy', and that 'individual freedoms ... depend on social and economic arrangements.' Walker is also careful to point out that schooling can reproduce existing inequalities, echoing Amartya Sen's (2009) argument that economic, cultural and political hurdles prevent the full participation of disadvantaged groups.

This research examines schooling at the micro level, using an in-depth qualitative study to paint a more detailed picture of the primary education landscape in one poor rural community. The study was guided by the following research questions:

1. What is the relationship between the government and private actors in providing primary education in Bangladesh, and how does this shape and define education options and opportunities for poor and marginalised communities?
2. How is quality best defined in the Bangladeshi primary-education system? Are traditional measures suitable, or are new/additional measures needed to best assess these institutions?
3. What factors limit or support access to these different schooling options in a poor rural community?

Methodology

The study used a mixed-methods approach, blending ethnography with quantitative and qualitative data from participant observation and interviews with head teachers, the sub-district education office, and non-governmental organisation (NGO) education officials. An in-depth look at different kinds of schools through observation and interviews with teachers, paired with focus groups with parents and long-term community observation, reveals insights into school qualities and the structural and social barriers to children's access and participation at school.

My research site, Dimla sub-district (one sub-district in Nilphamari district) was chosen because of its remote location and high incidence of poverty, along with the logistical support available. Nilphamari is among a handful of districts with the country's highest incidence of poverty at 52% in 2005, compared to a nation-wide average of 40% (Bangladesh Government, General Economics Division Planning Commission, 2008).

In total, I completed an observation schedule and conducted semi-structured interviews with headmasters at 26 schools, interviewed local education experts from the government and NGOs, held focus groups with parents, and engaged in participant observation at two schools by teaching daily for a month. I worked primarily in Bengali with a local translator/research assistant.

Bangladesh Primary-Education School Types

This research focused on four general school groups in Dimla sub-district; these are described in greater detail below:

I. Secular government-funded schools

   1.   Government schools
   2.   Registered non-government primary schools (RNGPS)
   3.   Community schools

II. Non-formal schools

   4.   BRAC (formerly the Bangladesh Rural Advancement Committee) or other NGO schools

III. Fee-charging schools

   5.   Private schools

IV. Madrassas (education with a focus on teachings on Islam and the Qur'an)

   6.   *Aliya* madrassas (or *Ebtedayee* madrassas at the primary level)
   7.   *Quomi* madrassas

Kind of school	Total number	Number in sample
Government	72	4
Registered non-government primary schools (RNGPS)	99	3
Community	3	2
Government affiliated but unregistered	9	0*
Temporary registered	1	0
Ebtedayee Madrassa	26	3
Quomi Madrassa	Unknown	1
Non-formal	25	6
Private	17	7

Note: *'Government affiliated but unregistered schools' and schools with temporary registration from the government represent a small fraction of the total schools and were not included in the sample due to logistical constraints.

Table I. Total numbers of each kind of school in Dimla.
Source: Interview with the Sub-district Education Officer on 31 July 2011.

Table I shows the total number of each kind of school in Dimla, as well as the number of schools that were included in the sample. While it was not possible to get sub-district-wide numbers of students at each kind of school, Nath and Chowdhury (2009) indicated that 57% of rural primary students attend government schools, 20% at registered non-government primary schools (RNGPS), 1% at community schools, 10% at non-formal schools, 3% at private schools and 8% at *Aliya* madrassas.[1] In the region of study, fewer than 50% of students attend government schools, amplifying the necessity of exploring the implications of such a multifaceted system. Interestingly, many parents said that they sent their children to different kinds of schools: children in one family may attend a madrassa, a non-formal school, a private school and a government school.

Secular Government-Funded Schools

Secular government-funded schools are defined as those which are non-religious, registered with, and administered through the government. These schools use the national curriculum and receive funds for operating costs and teacher salaries from the government. In Dimla this includes those schools that are referred to as 'government schools' and also registered non-government primary schools (RNGPS), and community schools. The latter two actually form second and third tiers of government primary schooling. All children fall within the catchment area of one government-funded school, whether a government, RNGPS, or community school.

Nationally, the number of government schools barely increased between 1990 and 2008, from 37,655 in 1990 to 37,672 in 2005 (Ahmed et al, 2007). The number of registered and non-registered primary schools, however, increased more than fivefold in the same period, from 8262 in 1990 to 43,762 in 2007 (Nath & Chowdhury, 2009). RNGPS and community schools have driven the increases in primary enrolments for the last two decades during the Bangladeshi government's push to achieve education for all.

These three kinds of government-funded schools fall under the oversight of the sub-district education officer, whose supervision includes monthly visits and meetings. In addition to exams three times a year for all students, all Class 5 students must sit for the government-administered terminal exam in order to pass to lower secondary school. In Dimla, none of these three kinds of schools receives any funding from non-government sources. These schools distribute free books to students and do not charge fees for tuition, though students may be required to pay exam fees (12 Tk/$US 0.16 three times/year) or other small fees throughout the year, in addition to purchasing school supplies (such as notebooks, pens and uniforms).

The Primary Education Stipend Programme (PESP), a government-funded initiative which started in 2002, nationally provides a stipend of Tk. 100/month (US$1.33) to 40% of primary-school-age children coming from poor rural households attending government-funded schools (Ahmed et al, 2007). In theory, students must meet minimum standards of 85% attendance and achieve 33% marks on term examinations in order to qualify. Because of the high level of poverty in Dimla, 90% of students at government-funded schools meeting the attendance and marks criteria are eligible. Eligible families with two children receive a maximum of Tk. 125/month, while families with three children in primary school receive no additional stipend.

Teachers at government schools are hired as civil servants at the district level with full civil-servant benefits, including full medical and housing allowances and pensions, whereas teachers at RNGPS or community schools are hired at the sub-district level and receive much lower pay and benefits. All teachers at government-funded schools are eligible to attend a one-year, full-time, residential teaching-training course at a district-level Primary Training Institute (PTI). Teachers undertake basic in-service and subject-based training developed at the national level.

Government-funded schools are also eligible for significant additional financing for infrastructure, administrative costs and teaching materials, much of which was funded through the Second Primary Education Development Project (PEDP II), Bangladesh's multi-donor-funded education-improvement initiative from 2004 to 2011. Government-funded schools' infrastructure fits a national standard model, constructed using solid materials (such as bricks and concrete) with at least one and sometimes two classrooms per grade with bench seating behind long desks with wells for drinking water on-site.

Non-formal/BRAC Schools

Nath and Chowdhury (2009) report that non-formal schools accounted for 9.6% of total primary enrolments in 2008. These schools are managed and funded by NGOs and/or international donors and do not receive government support. Across Bangladesh, BRAC runs more than 24,000 one-room, single-grade, single-teacher, non-formal primary schools serving 750,000 students (BRAC, 2011).

BRAC targets poor students who have dropped out of government-funded schools, ethnic minorities, students in rural areas, and students who are vulnerable, marginalised or excluded due to special needs or other reasons. Students are not charged any tuition or fees and most of their learning materials are provided by BRAC. Sixty-five per cent of BRAC's primary students are girls (Nath, 2005). BRAC works with local communities to plan the school hours and annual calendar, aiming to be flexible and responsive to communities' needs. Students complete the primary cycle in just four years, compared to five years in mainstream schools.

BRAC teachers are mostly locally hired women who have a minimum of 10 years of schooling. Pre-service training consists of an initial two-week course, and teachers subsequently meet monthly for one-day, experience-based refresher training sessions. Supervisory staff from the branch and regional BRAC offices visit each school monthly, and each school has a parent–teacher committee that helps monitor schools' daily activities.

While other organisations run non-formal schools in Bangladesh, BRAC is the only organisation funding non-formal schools in Dimla. Each school has a single class limited to 33 students and one teacher. Students sit on the floor around the perimeter of the classroom with their materials placed in front of them. Classrooms are colourfully decorated with printed learning materials and the students' own work, and BRAC staff talk persistently of creating a 'joyful learning environment', both in terms of the physical space and the learning methods.

The BRAC Education Programme (BEP) describes its teaching methodologies as 'learner-centred', 'interactive', 'gender-sensitive', 'pro-poor' and 'child-friendly'. BRAC has created its own books for use in the first two classes, and the National Curriculum and Textbook Board (NCTB) curriculum and books are used after that with supplemental BRAC learning materials. BRAC students sit for the government terminal exam at the end of Class 5, achieving a higher pass rate than the national average. Over 90% of BRAC school graduates enrol in formal secondary school (Nath, 2005).

Private Tuition-Charging Schools

Private schools throughout Bangladesh are mostly unregulated by the government. While private schools in urban areas are often English-medium, all the private schools in Dimla are Bangla-medium and charge low fees. In Dimla, all private schools offer classes 1 to 5, as well as pre-primary classes for younger students. Monthly tuition fees range from Tk. 80-150/month (US$1.06 to US$2), with supplementary books, fees for registration, examinations and other various charges.

All headmasters in the private schools stated that their schools operated completely independently of the government; however, as of 2010 private schools are required to teach the national curriculum. All sample schools said that they complied with this rule, despite no apparent follow-up. Private schools submit enrolment lists to the sub-district education office in order to receive the requisite number of government textbooks for free, but this tends to be the extent of their official involvement with the government.

Private schools had school-managing committees (SMC), though the SMC's responsibilities varied on a school-by-school basis. In several sample schools, the founders, head teachers or members of the SMC were current teachers or retirees from the government school system.

Infrastructure among private schools varied greatly, though most were rudimentary, with bamboo or straw walls and classroom partitions and roofs made from tin sheeting. Others were operating in unfinished brick-and-concrete buildings. Blackboards were often small and shabby, and students sat at a combination of chairs and benches at various schools.

Madrassas

There are two kinds of madrassas: *Aliya*, in which the primary-school section is called *Ebtedayee* and which are reformed/registered; and *Quomi*, which are unreformed/unregistered. These differ from secular schools in their focus on Islamic education, but are quite different from each other in degree of integration with and oversight from the government and the national education system.

The National Education Policy 2009 provides a plan for *Aliya* madrassa reform; *Aliya* teachers' salaries are paid at least in part by the government, and they have used NCTB books for secular subjects since 2012. Unlike government-funded secular schools, however, *Aliya* madrassa students are not eligible to receive the monthly government stipend. There is no government support for the training of madrassa teachers. Asadullah and Chaudhury (2008, p. 225) state that reformed madrassas 'contribute significantly to the government's efforts to expand female education, because they serve the poor, are inexpensive, and operate in rural and isolated areas that offer few other educational opportunities'; however, Asadullah and others (2006) find that graduates of *Ebtedayee* have significantly lower test scores in secondary school than their peers who attended secular institutions.

The *Quomi* institutions are entirely outside of mainstream education and reform efforts. *Quomi* madrassas do not operate under the auspices of the Bangladeshi government at all; they are often funded through private or community donations, and they do not follow the national curriculum. Most *quomi* students are male and most institutions are single-sex and residential; students are split into different streams focusing either on *Qur'an* memorisation or other basic subjects with a heavy focus on Islamic education.

School Comparisons

Table II is a tool for making comparisons among different schools.

Analysis

Defining Quality and Access

The rapid expansion of primary schooling succeeded in increasing access and enrolling large numbers of students in the past two-plus decades. However, average drop-out and repetition rates in the primary grades skyrocketed from 5.6% and 8% in 1998 to 11.5% and 10.9% in 2008, respectively (Nath & Chowdhury, 2009). Official statistics indicate that only 50.1% of students enrolled in class 1 ever complete the full cycle of primary education. These figures show that many children face serious problems attending school and learning over the course of the primary cycle. Pairing an examination of school quality with an assessment of access specifying which children go to which kinds of schools helps to understand what is actually occurring in classrooms and why students' experiences may differ both between and within schools, shedding light on what capabilities students cultivate at school.

	Government	RNGPS	Community	Non-formal / BRAC	Private	Ebtedayee Madrassa	Quomi Madrassa
Full government salaries	■						
Partial government salaries		■	■			■	
Full government benefits	■						
Reduced government benefits (Tk. 449 – 775/mo)		■				■	
Teachers paid an average of <1500 taka				■	■		
Gov't-provided contingency fee of ~Tk. 500/mo	■						
Gov't-provided contingency fee of ~Tk. 200/mo		■					
Gov't-provided contingency fee of ~Tk. 30/mo			■				
School charges monthly tuition fees					■		
School charges tri-annual exam fees	■	■	■	■	■	■	
Students required to buy uniforms*	■				■		
Teachers trained at Primary Training Institute	■	■	■				
Teachers receive subject-based training	■	■	■				
Teachers receive systematic training from NGOs				■			
Use NCTB books and curriculum	■	■	■	■	■	■**	
Use supplemental books and materials				■	■		
Class 5 students take government terminal exam	■	■	■	■	■		
Class 5 students take terminal exam						■	

designed by Madrassa Education Board								
Mostly (more than 90%) female teachers				■				
Mostly (more than 90%) male teachers							■	■
Students eligible for Tk. 100/month stipend	■	■	■					
Majority of students are residential/live at school								■
Periodic monitoring visits from sub-district Education Office	■	■	■					
Habitually offer pre-primary for students <6 years	■	■			■			
Received PEDP II infrastructure improvements	■	■						

Notes: *This is based on whether or not students were actually wearing uniforms during the school visits, not the schools' official uniform policy; **Starting in 2012.

Table II. Comparative matrix of school types. *Source*: Personal research, including interviews with head teachers and education officials.

At the outset of my research, I envisioned using standard input and outcome metrics to define quality; these include a combination of student achievement, teacher qualifications and years of experience, as well as infrastructural quality (Pigozzi, 2006 and others). However, I found these metrics either to be impossible to obtain or lacking in significance in terms of the individual children's experiences at school; quality varied among different kinds of schools and from one child to the next in the same school. Test scores, for instance, were not always available and were often illegible paper records; I questioned their validity and relevance as an indicator due to widespread reports of cheating. Teacher qualifications and years of experience seemed to give an incomplete picture of teachers' attendance, motivation and behaviours at school. The achievements of both non-formal and private schools without traditional infrastructure (desks and benches, gender-specific toilets, open space and so on) indicated that conventional infrastructure measures are also less relevant as a measure of learning.

As such, I adapted a new set of quality measures relevant to this particular context. I considered the literature on quality, available data, relevance to the context and quality as it was defined by the local community (in interviews and focus groups). The revised view of a quality education in this context, thus, is four-fold, including: (1) students who are physically and mentally ready for school; (2) motivated teachers who attend school and their classrooms; (3) effective teaching methods and materials; and (4) perceptions of a particular's school quality by education stakeholders, including teachers, parents and education officials. While this list lacks precise quantitative metrics for assigning values to these four points, a wealth of qualitative data allows for making informed observations regarding school quality. A simple matrix of these qualities is expanded in Table III.

Access shapes children's participation and capability development within the education system. While access is often defined by gross and net enrolment figures and completion rates, Lewin (2007) put forth a conceptual framework that adds depth to an understanding of access by characterising exclusion from primary education according to four zones: children who (1) never attend primary school; (2) drop out before completing primary school; (3) are enrolled but who do not regularly attend and who are not engaged in learning (silent exclusion); and (4) do not make the transition to secondary school after completing the primary cycle. This is useful when examining the factors affecting quality and access below, as they facilitate an understanding of students' degrees of participation at school. Poverty and exclusion from education have been strongly correlated, and Hossain and Zeitlyn (2010) offer an extensive discourse on access and equity in Bangladesh for those interested in further exploring this topic.

Quality in Context

The matrix in Table III offers an overview of how the four quality metrics described earlier manifest in each schooling option.

	(1) Student readiness	(2) Teacher behaviour	(3) Teaching methods	(4) School perceptions
Government schools	Long hours for class 3-5 students problematic without food at schools.	More frequent visits from government education administrators results in oversight and relatively greater accountability to government standards. Questionable teaching activity in classrooms.	Teachers receive standardised training at PTI; teaching methods focus on rote memorisation and are often not learner-centred.	Perceived corruption in teacher hiring among teachers and parents. Perception among parents that children at government schools must attend private tutoring in order to learn well.

RNGPS	RNGPS serve many poor children; many families reported not eating three meals/day. Many students inappropriate age for their grade. Rates of student absence are very high.	Teacher motivations affected by tiered salary system (see below). High rate of tardiness and absence. Low teaching activity among teachers present.	Government training and materials provided, though RNGPS teachers are behind government counterparts in line for training. Similar to government schools, teaching methods are rote and not learner-centred.	Last choice for parents among mainstream government-funded schools. Perception among parents that children at government schools must attend private tutoring in order to learn well. Perceived corruption in teacher hiring.
Community schools	Located in remote areas with high incidence of poverty. Malnutrition among students a big problem.	As above, teacher motivation impacted by tiered system. Frequent tardiness and absence.	As government and RNGPS, but teachers' time was further strained with insufficient staff. Teaching quality suffered as a result.	Perceived corruption in teacher hiring. They were often the only option in the area given their remote locations. Parents reported low quality.
Nonformal/ BRAC Schools	Students and families supported with school scheduling responsive to their needs. Special provisions and assistance for disabled or grade/age-inappropriate students.	Teachers are hired from local community and are trained, supported and monitored significantly by branch and regional offices.	Community awareness that BRAC teaching methods are 'different', integrate song, dance and rhyme. Attempt to create 'joyful learning environments'; use of colourful materials.	Top choice among focus-group parents. Seen as providing quality education at no cost; manageable for poor families. Complaints that spaces or schools do not meet demand.

Private schools	Students generally clean and well dressed in uniforms. Malnutrition less a problem among socio-economic group that can access these schools.	Teacher accountability to parents and administration results in fewer absences and more teaching time. Some teachers hold private tutoring sessions outside of school.	Teachers are untrained, but monitored by school administration, many of whom have teaching experience. Supplemental books enhance mandatory government curriculum.	Focus groups report quality at private schools in association with payment for tuitions. Seen as schools for those with the means only, not accessible to all.
Aliya madrassa	Poor students more likely to attend.	Teachers are untrained. No exterior accountability mechanism from government or other.	Teachers don't receive training. Standardised materials from the government.	Parents reported that students with less ability are sent to madrassas.
Quomi madrassa	Students living away from their families. Room and board facilities imply regular meals for students. Camaraderie among boys studying together.	Unknown. Teachers may receive some training in specialised Islamic subjects though this is not standardised. No practical, skill-based training.	Teaching methods are often rote memorisation. Teaching materials limited to Qur'an and Islamic subjects; no other skills training.	As many rural *quomi* madrassas are also orphanages, they are seen as an option for families who cannot tend their own children. Religious education only.

Table III: Qualitative quality matrix.

Factors Affecting Quality

Contact hours, attendance and teaching activity. Bangladesh's average annual classroom contact time in government-funded schools is one of the lowest in the world, at 587 hours/year (OECD, 2011). In addition to official contact hours, unofficial days off from school or early dismissal, and school closings due to extreme weather, teacher and student truancy and tardiness affect the quality and quantity of schooling that children receive. Schools with limited classroom space, especially RNGPS and community schools, almost always run classes in a shift system, effectively cutting down on students' classroom hours. Parents, teachers and administrators reported that schools were closed entirely in December and that they were very slow to reopen in January. The fasting month of Ramadan and the following Eid-ul-Fitr holiday marked school closings for most or all of that month. UNICEF (2009) cites student absenteeism in Bangladesh at 19%; Nath and Chowdhury (2009) cite teacher absenteeism at 12-13% (with half on leave) with additional high levels of tardiness among rural primary-school teachers.

BRAC schools avoid many of the scheduling problems that government schools face by setting an annual school calendar in collaboration with local communities, working to create school hours and an annual calendar that responds appropriately to families' need to have their children helping around the house and in the fields, especially during harvest time.

Teacher motivation and benefits. Teachers interviewed at all the school types indicated that their level of motivation was linked to their pay. This was especially acute at the government-funded schools, with teachers at government schools, RNGPS and community schools compensated with pay and benefits at different rates despite doing essentially the same job. These policies create a tiered system of government-paid teachers with the same job but different status, thus negatively affecting these RNGPS and community-school teachers' motivations and school quality. It was clear that individuals within the government system had expectations of a certain level of compensation that did not exist outside of the government sector.

BRAC teachers are almost entirely women, and almost none of them would have jobs if they were not teaching for BRAC. Their classroom hours were limited to mornings and they still had time to attend to their households during the day; they had no expectation of the salary or benefits of a government employee. Furthermore, many of these women stated that they felt empowered in their position as teachers, gaining a role and a voice within their communities.

Private-school teachers were also paid low salaries and lamented that they did not make more money. I heard private-school teachers say repeatedly that they were grateful to have work, however, and like BRAC teachers, their teaching time was officially over at or around noon, leaving the afternoon free for them to pursue other concurrent economic opportunities. This included private tutoring, working in shops or medical dispensaries, doing agricultural work or working at home.

Parents felt that private-schools teachers were more accountable because their salaries were being paid through students' tuitions, and that they had an imperative to cover all of the material as such.

Factors Affecting Access

Schooling expenditure. Despite Bangladesh's commitment to free primary education, much of the cost of primary education falls on the parents, an unmanageable burden for the poor in this community. With just 2.4% of gross domestic product (GDP) expenditure on education, Bangladesh ranks in the bottom tier of government spending for education internationally, and a majority of the cost of primary education is met by families.[2] While no schools, save private ones, charge tuition, families face many other costs in sending their children to school, including exam fees three times per year, as well as school supplies. Widespread supplemental private tutoring adds additional costs.

Sabates and others (2010) cite the importance of reducing direct and indirect costs of education to zero for the poorest; subsidies are one possible element to ensure sustained enrolment of these students. The current stipend programme is poorly targeted and insufficient, thus not fully removing cost barriers to schooling for the poorest (Hossain & Zeitlyn, 2010). Parents and teachers alike lamented that this money, which was cash dispersed to parents in tri-monthly intervals, was not spent by families on education and was not a sufficient amount for meeting families' education expenses. Parents and teachers agreed that the direct distribution of school supplies (including pens, notebooks, bags and uniforms and/or school feeding programmes) would be a more efficient means of ensuring that dedicated funds directly met educational needs.

Poverty and vulnerability. Poverty has a considerable impact on children's schooling, in terms of enrolment, participation, attendance and success. Poor parents must consider the actual and opportunity costs of school. Parents and teachers at government-funded schools reported that many students missed class for want of basic school supplies or were absent during harvest or other work-intensive times.

While poverty affects student enrolment, children 'who have poor health, lack basic school equipment and live in the catchment areas of non-government schools (who are also often the poor) are more likely be silently excluded – that is enrolled and overage, attending irregularly or poorly achieving' (Hossain & Zeitlyn, 2010, p. vii). Poor students' silent exclusion considerably impacts their participation and achievement at school.

Parents' education levels correlate with students' participation, and marginalised families are less willing and/or able to prioritise and provide financial and academic support towards their children's schooling. The logistics of school administration are also affected by poverty. Poor families are less likely to have their children's birth registration or other formal record of their children's ages; misconceptions of children's age-appropriateness are common (Nath & Chowdhury, 2009), leading to difficulties with school registration and placomont.

The poor tend to be most vulnerable to *monga* (seasonal hunger), malnutrition, natural disaster and seasonal variations for employment. Mothers in focus groups reported eating one meal per day during *monga* time for several months of the year, with their children missing school in favour of fishing or otherwise searching for food. Some students' education was interrupted by families' seasonal migration in search of work.

Private tutoring. Private tutoring (supplemental paid study of academic subjects outside of school hours) is a critical element of many households' financial burdens for education. Some estimates state that the cost of tutoring makes up the largest percentage of private expenditure on schooling (Ahmad, 2007). Parents say that children attending government-funded schools need to pay for additional private tutoring in order to learn, but students at these schools (particularly RNGPS and community schools) are often least able to afford that additional expense. Families reported private tutoring costs of at least Tk. 100/month per subject, with most students taking two subjects or more. Costs for private tutoring tend to increase with the teacher or tutor's credentials or reputation, and teachers may be negatively incentivised to teach well during school time by the possibilities of earning outside of regular classroom hours.

Gender and poverty. Students' genders play an important role in poverty and schooling choices. During a focus group, one parent informed that 'parents' preference is for boys; girls will leave the home to go to their in-laws' home [after marriage].' While Ahmed and others (2007) concluded that parents no longer discriminate against girls because family per student expenditure for boys and girls is about the same, I found higher enrolments of boys across the board in the private schools, and was told by headmasters that boys are preferred for education in the better private schools as they will bear the brunt of supporting their parents later in life. This inequality is likely more pronounced in a region where early marriage is still prevalent, with the youngest girls married before the end of the primary cycle (despite a legal marrying age of 18 for girls).

103

Case Studies

To gain depth of understanding and analysis, I selected one private school and one RNGPS for closer study so as to better understand the difference between public and private options. I made advance arrangements with school headmasters to teach Class 3 English at these two schools six days a week for a month.

The Private School

The private, low-fee-charging school (monthly tuition between US$1.30 and US$2, depending on which class students attend) was established in 2008 by a retired government high-school headmaster with 37 years of experience. He donated the land that the school sits on just one kilometre north of Dimla town, and donations of Tk. 70,000 (US$933) from local development funds from a Member of Parliament over the past two years helped to establish the school's infrastructure (indicating the benefit of local power networks). The headmaster claims not to draw a salary but is present each morning, walking to every classroom to see that classes have begun; he stated that he personally offers free coaching/private tutoring to students in Class 5 after school. As a well-known figure in the community, he said that many parents want to send their children to his school. The school currently offers pre-primary classes for students age 4 and 5 as well as Classes 1 to 8.

Teachers at this school were hired *ad hoc* and work without contracts or benefits, although their salaries are above the average among private schools in the sample. The teachers' attendance at school was regular, with classes starting by 8:40 am (ten minutes after the official start time of 8:30 am) at the ring of a large brass bell. The administrator stated that the teachers are accountable to the parents, whose tuition money pays their salaries, as well as to the headmaster, who relies on their performance to uphold the school's reputation.

This school's infrastructure is rudimentary: simple mud floors and thatched bamboo walls that don't keep out the voices of the students next door. However, Class 3 students wear neat uniforms, always have notebooks and pens on hand, do extra handwriting practice every night, and know how to read and write in English, a required subject from Class 1 in Bangladesh. On my first day, the teacher informed me that the students had already finished the government textbook, so we could start again from the beginning with a review. The students were most comfortable repeating rote sentences and vocabulary and were obviously not used to learner-centred teaching styles; they were uncomfortable learning grammar that had to be applied outside of memorised examples. The limitations of this pedagogical practice was clear, in that students did not have the capacity to build new sentences with the words that they had learned or use their knowledge outside of the teacher's examples.

The Registered Non-government Primary School (RNGPS)

A second-tier government-funded school with civil-servant teachers located next to the hospital in Dimla town, this school runs classes in two shifts to manage its limited number of three classrooms: Class 1 and 2 attend in the morning and Class 3, 4 and 5 officially attend from noon until 4:15 pm. To contrast, Class 3, 4 and 5 students at the nearest government school are in session from 9:30 am to 4:15 pm; the government-school students have nearly three more contact hours than their counterparts at the RNGPS each day.

The headmaster was present only a handful of days over the course of the month that I spent there, and I saw him engaged in teaching activity just once. The three other teachers' attendance was marginally better; most days two teachers were present, though they were engaged in teaching activity less than half of the time that I was at the school. The former teachers' room had been converted into a safe, lockable space for a well for water; the headmaster reported the well's pump had been stolen twice before. Space for the teachers had been relocated to a few tables in the largest classroom. I found the teachers sleeping with their heads on the table as an unattended class of fourth graders ran wild and there was no chalk. Two of the teachers' young children also went to school with their mothers, providing many distractions.

On my first day at the school, the teacher informed me that the students were about three-fourths through the government textbook. When I started the lesson, it quickly became clear that the students could not understand or read, and most could not write the letters of the English alphabet. Of the 68 students on the official register for Class 3, nearly all were consistently marked present but I never saw more than 37 students in attendance. It would have been impossible for the classroom to hold additional dozens of children. The students who do attend are a wily bunch, especially the boys, punching each other, shouting and imploring me to hit other children who are misbehaving. At least a third of each class was wasted in attempts at discipline. Many students were grade-age inappropriate; students in Class 3 were as old as 14. These children often sat in the back of the classroom and were most reluctant to participate. On several occasions students were unable to do assigned exercises for lack of paper or pens. Less than 15% of students wear uniforms. A minor Hindu holiday for which the school closed officially for one day resulted in an unofficial three-day holiday as the school lacks structure and teachers and students seem to use any excuse not to come to school.

Christine Sommers

Comparisons

My experience in these two schools unearthed several revelations about quality and access at schools in Dimla. Table IV sums up some important dimensions in understanding the student experience in the two case studies. It is clear that students who can afford investments in primary school do so beyond just paying for tuition at a private school. Many of these students live outside of walking distance from school and have the resources to travel to a school of their choice by rickshaw, motorcycle or other means. They pay for supplemental education outside of school hours using private tutoring, and they benefit from smaller class sizes with teachers who have greater accountability to their parents who are paying the tuition fees.

	Private school	RNGPS
Average student attendance	86.2%	46.7%
Class size (official register)	29 students	68 students
Percentage of age-grade inappropriate students	4%	62%
Percentage of students taking private tutoring	63%	36%
Percentage of students who walk to school	44%	100%

Table IV. Comparative matrix of sample private-school and RNGPS students. *Source*: Interviews among present students in Class 3 on 30 October 2011.

The private-school students experienced benefits in each of the quality indicators outlined above. While not all students had attended pre-primary, many had and they were at an institution where pre-primary was considered standard. Monitored by both the school administration and the students' parents, the teachers' attendance and behaviour at school was regular and scheduled class time was more or less respected, resulting in students being engaged in learning a high percentage of the time. Students were more disciplined all-around, in part because of the clearly established norms around appropriate student behaviour. Corporal punishment was still a threat, but students respected behaviour norms for the most part. Teaching methods were not dissimilar to those rote methods used in government-funded schools and this certainly impacted students' autonomy and learning and empowerment, but this reflected the norm I saw in all school types except the non-formal schools, which purposefully integrate learner-centred pedagogy.

The RNGPS, on the other hand, failed students in all of the quality measures I identified. Students were not ready for school; the absenteeism of more than half the class on most days clearly indicated

106

that students and/or their families did not prioritise, were not ready for, did not value, or were otherwise not able to attend school. No pre-primary courses were available. The teachers' behaviour was appalling; it is easy to understand why children would stop attending if their teachers have irregular attendance or if they are not engaged in teaching most of the school hours. This begins to explain why a one-day holiday expanded to three days with no notice. While I did not witness corporal punishment first-hand, the teachers' threats to beat the students as well as the students' insistence that I beat children who were misbehaving would indicate that they were accustomed to this method of discipline.

Regarding access, however, it was clear that the private school was not accessible to students who could not afford the tuition as well as the cost of uniforms and other supplies. Private-school students received free government-issued textbooks but were required to purchase several additional supplemental books. These costs significantly increased the total that parents had to pay. Additionally, 63% of the students from my Class 3 section were already taking private tutoring, demonstrating their increased access to valuable supplemental education services. This school did not have any scholarships or other means of accommodating poor children and made no provisions for disabled children.

The RNGPS, on the other hand, was accessible for enrolment to anyone living in the catchment area. This option came at very little cost, primarily the cost of notebooks and pens, especially given that most students did not carry a bag or wear a uniform. Many students were lacking even in the most essential school supplies. For the 36% of students that did pay for private tutoring, this likely comprised the bulk of their expenditure on education. All parents from this school community said that their children attended this school because they could not afford anything else.

Beyond enrolment, though, it was clear that the significant majority of students remained in the third zone of exclusion, meaning that they were 'silently excluded' from educational access and thus learning minimally or not at all at school; nearly half the students on the register were always absent, students above their age/grade level did not participate, and the school environment was not conducive to learning with the multitude of discipline issues. These observations are consistent with the findings from the CREATE survey data, where silent exclusion was indicated by poor attendance, low attainment, repetition, and students overage for their grade (Sabates et al, 2010). The private school does provide its students with an education that serves as a basis for continuing their schooling in the higher grades. The RNGPS fails to develop the minimal capacity to read and write, with considerable consequences in the short and long term.

Conclusions

The 16.5 million primary-school-aged children in Bangladesh have a right to education, and the country's future will be shaped by today's education policies and practices. Bangladesh's successful commitment to enrol children in primary school must be followed by an earnest dedication to quality improvements among all primary-education providers. Poor and vulnerable students are still left out or left behind, by failing to enrol, dropping out, or joining the ranks of the 'silently excluded' who fail to learn. The current system does indeed reinforce systemic inequalities based on poverty, where those who can afford it purchase as high a quality of education as is available, while those who cannot pay suffer in low-cost, low-quality alternatives.

Government-funded schools are the default providers of education, particularly the poor. The quality of government-funded schools seems to decrease in pockets of geographically distant or poor communities, thus leaving the most marginalised communities with the fewest options and least agency. The multi-tiered government-funded system with three levels of government funding and support magnifies the inequalities in the government system. Inadequate resources, management capacity and lack of commitment are all obstacles to strengthening the national education system to ensure a sustainable means of providing quality primary education for all (Nath, 2005).

The establishment and implementation of PEDP III in 2011 marked a critical attempt by the government to improve its public primary schools and a real opportunity to provide a higher standard of education through improvements to the multi-tiered mainstream education system. PEDP III's strategies to increase participation of poor and disadvantaged children, improve access and reduce social and regional disparities include expanding pre-primary education, improving physical school facilities, integrating health and nutrition programmes into schools, revamping the stipend programme, creating more inclusive policies for disadvantaged children, and coordinating more closely with alternative education providers. These are important steps in tackling the inequities in the current system, but achieving these goals will require accountability mechanisms and real financial commitment nationally as well as a willingness to invest time and embrace change locally.

The multiple-tiered system and all the factors affecting quality and access have significant implications. If social justice is defined as 'parity of participation' as referenced earlier, it is quite clear that students at different school types participate unequally in education and schooling both in and outside school structures, and that the difference is largely based on levels of income and agency. The government-funded schools, and RNGPS in particular, often fail to develop students' abilities to read and write, with considerable consequences for their ability to continue schooling or move ahead. Community perceptions of the school's poor quality also impacted the enrolled students' social standing.

The growth of *Ebtedayee* and *Quomi* madrassas indicates that religious education must be included in dialogue on education policy, and the government's gains in bringing *Ebtedayee* under closer government regulation is a positive step to ensuring that students at those institutions receive a standard education. The opaque nature of *Quomi* institutions, including funding sources, presents the government with the tricky and politically sensitive challenge of maintaining their responsibility to ensure quality education for *all* children.

While non-formal schools reach some marginalised or at-risk communities and certainly enhance the individual children who attend them, they will never expand to meet the needs of all poor students. BRAC schools play an important role in developing innovation in education, piloting different learner-centred teaching methods, creating supplemental curriculum and teaching materials, adapting school schedules to local needs, and experimenting with new models for recruiting and training teachers.

Private schools in rural areas similarly serve a niche market, meeting the demand of families who can afford additional education expenses. Private tutoring, too, provides additional education *à la carte* for those who can afford it. These options only serve to increase inequalities between those who can afford it and those who cannot. The responsibility lies with the government to create practices and policies that provide primary schooling that is affordable and properly prepares children for the future.

Notes

[1] *Quomi* madrassas were not included in the calculations.

[2] Chowdhury and Nath (2009) cite an average government expenditure of 1253 TK (US$17)/student/year at government and registered non-government schools, whereas the household costs are estimated to be 2500TK (US$34)/student/year.

References

Ahmad, Q.K. (2007) Education Watch 2006: financing primary and secondary education in Bangladesh. Campaign for Popular Education (CAMPE), Bangladesh. http://www.campebd.org/download/EW2006FullReportEnglish.pdf (accessed May 20, 2011).

Ahmed, M., Ahmed, K.S., Khan, N.I. & Ahmed, R. et al (2007) Access to Education in Bangladesh: country analytic review of primary and secondary school. http://www.create-rpc.org/pdf_documents/Bangladesh_CAR.pdf (accessed January 10, 2011).

Asadullah, M.N. & Chaudhury, N. (2008) Holy Alliances: public subsidies, Islamic high schools, and female schooling in Bangladesh, in M. Tembon & L. Fort (Eds) *Girls' Education in the 21st Century: gender equality, empowerment, and economic growth,* pp. 209-237. Washington, DC: World Bank.

Asadullah, M.N., Chaudhury, N. & Dar, A. (2006) Student Achievement Conditioned upon School Selection: religious and secular secondary school quality in Bangladesh. Queen Elizabeth House Working Paper 140. University of Oxford. http://ddp-ext.worldbank.org/EdStats/BGDwp06a.pdf

Bangladesh Government, General Economics Division Planning Commission (2008) A Strategy for Poverty Reduction in the Lagging Regions of Bangladesh. http://www.undp.org.bd/mdgs/full%20report-reduced.pdf (accessed May 30, 2011).

BRAC (2011) Stay Informed: BRAC at a glance. http://www.brac.net/content/stay-informed-brac-glance#Education%20Programme (accessed July 15, 2011).

Fraser, N. (2008) *Scales of Justice: reimagining political space in a globalizing world.* Cambridge: Polity Press.

Hossain, A. & Zeitlyn, B. (2010) *Poverty, Equity, and Access to Education in Bangladesh.* CREATE Pathways to Access Research Monograph 51. Brighton: University of Sussex.

Lewin, K. (2007) *Improving Access, Equity and Transitions in Education: creating a research agenda.* CREATE Pathways to Access Research Monograph 1. Brighton: University of Sussex.

Nath, S.R. (2005) Reaching Primary Education at the Doorstep of the Poor: the BRAC experience. BRAC Research Report, BRAC Research & Evaluation Division. http://www.bracresearch.org/reports/reaching_primary_school.pdf (accessed July 10, 2011).

Nath, S.R. & Chowdhury, A. (2009) Education Watch 2008: state of primary education in Bangladesh: progress made, challenges remained. Campaign for Popular Education (CAMPE), Bangladesh. http://www.campebd.org/download/EW2008FullReportEnglish.pdf (accessed February 20, 2011).

OECD (2011) *Education at a Glance 2011: OECD indicators.* Paris: OECD Publishing. http://www.oecd.org/education/highereducationandadultlearning/48631419.pdf (accessed July 20, 2012).

Pigozzi, M.J. (2006) What is the 'Quality of Education'? (A UNESCO Perspective), in K. Ross & I.J. Genevois (Eds) *Cross-National Studies of Education: planning their design and managing their impact.* Paris: International Institute for Educational Planning. http://www.sacmeq.org/downloads/Ross-Genevois_Cross_National_Studies_Quality_of_Education.pdf (accessed September 15, 2011).

Sabates, R., Hossain, A. & Lewin, K. (2010) *School Drop Out in Bangladesh: new insights from longitudinal evidence.* CREATE Pathways to Access Research Monograph #49. Brighton: University of Sussex.

Sen, A. (2009) *The Idea of Justice.* London: Penguin.

UNICEF (2009) Quality Primary Education in Bangladesh. Key statistics. United Nations Children's Fund (UNICEF). http://www.unicef.org/bangladesh/Quality_Primary_Education(1).pdf (accessed June 10, 2011).

Walker, M. (2006) Towards a Capability-Based Theory of Social Justice for Education Policy-Making, *Journal of Education Policy,* 21(2), 163-185.

CHAPTER 6

Dimensions and Implications of Privatisation of Education in Nepal: the case of primary and secondary schools

GOVINDA SUBEDI,
MANDAN GOPAL SHRESTHA
& MUKTI SUVEDI

Introduction

In the last four decades the number of schools in Nepal increased 5-fold and students 14-fold. Increased awareness of the value of schooling, rights-based advocacy and population growth have contributed to this rise, but there remain 4.9% of appropriately aged children out of school at primary level, with most of these from disadvantaged groups. In 1971, when the Government decided to take over the management and financing of all community-supported schools, it did not foresee the magnitude of the future financial commitment for the development of the education system. The increased number of schools and students meant that the limited available government funds had to be distributed very thinly, and inexperienced personnel found it difficult to supervise and manage public schools. In this context the government opened the door to the private sector to operate for-profit schools, with the result that the private sector now provides for 14% of basic-school students (grade 1-8) and 15% of secondary-school students (grade 9-12) (DOE, 2011a). Schools in Nepal now seem to operate under a dual system – one for the rich and another for the poor (Mathema, 2013).

The Research Context

Research in education in Nepal primarily focuses on the status of education. The Department of Education (DOE) publishes a half-yearly *Flash Report* showing the status of education; it does not analyse the educational performance of private and public schools, the role of the private sector in quality education, or the implications of mushrooming private schools on social cohesion in an already highly stratified society. The Nepal Living Standards Survey published by CBS (2011) – a nationally representative household survey – has also collected information about current school attendance by types of school, but has not analysed the data in detail (CBS, 2011). Martha Caddell (2007) discussed how private schools faced challenges in the early 2000s, when instability and threats led to private schools agreeing to reduce their fees by 15-20% and to registration of schools under the Company Act. However, she did not discuss in detail how private schools were concentrated in more prosperous areas and how it was that relatively better off families send their children to private schools.

Three perspectives related to the privatisation of education in Nepal prevail. One bluntly opposes the privatisation of schools, arguing it has perpetuated inequality in education and reinforced prevailing social stratifications. The second claim is that privatisation of schools has contributed to enhancing the quality of education, and to achieving Education for All. The third perspective supports limited not-for-profit privatisation but opposes commercialisation in education.

The Study and Objectives

With an overall objective of analysing the nature and size of private education in Nepal and examining the parents' perception of private education, Friends of Sankhu conducted a study during January–December 2011, with the financial and technical support of the Privatisation in Education Research Initiative (PERI).

The specific research questions were: (1) What is the management and operation modality of private schools? What are the magnitude and processes of privatisation, especially in the less prosperous areas? How do private schools align their interests with government policies?; (2) How do people, especially the middle class, view the importance of education for their children? Has education provided a means of social mobility?; and (3) What, if any, are the good practices of privatisation of education that can be adopted by public schools?

Methodology

The study was cross-sectional and exploratory and employed a household survey which generated data to attempt to explain the dynamics of privatisation in education and community perceptions about private schools. Secondary data were reviewed from Flash Reports, raw data from the Nepal Living Standards Survey (NLSS) 2010/11 (Central Bureau of Statistics [CBS], 2011), and other relevant reports. Primary data, which was both quantitative and qualitative, were generated through a household survey, school surveys, key-informant interviews (KIIs) and workshops. For the household survey, districts were grouped into six regions on the basis of prevailing regions (Table I): Eastern; Central (excluding Kathmandu Valley); Kathmandu Valley; Western; Mid-Western; and Far-Western. Two districts with the largest number of private schools in each region were selected to ensure diversity of responses in terms of types of private school, as well as social and economic group. The sampling scheme represented all development regions and two ecological zones (Terai and Hills) among the three zones.[1]

Region	Terai District	Hill District	Basic educational levels	Secondary level	Higher secondary level	Total
Eastern						
	Jhapa		7	17	3	27
	Sunsari		6	17	3	26
Central						
		Kavre	1	2	2	5
	Chitawan		0	3	0	3
Kathmandu Valley						
		Lalitpur	0	6	1	7
		Kathmandu	2	17	4	23
Western						
		Kaski	0	7	8	15
	Nawalparasi		3	3	5	11
Mid-Western						
		Dang	0	5	0	5
	Banke		1	2	1	4
Far Western						
	Kailali		0	2	1	3
	Kanchanpur		0	1	2	3
Total			20	82	30	132

Table I. Sample regions/districts and number of private schools selected/visited by districts/regions, Nepal.

115

The required households [2] were selected by a systematic sampling procedure and, to reduce the cluster effect of three-stage sampling, a sample size of 1224 households with 36 households in each of 34 clusters was made. A total of 132 private schools (14 primary, 6 lower secondary, 82 secondary and 30 higher secondary) were surveyed at sites of the household survey.

The study used desk reviews, household questionnaires, survey instruments for schools, key informant interviews (KIIs), a workshop with key stakeholders and a feedback workshop; the preliminary draft report was presented to the regional seminar organised by PERI in Kathmandu in August 2011. The quantitative data were thoroughly edited, recoded and entered in SPSS/PC software and analysed, regrouped and contextualised. Simple frequency tables, cross-tabulation methods, and, where relevant, chi-squared (X2) tests were used.

Reviewing the School Education System in Nepal

Until 2009, schools in Nepal consisted of primary (grades 1-5), lower secondary (grades 6-8), secondary (grades 9-10) and higher secondary (grades 11-12) levels (DOE, 2009). Since the introduction of the School Sector Reform Program (SSRP) in 2009, school education has been categorised as basic education (grades 1-8) with primary and lower secondary levels; and secondary education (grades 9-12) with secondary and higher secondary levels. The government of Nepal has classified schools into three broad categories: (1) government/community schools; (2) institutional schools; and (3) religious schools (DOE, 2010). Community schools are further categorised based on funds they received from government as: community-aided schools; community-managed schools; and community-unaided schools. For this study all these types of schools are categorised as public schools.

Institutional schools, not funded by government, depend on parental support and are managed and owned by individuals or private/public trusts. These are further categorised as: public trust schools; private trust schools; and private schools – registered under the Company Act. These comply with tax requirements, remain the property of the investors and require registration with the Ministry of Education; a 1% tax on the school's income is levied to contribute to a fund aimed at improving rural community schools.

The education regulations establish four classifications within private schools based on their physical facilities, the skill of the teachers (human resources), responsibility and transparency, school-operating processes, performance and results, and other outcomes. Private schools with score of 80% and above across these six areas are classified as grade A; 60-79% as grade B; 40-59% as grade C; and less than/equal to 39% as grade D. This classification determines the fee that they are allowed to charge. In each academic year, a private school may request to be upgraded by the District Education Office (DEO).

Religious schools are categorised as: madrassas (Islamic education); gumba/vihar (Buddhist education); and ashram/gurukul (Hindu tradition education). These schools receive government grants if they align their curriculum with the formal education system.

Many of the details of the Education Act and Regulations apply to both private and public schools. For example, the school calendar, registration process, students' evaluation system and required teachers' qualifications are the same for both types of schools. However, there are key differences in the grading systems, provision of government funds, the payment of education tax and registration deposits.

Evolution of Private Schools in Nepal: policies and legal context

Private schools have evolved since the late 1980s when Nepal entered into a neo-liberal economic regime and multi-party democracy. Education Regulation, 1981 allowed for the establishment and operation of private and/or boarding schools. The Royal Higher Education Commission, 1984 recommended promoting private education from primary to higher education to enhance the quality of education. The National Education Commission, 1993 emphasised private-education policy in the changing political context following the 1991 People's Movement for the re-institutionalisation of multi-party democracy. Foreign educational institutions were allowed to open affiliated schools in private management. The Eighth Amendment of the Education Act, 2004 promoted the establishment of private schools.

The Eighth Plan (1992-97) and subsequent plans, including the current Three Year Plan Approach Paper (2010/11-2012/13), emphasise the promotion of private education for meeting the need for basic education (NPC, 1992, 2010).

It was evident from the key-informant interview's information, especially with private-school organisations, that a deterioration in the quality of education in public schools created an environment for the growth of private schools, which helped to release the pressure of education demand not met by public schools in terms of the perceived needs of parents for quality education.

Private schools should comply with: minimum educational qualifications for teachers; teaching licences; School Management Committees (SMCs); giving 10% of all students scholarships; and a 1% service tax to the government. The DEO is mandated to provide permission for establishing, registering and monitoring private schools.

Findings: status of compliance of
legal requirements in private schools

Minimum Qualification and Training of Teachers

Qualifications of teachers in private schools should be same as required for public schools. This study found that in A- and B-classified schools, teachers were generally qualified while in others they had minimal qualifications and the majority of teachers were untrained. Some private schools were providing training to teachers at their own expense, and private-school organisations occasionally organised necessary training for teachers.

Salaries and Benefits of Private School Teachers

Only 20% of private-school teachers received the government-determined salary. In many schools teachers' salaries were as low as 50-60% of it, and there were no provident funds, promotion facilities, job security, paid leave or incentives for refresher/ orientation training.

Licence Holding

According to the President of the Institutional Schools Teacher Union (ISTU–Nepal), only 5% of teachers in private schools held teaching licences, as schools are less concerned with appointing licence-holding teachers than those who are able to teach well.

School Management Committees

Only 5% of surveyed private schools had School Management Committees as required.

Curriculum

The curriculum and textbooks are the same for both private and public schools. Almost all private schools surveyed had introduced additional courses related to English, Maths and Moral Studies, as well as extra-curricular activities. As there is a board-exam system [3] in grades 5, 8 and 10, schools were using government textbooks in those grades.

Determination of Student Fee Structure

The government has categorised grade-C schools as the basic level for determining fee structure. Grade-D schools have to charge 25% less than grade-C schools. Grade-A schools may charge a fee 50% higher than that of grade-C schools, plus 72% for other expenses. Similarly grade-B schools may charge additional fees of 25% and 50% respectively. Some grade-A schools in this study were charging 45-51% more than the government-determined fee; students paid 44% more in a grade-C school.

Conflicts of Interest between Government, Private Schools and Teachers

Private schools are demanding a separate Act and Regulations, as the current one does not explicitly include issues relevant to them. After long debates, private schools agreed to pay a 1% education tax and claim that the government should provide facilities and benefits for them such as soft loans, land, curriculum materials, reference books, equipment and provision for teacher training.

The key demands of private-school teachers from school management are: teachers' representation on SMCs; making school records public; providing regular salaries, holiday and other benefits; social security, teacher training, and appointment letters as required by government.

Findings: number of private schools and trends

Number of Private Schools

By April 2011 there were 3656 private schools in the country; a total of 15% of primary schools, 25% of lower secondary schools, and 32% of secondary schools are private (DOE, 2010). All districts in Nepal have at least one private school. One fifth of the private schools are in Kathmandu district alone and eight districts have 37% of the total number of private schools (DOE). The number of private schools established is largely associated with the income level of districts (gross domestic product [GDP] or purchasing power parity [PPP] per capita in USD) (UNDP, 2009). Districts with the highest GDP per capita have generally high numbers of private schools. It can be inferred that the majority of private schools are operating in relatively more prosperous economic areas.

Proportion of Private-School Teachers

Data reveal that the share of teachers in private schools is nearly one quarter at primary level. At lower secondary level the share declined from nearly 35% in 2006 to 29% in 2010; at secondary level the share has remained at around 32% although the number of teachers in public schools has increased from 11,113 in 2006 to 67,280 in 2010. (The government has appointed 40,000 teachers or relief teachers on a temporary basis).

119

At the primary level, the share of female teachers is 57% in private schools and 37.5% in public schools. At the lower secondary level, the female share in private schools was almost double that in public school; at the secondary level the share is much lower in both public and private schools. This reveals that the proportion of female teachers tends to decline as the level of education increases.

Student Enrolment Rates in Private Schools

The proportion of enrolment in private schools at all levels of education declined from 2003, especially in 2005 and 2006 (Table II), which is mainly attributed to Maoist threats to private schools and to parents sending children to private schools.

Year	Primary schools		Lower secondary schools		Secondary schools	
	Public	Private	Public	Private	Public	Private
2003	89.2	10.8	86.7	13.3	84.6	15.4
2004	85.5	10.5	89.7	10.3	86.7	13.3
2005	94.0	6.0	92.4	7.6	90.3	9.7
2006	91.4	8.6	87.2	12.8	87.4	13.0
2007	89.8	10.2	87.0	13.0	85.1	14.9
2008	89.7	10.3	86.1	13.9	84.3	15.7
2009	86.8	13.2	85.2	14.8	83.1	16.9
2010	88.1	11.9	86.4	13.6	83.7	16.3

Table II. Share of enrolment by levels and types of schools, 2003-10.
Source: DOE (2008, 2010, 2011).

Year	Primary level		Lower secondary level		Secondary level	
	Girls	Boys	Girls	Boys	Girls	Boys
2003	10.0	11.5	11.7	14.4	14.3	16.2
2004	9.7	11.3	9.4	11.0	12.4	14.1
2005	5.3	6.6	6.9	8.3	8.9	10.4
2006	7.6	9.5	11.6	13.8	12.0	13.9
2007	8.9	11.5	11.7	14.2	13.6	16.0
2008	9.0	11.6	12.3	15.3	14.3	17.0
2009	11.3	15.0	13.0	16.6	11.7	15.4

Table III. Percentage share of enrolment in private schools by gender and level of education, Nepal. *Source*: DOE (2008, 2010, 2011).

Save the Children (2002) argued that from 2000 the Maoists intensified their attack against private schools, which caused the closure of about 500 of them; around 100,000 students and 9000 teachers were displaced by 2002. Enrolment in private schools started increasing again from 2007, following the end of a 10-year (1996-2006) armed struggle between the State and the Maoists. Relatively more boys are sent to private schools compared to girls (Table III) indicating gender bias among parents in providing education to their children.

Findings: socioeconomic differentials among students attending public and private schools

Rural–Urban Differentials in School Attendance by Types of Schools

Data from NLSS 2010/11 shows that the share of students in private schools at primary, lower secondary, and secondary levels is 22%, 17% and 20% respectively. The differences in attendance between rural and urban private schools are very high at all levels. At primary level, 57% of students are in urban private schools compared to 16% in rural areas. At lower secondary level the proportion of students in private schools in urban areas is almost five times that in rural areas, and at secondary level it is more than four times.

Types of school	Kathmandu urban	Other urban	Rural	Total
Public	21.3	53.5	84.9	78.7
	(0.8)	(6.5)	(71.3)	
Private	78.4	45.6	13.9	20.2
	(3.0)	(5.6)	(11.7)	
Others	0.3	1.0	1.2	1.1
	(0.0)	(0.1)	(1.0)	
Total	100.0	100.0	100.0	100.0
	(3.8)	(12.2)	(84.0)	
Estimated number of students (in '000)	296	942	6497	7735

Note: Figures in parentheses indicate percentage of total while figures outside of parentheses indicate percentage within the group. The p value of the chi-square test = .000 ($p < .001$), df= 4.

Table IV. Percentage distribution of individuals currently attending school (grades 1 to 10) by place of residence and types of school attendance.
Source: CBS (2011a), raw data from the Nepal Living Standards Survey 2010/11.

Govinda Subedi et al

Of total students in rural areas, 14% are in private schools: this is about
12% of the total number of students in the country (Table IV). Given that
83% of the population is in rural areas (according to the population
census of 2011), the share of students in private schools in rural appears
to be very low. It implies that there is an association between types of
schools attended by students and their place of residence.

Gender Variation in School Attendance by Type of School

NLSS 2010/11 data reveal that variation in school attendance by sex is
evident. The proportion of girls in private schools is consistently lower
than that of boys for all levels of schools; it is 68, 71 and 77 girls per 100
boys in primary, lower secondary and secondary level respectively.
Conversely, the proportion of girls in public schools is higher than that
of boys at all levels; it is 116, 105 and 102 girls per 100 boys in those
levels respectively.

Of the estimated 7.7 million students, 50.3% are girls and 49.7%
boys. Of the girls, 17% are in private schools, while it is 24% of the boys
(Table V). This suggests that there is a link between types of schools
attended by students and students' gender.

Types of school	Boys	Girls	Total
Public	75.1	82.1	78.7
	(37.3)	(41.3)	
Private	23.9	16.6	20.2
	(11.9)	(8.3)	
Others	1.0	1.3	1.1
	(0.5)	(0.7)	
Total	100.0	100.0	100.0
	(49.7)	(50.3)	
Estimated number of students (in '000)	3843	3892	7735

Note: p value of chi-square = .000 (p < .001), df = 2.

Table V. Percentage distribution of individuals currently
attending school (grades 1 to 10) by sex and types of school, Nepal.
Source: CBS (2011a), raw data from the Nepal Living Standards Survey 2010/11.

Income Variation in School Attendance of Types of School

NLSS 2010/11 data shows that the proportion of students currently
attending private schools tends to increase with the variation in
households from the bottom consumption quintile to higher ones. Ratios
of students attending private schools for the poorest 20% of households
to the richest 20% are 13%, 2% and 1% at primary, lower secondary and

secondary level, respectively, while the ratio for the poorest 40% of households to the richest 40% are 22%, 6% and 5% respectively. Inequality tends to increase with an increase in educational levels, implying that there are few children from the poorest households in private schools.

The data also reveal that the majority of students studying in public schools in rural areas are from low-income households. However, in private schools, the proportion of students in rural areas increases with the variation of households from lower to higher consumption quintiles, implying that the wealthier the household, the more likely children will be to attend private schools.

Variation in Attendance of Types of School by Social Groups

Brahmin/Chhetri make up 31% of the population, Hill and Terai Janajati 36.4%, Hill Dalits 8.11%, Terai Dalits 3.9% and Muslims 5%; the rest consists of Terai caste groups and others (Population census, 2001 – CBS, 2003). Among social groups, Brahmin/Chhetri (relatively advantaged) has the highest proportion of students, followed by Hill Janajati, Terai caste groups (disadvantaged groups) and Hill Dalits and Terai Dalits (so-called untouchable and most disadvantaged). This pattern holds according to types and levels of schools too (Table VI).

Types of school	Brahmin/ Chhetri	Hill Janajati	Hill Dalits	Terai caste groups	Terai Janajati	TeraiDalits	Others	Total	Number (in '000)
Pre-primary									
Public schools	24.3	20.6	13.6	22.1	6.9	6.5	6.0	100	514
Private schools	30.8	21.6	5.3	23.1	11.1	2.7	5.4	100	683
Other schools	1.8	1.8	2.9	10.2	3.7	0.0	79.7	100	25
Primary									
Public schools	24.6	27.0	14.2	14.6	9.9	5.4	4.3	100	3440
Private schools	37.4	25.3	4.5	18.6	5.5	1.8	7.0	100	971
Other schools	8.6	3.4	0.0	1.3	2.7	0.0	84.1	100	70
Lower secondary									
Public	34.9	28.1	9.5	10.3	10.9	3.0	3.2	100	1591

Govinda Subedi et al

schools									
Private schools	47.5	29.6	2.5	13.3	4.3	0.0	2.8	100	328
Other schools	15.8	4.2	16.2	8.7	11.4	0.0	43.8	100	10
Secondary									
Public schools	39.3	26.4	8.0	10.2	11.5	1.7	2.9	100	1052
Private schools	44.8	36.8	2.7	7.9	4.8	0.6	2.4	100	265
Other schools	16.6	51.0	0.0	22.6	9.9	0.0	0.0	100	7
Primary to secondary									
Public schools	29.8	27.2	11.8	12.7	10.5	4.1	3.8	100	6083
Private schools	40.8	28.2	3.8	15.7	5.1	1.2	5.4	100	1564
Other schools	10.1	7.4	1.9	3.9	4.3	0.0	72.4	100	87
Total	31.8	27.2	10.1	13.2	9.3	3.5	5.0	100	7745

Note: Chi-square test comparing social groups and proportion of students in schools (primary to secondary level): p value of chi-square = .000 (p < .000), df= 12.

Table VI. Percentage distribution of individuals currently attending school by social groups and types of school, Nepal.
Source: CBS (2011a), raw data from the Nepal Living Standards Survey 2010/11.

Interface between Social Groups and Consumption Quintile and Type of School Attended

The percentage distribution of students currently attending a public or private school by social groups and consumption quintile (NLSS, 2011) shows that caste/ethnicity is not the only factor that determines the attendance of students at private schools, as the Brahmin/Chhetri children attending private schools come from a range of consumption quintiles; this is also the case among other disadvantaged groups. The proportion of children attending private schools increases with a shift from lower to higher-consumption quintile levels, between Brahmin/Chhetri and Hill Janajati. This relationship suggests that the likelihood of children attending private schools among these social groups tends to increase when households are wealthier. Among other groups, opposite relationships exist between the proportion of children

124

attending private schools and consumption quintile. This relationship suggests that the share of these groups in private schools is very low, especially in higher-consumption quintile households.

Results of the School Survey

Profile of private schools. Data from the 132 private schools surveyed reveal that almost two thirds of schools have their own buildings and have libraries (86%); almost all schools have drinking-water facilities, lunch provision (51%), separate toilet facilities for girls and boys (94%), a science library (83%), computer facilities (92%), a playground (95%), separate hostels for boys and girls (84%) and a canteen (73%). These private schools also have music teachers (46%), dance teachers (61%), sports teachers (91%), first-aid facilities (89%), security personnel (81%), audio-visual materials (70%), Internet facilities (42%) and transport facilities (83%). These facilities are more prevalent in secondary and higher secondary level schools.

Student-teacher ratio. In the surveyed schools the student–teacher ratio at the basic education and secondary level is 16 and 21, which is much lower than the government provision of 44 and 27 respectively; it is 21, which is almost the same (20), at the higher secondary level.

Results of Household Survey:
people's perceptions of private schools

Perception of private schools. In total 53.4% of respondents selected private schools as they believed that they provided quality education, while the other main reasons included: English-medium teaching (21.5%); good discipline of students (8%); good care of children (6%); the prospect of a bright future for children (5.8%); prestige (2.9%); regular classes (1.6%); provision of extra-curricular activities (0.6%); and school-bus facilities (0.2%).

Parents' perception of private schools varied depending on whether their children were currently attending private or public schools; a full 75% of parents whose children attended private schools regarded private schools as 'good' while the comparable figure for those parents whose children attended public school was 40%. Parents' perceptions varied according to development region, ecological zone and social group.

Perception of public schools. Overall, 27% of those parents whose children attended private schools regarded public schools as 'good', 64% as 'average' and another 9% were undecided. In contrast, 44% of the parents whose children attended public schools regarded public schools as 'good' and 55% as average.

Reasons for preferring private schools to public schools. Workshop participants outlined the characteristics of parents' perceptions of and preferences for private school (Table VII).

Private schools	Public schools
English-medium teaching	Nepali-medium teaching
Quality education	Lower-quality education
Disciplined students	Difficult to maintain discipline
School environment is quite good	Not conducive to learning because of the politicisation of schools
Dedicated and qualified teachers	Not fully dedicated
Frequent evaluation and feedback system	No such provision
Parents take responsibility for children's education	Parents don't take responsibility
Teachers accountable to students	Teachers not accountable
Limited number of students per classroom	More students per classroom
Attendance brings the family prestige	Attendance does not bring the family prestige
Offers prospects of a bright future for children	Few prospects of a bright future for children
Have extra-curricular activities	No extra-curricular activities offered
Strong in Math, Science and English	
Less politicised	Highly politicised: unionisation of teachers, election of SMCs

Table VII. Characteristics of parents' perceptions
of private schools and public schools, Nepal.
Source: Based on a workshop in Sindhupalchok district, 2011.

A government authority in KII, also confirmed this:

> I believe that it is the age of competition. Parents expect quality education and are prepared to cut their two meals a day to get it. Public schools are not responsible; there is no regular class. There is a high level of politicization of teachers and teachers cannot be hired or fired on the basic of performance. (Local development officer, Sindhupalchok district)

Parents' involvement in school activities by types of school. In public schools, parents' involvement in school activities was relatively higher among the Brahmin (23%), Janajati (18%) and Chhetri (16%), as well as in eastern (43%) and western (20%) development regions. In private schools, relatively more Brahmin, Chhetri and Janajati than Dalits tended to participate in school activities as well as in western (25%), mid-western (22.5%), and eastern (21.5%) regions. In Kathmandu Valley, in both types of schools, parents' involvement in school activities was reported to be minimal.

Parents' perception of children's achievement in private schools. The majority of parents viewed their children's educational achievement as 'good' (54%) or 'very good' (11.5%). The main criteria for the judgment were: ability to read and write proficiently in English; being good at studying; regular class attendance; intelligence; and being top of the class.

In relation to perceptions of the educational activities of the private schools, the majority of parents reported them to be 'good' (44%), 'very good' (9%) and 'average' (37%). The main reasons were: having a regular evaluation system; the conduct of meetings with parents; the conduct of extra-curricular activities; better rules and regulations; the availability of computers; and cleanliness.

Description	Primary		Lower secondary		Secondary	
	Public	Private	Public	Private	Public	Private
Monthly fee	116	4,841	235	7,985	554	10,640
Exam and admission fees	119	1,469	324	2,369	795	4,901
Uniform	342	936	546	1,135	675	1,131
Textbooks and other	379	1,704	766	2,346	1,424	2,582
Transportation	7	371	7	611	28	1,008
Tuition/coaching	84	367	152	756	882	2,353
Tiffin	286	1,477	475	2,065	1,029	2,521
Total	1,332	11,164	2,504	17,267	5,387	25,134
Percentage higher for private schools compared to public schools		8.4		6.9		4.7

Table VIII: Per capita annual education expenditure
by level of education, Nepal (in Nepali rupees).
Source: CBS (2011a), raw data from the Nepal Living Standards Survey 2010/11.

In total 43% of parents viewed the physical facilities of their children's schools as 'good' and 9% 'very good'; more than one third of parents reported the facilities as being 'average' or were undecided. There were also parents who reported that the building was in poor condition, or that drinking water and toilet facilities were lacking.

Fully 75% of those parents interviewed (whose children attend public or private schools) firmly believed that graduates of private schools were better than those of public schools.

Household expenditure on education. Per capita annual expenditure in private schools is higher by eight, seven and five times than that of public schools at primary, lower secondary and secondary level respectively (Table VIII).

Education as a Means for Social Mobility and Social Capital

Based on information on social mobility gathered from interviews with principals, leaders of teachers' unions, school-management committees and government authorities it is reported that the majority of high-school graduates of private schools are attracted to technical subjects as well as finance and banking in higher education. In job markets, careers in government are still dominated by public-school graduates. Private-school graduates are found engaged in international/national non-government organisations (I/NGOs). Increasing numbers of youth are attracted to foreign employment, which has resulted in an outflux of many private-school graduates to developed countries. This was confirmed by the following observations from key informants:

> Products [graduates] of public schools move to the government jobs. They pass the Public Service Commission (PSC) examination; while I think less than 1 percent private school products take in PSC exam. Private school products are working in industries, banking and health sectors and more go overseas. I find that technically skilled human resources such as Computer Engineers are also products of Private Schools. (DEO, Kaski)

> Almost half of the products of private schools leave the country. What is the use in investing in private education in the country? (National President, ISTU-Nepal)

> Nearly 60 percent of graduates of this school go to USA, 5 percent go to UK and 5 percent go to other developed countries including Europe. This holds for both girls and boys. In terms of jobs, the very limited number of products of this school has joined in the Nepal Police; some have joined in the Nepal Army, few have joined Management and almost none has fought for PSC. (Teacher at Nepal Police Higher Secondary School, Sanga, Kavre district)

Findings: implications of the privatisation of education in Nepal

Contribution to Achieving Millennium Development Goals (MDGs)

A member of Private and Boarding Schools' Organization Nepal (PABSON) in Nawalparasi district stated:

> Had there been no private sector in education, the Government would have to spend much higher budget compared to today. This surplus budget should be spent for education in remote, deprived, marginal and indigenous groups. Private schools are also supporting the poor, marginalized and talented students, which helps to achieve the goal of education for all. (PABSON, 2011)

On the other hand, some government officers did not recognise the role played by private schools in achieving MDGs. They claimed that private schools were engaged in business and charging excessive fees. Government authorities' perceptions of private schools reflect the conflict of interest between government and private schools, as they would like to see private schools under their close surveillance, as with public schools, while this is not the case for many private schools in Nepal.

High Degree of Stratification in Education

Nepal's school education system has a high degree of stratification as reflected in the enrolment rates of students in private and public schools with gender, economic and social group, and rural–urban differences.

In the household survey, 59% of parents believed that the dual-schooling system in Nepal was not conducive to the social cohesion of the country. However, one quarter of the parents accepted the system as the private sector was seen as contributing to increasing the quality of education in the country; one quarter was undecided.

One principal in Lalitpur commented:

> We are producing unequal citizens. From public school, weak students are produced especially in English language, but they are relatively independent. In private schools, we produce dependent students, as they are the readymade product, bookish knowledge rather than creative one; students are weak in Nepali language.

The DEO, Sindhupalchok district, commented:

> I do not accept that education is privatized. Public schools have not been privatized in Nepal but new schools are opening up as private schools. The government is focusing on increasing public–private partnership in the education sector.

But I would see that there should not be public–private partnership at least at the basic education level. All the responsibility for providing basic education should be of government.

Social Justice in Education: the provision of scholarships

The government provides scholarships to girls, Dalits, disadvantaged Janajati, disabled persons and people living in Karnali region in public schools to improve access and quality within education.

Characteristics	Public schools	Private schools
Level of education		
Primary	26.6	3.3
Lower secondary	22.6	5.5
Secondary	10.1	7.3
Residence		
Rural	22.8	3.7
Urban	21.0	5.4
Sex of students		
Boys	13.1	4.2
Girls	31.3	4.7
Consumption quintile		
Poorest	24.4	0.0
Second	23.9	0.8
Third	20.9	5.1
Fourth	24.2	4.2
Richest	14.1	5.2
Social groups		
Brahmin/Chhetri	19.6	5.2
Hill Janajati	18.0	4.7
Hill Dalits	54.1	4.8
Terai caste groups	9.1	2.9
Terai Janajati	20.1	3.0
Terai Dalits	38.4	7.5
Others	16.9	1.5

Table IX. Percentage of students who received any type of scholarship during the last 12 months by types of school (grades 1 to 10), Nepal.
Source: CBS (2011a), raw data from the Nepal Living Standards Survey 2010/11.

In the case of private schools, private schools' organisations aim to conduct programmes targeting students by establishing various types of public–private partnerships to improve access and quality of education; helping public schools in management/academics; and providing scholarships. In the school survey, 10.5% of students in basic-education schools, 11% in secondary schools and 9% in higher secondary schools were reported to have either a full or partial scholarship. NLSS 2010/11 survey data indicate that 23% of students in public schools and 4% in private schools receive some type of scholarship.

The proportion of students receiving scholarships in public schools tends to decline with an increase in the level of education and vice versa in private schools (Table IX).

Good Practices of Private Schools: can they be adopted by public schools?

Drawing from KIIs and workshop findings, it was evident that private schools have adopted some good practices from which public schools could learn. These include: advertising the school programme; regular monitoring and feedback to students; and a strong sense of ownership in school management among owners.

The schools survey showed that 83% of private schools had at least one type of advertisement per academic year. Private schools have also started making rules about advertising, as the case of a school in Chitwan district shows:

> Advertisement and publicity are measures to attract the
> students in private schools. We are encouraging
> advertisements through electronic and paper media and
> discouraging the statements like 'Day meal free', '100% passes'
> which are produced by some private schools in our district.

Private schools call parents from time to time to report on the strengths and weaknesses of their children and for the counselling of parents. In every private school it was reported that they conducted parents' meetings at least once a year.

In private schools, there is strong feeling of ownership among founders and shareholders. This in turn leads to the good management of schools: running schools on time; ensuring teachers attend classes on time; less politicisation; and making teachers more focused on students' achievement. Almost 86% of students in private schools passed SLC Examination 2011; the figure for those in public schools was 47%.

Despite these positive aspects of private schools, most key informants reported that there are areas for improvement, such as reaching out to poor and marginal communities and remote areas, subsidising the fees and creating scholarship funds in and among the private schools.

Summary

Understanding Private Schools

Both private and public schools are regulated by the same Education Act and Regulations; key differences are in the grading system, the provision of government funds, the payment of education tax and the deposit required for registration. Private schools have evolved since the late 1980s. Current development plans aim to maintain coordination and build partnerships between public and private schools to increase the quality of education in public schools and for each to learn the good practices of the other.

The budget allocation for the education sector increased from 17.6% of gross national product (GNP) in fiscal year (FY) 2001/2 to 21.4% in FY 2008/9 indicating the high priority given to education by the government. Private schools do not receive funds from the government.

Except in a few cases, many teachers in private schools have low qualifications and are untrained, with a high turnover rate. Only 20% of private-school teachers receive the appropriate government-determined salaries, and in many schools payment is as low as 50% to 60% of that figure. Only 5% of teachers hold teaching licences. Only 5% of surveyed schools have SMCs, as required by the regulations. Many private schools do not comply with the government's determined fee structure. Almost all private schools surveyed have good infrastructure and have introduced additional courses and extra-curricular activities that are not generally found in public schools.

Attendance Figures for Private Schools

More than 20% of the students in Nepal are currently attending private schools (primary 22%, lower secondary 17% and secondary 11%). A wide variation in types of school attendance by place of residence, gender, economic strata and social groups was evident, although all categories of students are found in private schools. Gender inequality in attendance in private school is high at the primary level but tends to decline with an increase in the level of education.

A study conducted by Gayatree Timsina (2011) reveals that the patriarchal value system and prejudices regarding girls' education are still creating major barriers to girls' opportunities for education, with low caste disproportionately increasing discrimination towards girls compared to boys. The growth of private education is an added force for discrimination, with boys far more likely than girls to be supported by their families at private schools.

Half the students in private schools are from the richest quintile and 41% are Brahmin/Chhetri, the advantaged social group. However, caste is not the only factor in determining the type of school attendance, as students attending private schools come from across the consumption quintile, from relatively advantaged social groups to more disadvantaged groups.

People's Perceptions of Private Schools

The majority of parents whose children attend private schools believe that private schools are 'good' in terms of: providing education; educational achievement; and physical facilities. A full 40% of the parents whose children attend public schools also feel that way. Both types of parents believe that private-school graduates are more qualified than those of public schools.

Current trends suggest that the majority of parents in the upper and middle classes (relatively advantaged social groups, the richest households and from urban areas) prefer to send their children to private schools. A study implemented by Amrit Thapa (2011) shows that students in private schools are usually from richer and middle-class families, and belong to the higher caste. Students in public schools are mostly from middle-class or poor families.

Nepalese households incur eight, seven and five times higher expenditure in the private primary, lower secondary and secondary-education levels than in the corresponding public schools. The majority of high-school graduates of private schools are attracted to higher education in technical subjects, finance and banking. Increasing numbers of young people are attracted to foreign employment.

Implications of the Privatisation of School Education

Private schools have contributed significantly to increasing enrolment rates and achieving Nepal's MDGs, but tend also to increase stratification in society. Studies by Save the Children (2002) revealed that the majority of private schools are profit oriented, and largely concentrated in urban, semi-urban and rural areas with sufficient transportation facilities, and thus cater to the needs of children from relatively well-off families.

The government has attempted to ensure educational equity by providing scholarships to children from disadvantaged social groups in public schools. Despite the government provision of scholarships of at least 10% of the total students enrolled in the private schools, data reveals that only 4% of students in private schools receive scholarships compared to nearly 22% in public schools. Private schools are less sensitive to social equity and they mainly provide scholarships on the basis of a student's competence.

Private schools have adopted some good practices which public schools can adopt for quality education that include: regular interaction with parents; the monitoring of students; and a strong sense of ownership among owners. Similarly, private schools could learn from public schools in terms of reaching out to poor and deprived communities as well as remote and targeted areas.

Conclusions

Current policy discourse on school education is likely to exacerbate social and economic inequality in Nepalese society. A considerable proportion of students (more than 20%) are in private schools, and this will inevitably produce a highly segmented and polarised society. Parents are increasingly aware of the importance of education and are investing in their children's schooling. Private schools have spread across society: rich, middle and even labouring and peasant classes. Elimination of private schools would not be acceptable for many parents and would also not be possible in the context of increasing globalisation. Thus, Nepal has to adopt measures that will follow the good practices of private schools in public schools and vice versa, thereby reducing inequality in education. In addition, the government needs to come up with a clear plan to utilise its 1% education tax to benefit marginalised people. Finally, both public and private sectors need to build partnerships with the aim of improving the quality of education in public schools.

Possible areas for public–private partnership in school education are as follows:

- From the government's side: formulate separate legislation to regulate private schools and develop separate institutional mechanisms for registration and monitoring; provide training to principals and teachers regularly, together with public-school teachers; and assist teachers to obtain their teaching licences.
- From the private schools' side: create an exchange programme between private and public schools for the sharing of administration/management skills, teaching and learning; increase the allocation of seats for girls, members of marginalised communities; and from remote areas; allocate scholarships to children from public schools in remote and disadvantaged areas; and cover the training costs of teachers.

Notes

[1] Note that there are a very few private schools in mountain ecological zones that were not included in the survey.

[2] The basic analytical unit of the survey was the household. Households are defined as a group of people who share a roof and a cooking pot, according to the definition in the population censuses of Nepal.

[3] In grade 5 and 8 it is the district-level standardised board exam, while in grade 10 it is the national-level standardised board exam. In the board exam, the subjects are the same for both private and public schools.

References

Caddell, M. (2007) Private Schools and Political Conflict in Nepal, in P. Srivastava & G. Walford (Eds) *Private Schooling in Less Economically Developed Countries: Asian and African perspectives*, pp. 187-207. Oxford: Symposium Books.

Central Bureau of Statistics (CBS) (2003) *Population Monograph of Nepal, Volume 1*. Kathmandu: CBS.

Central Bureau of Statistics (CBS) (2011) *Nepal Living Standards Survey 2010/11*. Kathmandu: CBS.

Department of Education (DOE) (2008) *School Level Educational Statistics of Nepal*. Consolidated Report 2008. Kathmandu: DOE.

Department of Education (DOE) (2009) *Flash Report 2008/09*. Kathmandu: DOE.

Department of Education (DOE) (2010) *Flash Report 2009/10*. Kathmandu: DOE.

Department of Education (DOE) (2011) *Flash Report 2010/11*. Kathmandu: DOE.

Mathema, K.B. (2013) The Great Equalizer, *Republica*, April 25, Nepal.

United Nations Development Program (UNDP) (2009) *Nepal Human Development Report 2009*. Kathmandu: UNDP.

National Planning Commission (NPC) (1992) *Eight Five Year Plan (1992-97)*. Kathmandu: NPC.

National Planning Commission (NPC) (2010) *Three Year Plan Approach Paper (2010/11-2012/13)*. Kathmandu: NPC.

Private and Boarding Schools' Organization (PABSON) (2011) 12 April. http://pabson.org.np/.

Save the Children (2002) The Private Sector as Service Provider and its Role in Implementing Child Rights. Save the Children UK, South and Central Asia. http://www.enterprisingschools.com/sites/default/files/library/documents/Private_Sector_Involvement_-_Nepal.pdf (accessed on February8, 2011)

Thapa, A. (2011) Does Private School Competition Improve Public School Performance? The Case Of Nepal. Doctoral dissertation, Columbia University, New York.

Timsina, G. (2011) Educational Participation of Girls in Nepal. An Ethnographic Study of Girls' Education in a Rural Village. Doctoral thesis, Canterbury Christ Church University, United Kingdom.

CHAPTER 7

The Shadow Education Sector in India and Pakistan: opening Pandora's Box

MONAZZA ASLAM & PAUL ATHERTON

Introduction

Education is a critical determinant not only of individual productivity and economic success, but also of a country's economic progress (Hanushek & Woessmann, 2008; Appleton et al, 2011). Rapidly increasing enrolments and financial constraints worldwide, however, have put intense pressure on state-sector provision of quality education, leading to an emergence of a private sector which has absorbed an ever-increasing proportion of children in South Asia (Andrabi et al, 2002; Kingdon, 2007; Aslam, 2009). This in turn has raised pertinent questions regarding equity, efficiency and social justice.

The emergence of the private sector, indeed a mushrooming in some countries in recent years, has been accompanied in some by the stealthy evolution of a parallel or 'shadow' education system that provides *paid* supplementary tutoring outside normal school hours (Bray, 2009). Large private-tutoring industries are now known to exist in economically and geographically diverse countries such as: Cambodia, Egypt, Japan, Kenya, Morocco, Romania, Singapore, the United States and the United Kingdom (Dang & Rogers, 2008); and in the transition economies of Azerbaijan, Bosnia and Herzegovina, Croatia, Georgia, Lithuania, Mongolia, Poland, Slovakia and Ukraine (OSI, 2006; Bray, 2009). There is substantial anecdotal evidence of the existence of large-scale private tutoring industries in India and Pakistan. To our knowledge, there have been no substantive studies to date that map out the extent of the shadow education sectors in the aforementioned countries. Using recent, large-scale surveys of children in the two countries, this study improves on the existing anecdotal evidence by providing a quantitative picture of the size, nature and the consequent equity effects of the private-tutoring industry in India and Pakistan.

It is surprising how little policy attention has been paid to what some academics now recognise as the 'third important education sector' (Dang & Rogers, 2008). The lack of existing evidence is worrying. The option of giving (for the teachers) and receiving (for the pupils) tuition outside of normal school hours changes the incentive structure of the provision of high-quality instruction within the standard school system, which in turn has implications for equity and social justice. The relationship between private tutoring and student achievement is also increasingly gaining policy attention as it calls into question the quality of schooling during usual school hours.

More general research stems from the need to understand the association between educational expenditures and student outcomes i.e. addressing the question: do monetary expenditures improve student learning? Studies investigating this link arrive at mixed conclusions. On the one hand, Card and Krueger (1996) and Krueger (1999, 2003) present evidence for the effectiveness of public-school expenditures. Betts (1996), Hanushek (1986, 2003) and Leuven and others (2007), on the other hand, cast doubt on these conclusions. More recent studies based on natural experiments or randomisation in developing countries continue to reveal conflicting evidence on the effectiveness of public-school inputs (Jacob & Lefgren, 2004; Glewwe et al, 2004, 2007; Lavy & Schlosser, 2005; Leuven et al, 2007; Kingdon & Banerji, 2009). Studies that focus on private schools (e.g. Catholic schools in the United States) seem to agree no more about the impacts of educational inputs. While Evans and Schwab (1995) and Neal (1997) show educational benefits of attending Catholic high school, Altonji and others (2005), Figlio and Stone (1999) and Goldhaber (1996) find no significant differences in test scores between public and private schools. Studies in South Asia report more consistent findings. Kingdon (1996) and Aslam (2009) for instance show that private-school students on average achieve more than their government-school counterparts, indicating that in these countries of the region, there may be a link between educational expenditures or a variety of other factors and student outcomes. However, the evidence from the South Asia region on the 'true' private school effect is, at best, mixed (see for instance Chudgar and Quin, 2012). More importantly, whether the apparent private-school effect is the effect of attending a private school or a private-tutoring effect has not been investigated rigorously in most studies. The only exception to that is a study by Thapa (2012) in Nepal that finds strong positive private-school premiums in achievement at the secondary level, even after controlling for private tutoring. Whilst the current study does not aim to isolate the 'real' private-school effect from a 'private-tutoring effect', it is a first attempt to identify the extent to which private tutoring exists in the two countries.

A major reason for the lack of attention to this issue in the literature particularly in South Asia is the shortage of quality data that allows addressing relevant questions. For the first time in India and Pakistan, the availability of quality data means that we are able to take a first step in filling this knowledge gap with solid statistical evidence on both the size of this industry and a picture of *who* takes tuition and the likely implications this will have on social justice and equity. We recognise that the data from both countries have their limitations – they cover only rural areas and have partial coverage (especially in India). However, the data are incredibly rich in variables that have not been available to researchers before and this allows us to provide a snapshot (if not a complete picture) of the shadow tutoring industry in the two countries.

This study proposes to address several questions. In the first instance, we are interested in mapping out the true extent of the private-tutoring industry in India and Pakistan. In doing so, we aim to underpin who exactly takes tuition in the two countries, i.e. is it linked to private schooling or a preserve of the rich? Interestingly, in some countries where the shadow education system has been studied it is believed that private tutoring caters to the needs of students trapped in poor-quality *state* schooling systems. This premise, however, has no basis in good-quality research in South Asia. Both India and Pakistan have seen a mushrooming of very low-fee-charging private schools (Aslam, 2009). The quality of schooling these schools provide is often no different to the poor-quality schooling provided by the state sector (Andrabi et al, 2002). There is, therefore, no reason to presume that only government-school students will necessarily engage in private-tuition-taking activities. Our study will allow the data to speak about the extent of tuition undertaken across the different school types rather than presume that children in one type of school necessarily undertake private tutoring more often than others.

Another key aim of this study is to discuss the potential equity implications of the findings that are eventually uncovered. The existence of a fee-charging shadow sector also has crucial equity implications, for instance if it consumes substantial proportions of family income and imposes a heavy burden on low-income families. It is also argued that tutoring exacerbates social inequalities if it becomes accessible only to the rich or to the children of more educated parents or if the quality of tutoring accessed differs by social class. These issues will be addressed by painting a comparative descriptive picture of the extent of private tutoring in the two countries.

This chapter is organised as follows. Section 2 discusses the data used from India and Pakistan. Section 3 paints a descriptive picture of the prevalence of private tuition in the two countries. It investigates critical hypotheses, including the extent to which children attending different types of schools in the region take out-of-hours paid tuition and the equity implications of private tuition. Section 4 discusses the key determinants of tuition-taking and possible impacts on student learning. Section 5 discusses the equity and social justice implications of the findings. Section 6 concludes.

Data Sources

This study uses individual-level quantitative data for India and Pakistan that allow for the first time to address issues pertaining to the shadow education systems that prevail in the two countries. For India, the study draws from the SchoolTells survey, a survey of primary schools in two north Indian states: Uttar Pradesh and Bihar. These are two of the most economically and educationally challenged states of India.[1] This survey was designed by Professor Geeta Kingdon of the Institute of Education, and funded by the Spencer Foundation, with the main aim of answering questions regarding the relative effectiveness of regular and contract teachers. The SchoolTells survey was carried out in the 2007-08 school year in 160 rural primary schools across 10 districts of the sample states. It yielded achievement data on over 4000 students of grades 2 and 4 as well as on their teachers and schools. Each school was visited four times in the school year. Students were tested in language and maths at the start and end of the school year, approximately nine months apart. The survey provides an unusually rich source of data with detailed questions on the children's personal traits (age, gender, height, illness); family background (caste, religion, parental education, household-asset ownership); teacher characteristics (qualifications, training, gender, age, regular/contract status, absence rate and time on task); and a wide range of school-quality factors. For the purpose of this study, we use reported responses to questions about whether they take any paid private tuition or not and how much is spent on it in a given year.[2]

For Pakistan, data from the Annual Status of Education Report (ASER), 2010 are used. Based on a household- and individual-level survey of rural regions undertaken across 32 districts in 5 provinces – Punjab, Sindh, Khyber Pakhtunkhwah (KP, previously the North West Frontier Province), Balochistan and Gilgit-Baldistan – as well as in Azad Jammu and Kashmir (AJK) and the Federal Capital, Islamabad. This survey covers more than 900 villages, no fewer than 19,000 households and more than 54,000 children aged 3-16 across the country. The data collection was undertaken during September-November 2010. For our purposes, these data are unique as they ask parents/adults in the household information about all children aged 3-16 within the household questions about: the type of school the child is enrolled in (with options ranging from private to madrassa, non-formal Education, non-government organisation (NGO) or government school as well as two questions pertaining to whether the child takes any paid private tuition and if so, how much is spent on it in rupees/month. In addition, the questionnaire asks questions about the household's economic status and parental education levels. In addition to gathering information about children, parents and the household from the adults/parents in the household, another key aspect of the data is that that the basic language, numeracy and English-language skills of each child (aged 5-16 only) are also individually tested.

The Shadow Education Sector in India and Pakistan

The objective of this section is to furnish a picture of the size and nature of the private-tutoring sectors of the two countries and provide a descriptive picture of the determinants of private tutoring. Embedded deeply is the concern about the equity implications. Using the available data, the analysis below provides a descriptive analysis of the extent and determinants of private tutoring in specific parts of the two countries. This analysis investigates the prevalence of tuition and monthly expenditure conditional on taking tuition by disaggregating across various dimensions including age, gender, region/province and school type.

What Is the Extent of the Private
Tuition Industry in India and Pakistan?

While anecdotal evidence suggests that private tuition is widespread, it is important to expand such evidence using survey data to substantiate the claims. Table 1 below reports tuition prevalence by age group, for school-aged children (defined as those who are aged 3-16) in rural India and Pakistan. There are some very striking findings emerging from these tables.

Firstly, a large proportion of school-aged children in both countries seem to be taking paid private tuition. Across Pakistan, almost 16% of rural children take paid tuition. This represents 5224 children in the sample of 33,290 children aged 3-16 in rural Pakistan. The proportion of children undertaking tuition is even higher in our Indian sample, where nearly a fifth of all children surveyed (i.e. about 20%) were taking private tuition. As our data are drawn from rural samples only, these are likely to be under-estimates of the true levels, as tuition-taking is often more prevalent in urban areas (Bray, 2009). In both countries the incidence increases with age, although the effect is more marked in Pakistan than India, where the incidence rises from 13% for younger children to nearly 20% for the oldest age group in our sample.

Secondly, the amount spent on tuition in a given month is also large: on average parents spend Rs. 293/month on private tuition in rural Pakistan. This equates to about US$3.4/month.[3] This is not an

141

insubstantial amount given that 60% of Pakistan's population reportedly lives on under US$2/day.[4] Table I also shows older children are more likely to be taking private tuition than younger children. The amount spent on tuition also appears to increase monotonically with age. In India, the average spend is 76 rupees per month, which is approximately US$1.7 per month, which again is not an insubstantial amount. We discuss in more detail later the proportion of average household earnings that seems to be spent on private tuition in the region.

India

Age group (years)	Proportion taking tuition	Monthly expenditure on tuition (Indian or Pakistani rupees)
3-8	21.9	71
9-12	23.2	74
13-16	23.9	100
3-16	22.6	76

Pakistan

Age group (years)	Proportion taking tuition	Monthly expenditure on tuition (Indian or Pakistani rupees)
3-8	13.3	203
9-12	16.2	264
13-16	19.7	453
3-16	15.7	293

Table I. Private-tuition prevalence by age group in rural India and Pakistan, ages 3-16. *Source*: SchoolTELLS (2008) for India and ASER (2010) in Pakistan.

Table II disaggregates the incidence of tuition and expenditures by province/region where data are available. Disaggregating by region allows a more nuanced picture to emerge: we find that Punjab and Islamabad (the Federal capital) have the highest incidence of tuition-taking in the country, with almost 30% of children taking tuition in Islamabad, followed closely by 23% in Punjab. Tuition-taking is lowest in Sindh (only about 6% or so of children aged 3-16 take tuition). In India we observe that children in Bihar are far more likely to be taking tuition than in Uttar Pradesh. In Bihar, 44% of children undertake private tuition in rural areas (again, the figure is likely to be higher in urban areas), while in UP just 6% of children undertake tuition. On average, parents in UP spend more on tuition compared to parents in Bihar – 26 rupees per month more on average – about US$0.60. In

Pakistan there are also substantial differences in the amount spent, with expenditure varying from 247 Pakistani rupees in the Punjab to nearly 600 rupees in Gilgit (US$6.80).

	Proportion taking tuition	Expenditure on tuition (rupees/month)
India		
Uttar Pradesh	6.5	97.4
Bihar	44.3	71.9
Pakistan		
Punjab	23.0	247
Sindh	5.6	275
Balochistan	9.9	276
KP (NWFP)	9.5	403
Gilgit	13.1	585
AJK	9.5	352
Islamabad*	28.5	432
Pakistan	15.7	293

Note: *Islamabad Capital Territory (ICT) is classified into urban and rural regions. The sample for ASER is drawn from rural ICT.

Table II. Private-tuition prevalence by province/ region in rural India and Pakistan, ages 3-16.
Source: SchoolTELLS (2008) for India and ASER (2010) in Pakistan.

It is clear from these tables that private tuition is quite a widespread phenomenon in the region, though the extent of its utilisation varies both across countries and within countries. In Bihar, nearly half of all children are undertaking some kind of tuition, while in the Sindh province of Pakistan, just 6% of children are.

All Children Are Equal, but Some Are More Equal Than Others

Private schools and private tuition. The expansion of private schooling in India and Pakistan is also a recent phenomenon that has changed the dynamics of education provision in the countries. Unconstrained expansion of fee-charging schools is questioned on equity grounds: that they cater to the elite in urban areas and marginalise the poor. These views have, however, been challenged in both India and in Pakistan. Studies reveal an unprecedented expansion of private schooling rather than just a 'peripheral' role serving only the urban few. Evidence suggests that private schools do not cater only to the urban elite but are also utilised by the poor (see for instance Alderman et al, 2001; Andrabi et al, 2002 and Aslam, 2009 for Pakistan and Kingdon, 1996 for India).

143

There is also evidence that private schools can bridge gender gaps, as even rural parents in Pakistan are seen as willing to send their daughters to private co-educational schools (Andrabi et al, 2002). However, this unimpeded expansion of private schooling has called into question the quality of schooling being imparted to students. Indeed, the poor quality of the government-school sector is described as a reason why the private sector has emerged as such a dominant player in the educational field. Within this context, one can place the establishment of a 'shadow' education sector; disillusioned by the poor quality of state provision and yet unable to undertake the burden of private schooling, parents may turn to a shadow education sector where poor-quality state education is supplemented by extra studying.

There is, however, no evidence to date that gives credence to the view that disillusioned state-sector pupils turn more to private tuition. A crucial hypothesis proposed in this study for the first time within the context of South Asia is to identify to what extent private tutoring is a 'complement' to or a 'substitute' to poor-quality state schooling. In other words, we question the extent to which students studying in different types of schools 'complement' their studies (of presumably reasonable quality) with extra tutoring or actually find that they are having to 'substitute' (presumably poor-quality schooling) with private tutoring. This question arises from a premise that private schools provide *relatively* better quality schooling compared to government schools in the two countries. There is substantial evidence to affirm this claim (see for instance Kingdon, 1996 for India and Aslam, 2009 for Pakistan). If this is the case, if private-school students undertake private coaching, they are likely 'complementing' relatively better quality schooling with tuition. However, if government-school students are found to engage more in tuition-taking and if government schools are relatively worse off in imparting learning (which they appear to be according to latest evidence), these students are presumably 'substituting' poor-quality schooling with tuition-taking in a bid to learn. We therefore wish to understand the extent to which children attending different school types engage in paid out-of-school hours tutoring. Interestingly, in some countries where the shadow education system has been studied, it is believed that private tutoring caters to the needs of students trapped in poor-quality state-schooling systems.

We do not presume that private tuition-taking is undertaken only by children studying in poor-quality government schools. Nor do we assume that it is only undertaken by the very rich i.e. those in the highest income quintiles who can easily afford to do so, as a complement to their schooling. As mentioned before, the existence of low-fee charging private schools is a phenomenon common to both countries. Therefore the prevalence of private tuition by school type is an empirical question, which we hope to answer using our rich data sources. We distinguish between only two types of schools: government and private. While data allowed distinguishing between other types of schools (such as madrassas and non-formal education [NFE] or non-governmental organisation [NGO], schools), the proportion of children in rural areas reportedly enrolled in these schools was too low to allow meaningful comparisons. For example, in Pakistan, 70% of rural children aged 3-16 were enrolled in government schools and 29% were in private schools. Only 1% were enrolled in madrassas and an even smaller proportion in NFE, NGO and other schools. In India, Kingdon (2007) found that in 2006, 20% of children in rural areas attended private schools, and that these figures are three times higher than the official government statistics. This indicates that disaggregating our sample by 'private' and 'government' should cover a majority of the schoolchildren in the rural samples in the two countries. In urban areas the figures are noticeably higher in official statistics, and the true numbers are likely to be higher still. Thus, when doing this comparison, only children enrolled in government and private schools are considered.

	Proportion taking tuition	Expenditure on tuition (rupees/month)
Uttar Pradesh		
Government	4.6	78
Private	13.5	121
Bihar		
Government	44.1	72
Private	45.7	72

	Proportion taking tuition	Expenditure on tuition (Pakistan rupees/month)
Pakistan		
Government	10.9	256
Private	26.9	329
Other	7.5	233

Table III. Private-tuition prevalence by school type in rural India and Pakistan. *Source*: SchoolTELLS (2008) for India and ASER (2010) in Pakistan.

To this end, Table III disaggregates the incidence of, and expenditure on, private tuition by school type. With the exception of Bihar, the incidence of paid tuition-taking appears significantly higher among students in private schools than in government schools. For instance, while almost 27% of all children in Pakistani private schools report taking private tuition, only about 11% of government-school students do so. In Uttar Pradesh, while only 4.6% of government-school pupils undertake tuition, 13.5% of private-school pupils do so. In Bihar, on the other hand, there is no (statistically significant) difference between government-school and private-school pupils in their tendency to take private tuition.

What do these findings suggest? Firstly, unlike what has been anecdotally believed, private tuition is not the preserve of students in government schools substituting the poor quality of state schooling with private provision. On the contrary, it may be the case that private-school provision is of an equally poor quality when compared to state schooling, which results in students attempting to complement it with further tuition-taking. Evidence from Pakistan in fact suggests that the quality of private provision is often not very different from inferior-quality state schooling available to a majority of the population, although students in private schools generally fare better in terms of achievement outcomes compared to their government-school counterparts (Aslam, 2009). That does not, however, explain the very large differential in the incidence of tutoring between the two school types in most areas. However, if we consider what is termed the 'selection effect' of private schooling, that is, children whose parents have a higher preference for education are more likely to compensate for deficiencies in the schooling system through private means, then it is quite understandable that children in private schools, which are often still of lower quality than is expected by parents, supplement this to a larger degree than parents of government-school children. In addition, these households often have higher ability to pay, making tuition more likely. This notwithstanding, the lack of a difference in Bihar between government and private schools suggests very complicated dynamics that are almost impossible to isolate in a descriptive study alone.

Money can buy schooling. In the main, pupils who attend private schools are more likely to have undertaken some private tuition. Previous studies in other country settings have found factors such as wealth/income, parental education and the existence of competitive examinations at different education levels, as well as regional differences and the quality of state-sector education to be important in determining the extent of private tutoring in a country (Bray, 2007; Dang & Rogers, 2008). We are not aware of any studies in India or Pakistan that address this question. We first extend our analysis by differentiating pupils on grounds of household wealth. We do so by creating quintiles of wealth, using data on household possessions. While ideally one would wish for complete data on expenditure and assets, this is seldom available and where available is often fraught with reporting bias. We therefore use a simpler method of evaluating wealth differences, by using household assets, following Filmer and Pritchett (1999), who show a very high correlation between asset indices and consumption patterns both internationally and within the South Asia region. For Pakistan, the *Annual Status of*

Education Report (ASER) (2010) questionnaire asked the household head questions about asset ownership for the household. This included asking (and visibly confirming where possible) whether the household lives in a *kuccha* (mud), *semi-pucca* or *pucca* (built with bricks and mortar) house, whether there is any electricity or a toilet within the house. The enumerators were also asked to note down how many of the following assets the household reported owning: mobile phones, televisions, bicycles, motorcycles, cars or tractors. For the purpose of creating a wealth index, binary indicator variables were created for each of the assets/household indicators. For example, whether the household lived in a *pucca* house was given a value of 1 and 0 otherwise. Similarly, if the household reported owning a mobile phone (even one), the binary variable denoting 'mobile ownership' equalled 1 and if the household did not own any, the 'mobile ownership' variable equalled 0. This list of assets/indicators was then used to assign weights (for example owning a *pucca* house was given a weight of 300 compared to owning a mobile phone which was given a weight of 5). An identical exercise was carried out using the Indian data. Wealth indices were then created by assigning weights to the different assets owned in the household. A given wealth index is then used to ascribe a quintile to the poorest 20% of the population, richest 20% and those in between the distribution.

Income quintile	Proportion taking tuition	Expenditure on tuition (rupees/month)
India		
1 = poorest	18.1	69
2	20.0	70.4
3	21.1	73
4	25.2	76
5 = richest	31.8	90
Pakistan		
1 = poorest	5.5	287
2	9.6	233
3	14.0	241
4	19.9	292
5 = richest	27.6	352

Table IV. Private-tuition prevalence by income quintile in rural India and Pakistan, ages 3-16.
Source: SchoolTELLS (2008) for India and ASER (2010) in Pakistan.

It is clear from Table IV that the incidence of private tutoring increases with ability to pay. Children belonging to the richest income groups in rural Pakistan are almost five times as likely as those in the poorest quintiles to be taking private tutoring. Notably, however, there is very

147

little difference in the amount spent on tuition across the different income quintiles. Persons in the poorest quintiles spend on average Rs. 287 per month compared to Rs. 352 per month spent by those in the richest quintile. This is a striking finding because it suggests that while the incidence of tuition-taking changes depending on how rich/poor you are, the amount actually spent is not dependent on socio-economic status.

Region	Average monthly income (2004/05 prices)*	Average monthly income in 2010 prices+	Average monthly expenditure on private tuition per child (aged 3-16) in 2010	Average household (HH) size**
	(a)	(b)	(c)	(d)
Punjab	9,488	16,604	247	7.0
Sindh	10,413	18,223	275	6.1
Balochistan	8,849	15,486	276	6.8
KP/NWFP	9,395	16,441	403	8.0
Pakistan	9,685	16,949	293	6.9

Region	Proportion aged<16 in rural areas	Average number of children aged <16	Average estimated monthly HH expenditure on tuition	Expenditure as share of HH income (if all children aged 3—16 take tuition)
	(e)	(f)	(g)	(h)
Punjab	0.44	3.1	766	4.6
Sindh	0.46	2.8	770	4.2
Balochistan	0.47	3.2	883	5.7
KP/NWFP	0.48	3.8	1,531	9.3
Pakistan	0.45	3.1	908	5.3

Table V. What proportion of rural household income is spent on private tuition?
Sources: *Pakistan Statistical Yearbook (2007), Government of Pakistan, Statistics Division, Federal Bureau of Statistics; + Column (b) shows column (a) figures inflated to 2010 prices using the Wholesale Price Index for Pakistan reported in Pakistan Statistical Yearbook (2007); Column (c) estimates based on ASER (2010) data; **Average household size and proportion of persons aged <16 as based on 1998 Census estimates reported: http://www.census.gov.pk/HousingIndicators.htm.; Column (g) = (c) x (f); Column (h)=(g)/(b)*100.

In India, the proportion of children taking tuition also increases with household wealth, and while expenditures increase, the average increase in expenditure between the poorest and the richest groups is just 21.3 Indian rupees (about a third more). To some extent, as in Pakistan, this reflects the heavy burden faced by the poorest persons in rural areas in educating their children.

One of the means of benchmarking the burden that private tutoring imposes on rural families is to compute the ratio of expenditure on private tuition per family to the per capita income. Table V does this with Pakistan as an example. Because the latest monthly income figures disaggregated by province/region are available in 2004/05 prices, column (b) inflates these figures to 2010 prices using the Consumer Price Index. Per capita income is estimated using the average household size reported in the 1998 Census; the proportion of persons below the age of 16 is estimated using the 1998 Census estimates. Assuming that all persons in the household take private tuition allows us to compute a very rough lower bound of the expenditure on private tuition as a share of household income. The estimates show that almost 5% of household income is spent on private tutoring alone. Given that government schooling is not 'free', with households incurring significant expenses on travel costs, uniform, books and so on, this figure is not insubstantial. Moreover, keeping in mind that the average monthly income estimates are for both rural and urban areas and that rural incomes are presumably substantially smaller than urban incomes, the estimates reported in column (h) are likely very largely under-estimates. Quite a substantial share of family incomes in rural areas appears to be diverted towards the shadow education sector in Pakistan.

The analysis so far has shown that the incidence of private tuition increases with ability to pay. However, quite a large proportion of lower-income families in both India and Pakistan choose to engage in extra tuition-taking, suggesting that it is not just a preserve of the rich. Indeed, when they chose to take tuition the differences in the amount spent on private tuition does not rise in line with income, indicating that it imposes a substantial burden especially on low-income families in the two countries.

Gender bias in private tuition provision. Gender bias in education expenditure is well documented in the South Asia region (Kingdon, 2005; Aslam & Kingdon, 2008). To fully understand the nature of private tuition in the region, we need to disaggregate our data by gender, to try to evaluate gender bias in both the undertaking of and expenditure on private tuition. We move beyond a simple discussion of gender bias in private tuition by considering the two stages separately, before aggregating them for an overall estimate of the gender bias. We build on the literature evaluating private schooling in Pakistan, which finds that

149

at the primary-school level there is a pro-male gender bias in the decision to enrol children in private schooling, but not necessarily a bias against girls in the amount spent on their schooling, once the decision to attend school has been made (Aslam & Kingdon, 2008). It is suspected that a similar mechanism may be at work in the decision to allocate household expenditure to private tuition. Table VI shows the proportion of children undertaking tuition, and their conditional monthly expenditure, by gender.

Age group	Proportion taking tuition				Monthly expenditure on tuition			
	All	Male	Female	*t*-test (b) - (c)	All	Male	Female	*t*-test (f) - (g)
India								
3-8	22.1	23.6	20.2	***	72	73	69	*
9-12	23.4	25.5	20.9	***	75	78	69	***
13-16	24.0	25.6	22.1	***	100	113	83	***
3-16	22.7	24.5	20.7	***	76	80	71	***
Pakistan								
3-8	13.3	13.3	13.4		203	205	201	
9-12	16.2	16.3	15.9		264	265	262	
13-16	19.7	19.6	19.9		453	461	439	
3-16	15.7	15.8	15.5		293	301	281	***

Table VI. Gender bias in private tuition.
Source: SchoolTELLS (2008) for India and ASER (2010) in Pakistan.

It is interesting to note that while there appears to be a pro-male bias in both stages of the private-tutoring decision in the Indian sample, in Pakistan it only appears to be significant in the expenditure decision. That is to say, males and females are taking private tuition in roughly equal proportions, but households are spending more on tuition for boys than for girls in the older age group. For the younger age groups (3-9, 9-12), there appears to be very little differential treatment in Pakistan, either in terms of the decision to undertake private tuition, or the monthly expenditure on tuition. As before, it is quite possible that these average figures mask gender bias in certain states, so we further disaggregate by state/province in Table VII.

While in India the pro-male gender bias is apparent for both decisions in both sample states, in Pakistan there is very little gender bias in terms of attending schools in the provinces. The exceptions to this are Gilgit and AJK, where a slight pro-male gender bias does exist, with boys being two to three percentage points more likely to attend private tutoring than girls in these states. When we disaggregate conditional expenditure by province, we do find gender differences, although they are not always pro-male. In Gilgit, while boys are more likely to be undertaking tuition, when girls take tuition they spend relatively more than boys, by some 130 rupees per month. A similar story is told for AJK. This suggests that gender bias in household expenditure is a very complicated dynamic, and influenced by local conditions. However, these figures are just descriptive, implying correlations between gender and taking tuition, and may be the product of other, unobserved factors, such as household wealth or maternal education. To fully isolate gender bias, we need to move beyond mere descriptive, something we turn to in section 4.

	Proportion taking tuition				Expenditure on tuition (rupees/month)			
	All	Male	Female	t-test (b) - (c)	All	Male	Female	t-test (f) - (g)
	(a)	(b)	(c)	(d)	(e)	(f)	(g)	(h)
India: state								
Uttar Pradesh	6.58	7.6	5.4	***	97	105	84	***
Bihar	44.3	46.2	42	***	71	74	69	***
Pakistan: province/ region								
Punjab	23.0	23.4	22.5		247	249	245	
Sindh	5.6	5.9	5.1		275	290	242	**
Balochistan	9.9	9.9	10.0		276	319	180	***
KP (NWFP)	9.5	9.7	9.1		403	430	354	*
Gilgit	13.1	14.4	11.1	*	585	541	671	*
AJK	9.5	10.5	8.2	*	352	332	380	
Islamabad	28.5	28.3	28.8		432	445	413	
Pakistan	15.7	15.8	15.5		293	301	281	***

*significant at the 10% level; **significant at the 5% level; ***significant at the 1% level.

Table VII. Gender bias in private tuition, by state/province.
Source: SchoolTELLS (2008) for India and ASER (2010) in Pakistan.

Exploring Further: who takes tuition and how does it impact learning

The natural question that follows from the discussion above is: are these factors just correlations, driven by unobserved factors? Are private-school children more likely to take tuition because they are rich? In a companion research paper, Aslam and Atherton (2013) estimate a model of who takes private tuition and unravel the extent to which private tutoring impacts student learning. In the first instance, the key factors determining private tuition-taking in Pakistan are: age and gender of the child (being male); belonging to a more educated mother; and wealth. Among all the factors, wealth is one of the largest determinants of tuition uptake: the rich are significantly more likely to take tuition compared to the poor. In India, the incidence of tuition-taking increases with age only for the oldest age group; unlike Pakistan, there is evidence of pro-male gender bias, although this bias is higher among the poorer households rather than the wealthier ones, contrary to what we find for Pakistan. Mothers' education has a small positive association with the incidence of tuition-taking and as in Pakistan, wealth has a strong effect in absolute terms (an effect that disappears when quintile-level analyses are done). Children in Bihar are also significantly more likely to undertake tuition than in UP.

We also delve deeper to investigate the extent to which private tutoring is associated with learning achievement (see Aslam and Atherton, 2013 for details). In both countries we find that private tuition has beneficial effects on all pupils, but the main beneficiaries are government-school pupils. Within government schools, it is the poorest section who gain the most from undertaking paid tuition, being far more likely to be at a higher reading or mathematics level (in Pakistan) and gaining the equivalent of 85% of a school year in India. Such large learning differences between those who undertake tuition and those who don't suggest that while there may be equity concerns if the poorest are simply priced out of the private-tutoring market, those who do chose to take tuition can compensate for low-quality schooling provided in government schools.

What Are the Equity Effects of Private Tuition?

The existence of a fee-charging shadow sector has crucial equity implications for users and non-users, for instance, if it consumes substantial proportions of family income and imposes a heavy burden on low-income families. It is also argued that tutoring exacerbates social inequalities if it becomes accessible only to the rich, or to the children of more educated parents, or if the quality of tutoring accessed differs by social class. There are also important implications from the point of view of providers and the role schoolteachers play in providing the extra tuition at a cost, as well as the impact it has for classroom teaching in general. The option of giving (for the teachers) and receiving (for the pupils) tuition outside of normal school hours changes the incentive structure of the provision of high-quality instruction within the standard school system, which in turn has implications for equity and social justice. It seems that parents in rural India and Pakistan are turning to private tutoring more frequently than thought. Also, given that our data are from rural areas, tuition in urban areas of the region is likely to be much more prevalent. The findings from the above analysis seem to suggest that while private tutoring is not necessarily just the preserve of the rich in rural Pakistan, being richer does help increase the likelihood that a child will take private tuition. Moreover, the above analysis has clearly shown that private tuition imposes a significant burden on relatively low-income families. There are also elements of gender-differentiated treatment apparent in the uptake of private tuition emerging from the empirical analysis, especially in India where in general a pro-male bias prevails in the decision to enrol a child in private tutoring as well as in the decision of how much to spend conditional on enrolment. This suggests that private tutoring in India and Pakistan is capable of exacerbating already-existing and deeply entrenched social inequalities.

In both countries we also find that while private tuition has favourable effects on learning and achievement for all pupils, the main beneficiaries are government-school pupils. Within government schools, it is the poorest students who gain the most, being far more likely to be at a higher reading or mathematics level (in Pakistan) and gaining the equivalent of 85% of a school year in India. It is the poor who are also least likely to be able to afford private tuition and hence to be priced out of the private-tuition market when faced with poor-quality general schooling in state schools. They are, however, also the most likely to benefit from any extra paid tuition in terms of achievement gains.

Conclusions

The South Asia region housed the largest proportion of primary-school-age children out of school – some 36 % – in 2001/2.[5] Despite progress in increasing access in recent years, a large proportion of children are still out of school in India and Pakistan. These countries also suffer from the problem of poor 'quality' schooling and many studies report the heterogeneity in schooling quality available and the resultant learning differences among graduates. There are known to be children studying in schools without the most basic facilities compared to schools that would compare to some of the best in the developed world. It is hardly surprising that one finds a cadre of school graduates barely able to read and write and another set who can compete internationally in any forum.

Within this context, there has been a stealthy evolution of the private-tutoring industry. The silence in policy documents, government statistics and research reports as well as the lack of attention that has been provided to this education sector is surprising as well as alarming: surprising because this study has shown convincing evidence to suggest that private tuition-taking is more widespread a phenomenon than believed in the region. It has also shown differences in the uptake of private tuition among the rich and poor and by gender in rural India and Pakistan. This has already raised some concerns regarding the exacerbation of existing social inequalities. The findings also suggest that there are even more far-reaching elements to social inequalities that may manifest themselves as a consequence of this phenomenon in the two countries. Children in government schools taking private tuition and especially those belonging to the poorest classes appear to perform better than those who do not take private tuition. This hints at the hugely inferior learning the poorest children in some government schools in rural India and Pakistan are receiving. It suggests that private tutoring does appear to complement poor-quality schooling for these children. This, however, comes at a cost. When rural incomes are so low, and especially among the poorest families, one wonders at the feasibility of this solution in the two countries' education systems.

Part of the explanation for the rise in private tutoring in the two SAR (South Asia Region) countries may rest on the poor quality of schooling that is provided to students *in* school. This may be due to several factors, including poor facilities, out-dated curriculums or untrained and even un-interested and incompetent teachers. It is harder, however, to reconcile many of the differential findings (such as differences in uptake of tuition by gender or by school type) on the basis of variations in schooling quality alone. An alternative explanation for the rise in private tuition is based on the argument that teacher salaries in India and Pakistan are lower compared to the salaries of people in other professions and with similar educational qualifications; this is cited as a reason why teachers turn to giving private tuition to supplement their incomes. Kingdon (2010) and Aslam and others (2011) argue that this is not entirely based on convincing evidence in the South Asia region. Their analyses suggest that not only are teacher salaries in India and Pakistan equivalent to those in other professions, but teacher salaries have risen more in real terms than salaries of persons in other professions. Teachers often get three to five times as much (and even more in certain regions/states) as multiples of per capita GDP in India and Pakistan.

Salary increases are intended to improve the quality of public services delivered to citizens. However, Kingdon (2010) argues that salary increases unrelated to performance are not necessarily efficiency-enhancing. The fact that most government-school teachers in India and Pakistan are hired 'permanently' and are therefore virtually un-sackable means that they can get away with a relatively high degree of shirking: evidence suggests high absenteeism among teachers in both countries. There is also the possibility that teachers are able to create a need for private tutoring either by encouraging their students to take it (from them or from others) or by not putting in enough effort while teaching in class, which may indirectly lead to the need for extra help outside the classroom. Thus, lax governance and accountability structures surrounding the teaching profession especially in government schools is a relatively convincing argument for the rise of private-tutoring industries in the two countries. However, it is again difficult to explain the heterogeneity in usage (by gender and school type for instance) on the basis of any of these arguments, suggesting a very complex interplay of factors that give rise to the demand and the supply of paid private tutoring in India and Pakistan.

Regardless of the reason for the rise of the shadow education sector in the two countries, it is prominent and has been documented to be large. The consequent implications for equality and social justice are numerous, ranging from issues of why a person chooses to pay extra for tuition when 'free' government education apparently exists, who the persons are who can access paid tuition and how it impacts their learning and other educational outcomes. Even more broadly speaking, there is now almost universal agreement that what is learnt (in school and out of it) matters as much as, if not more than, the years of schooling acquired. There is evidence that cognitive skills have economically large effects on individual earnings and on national growth. This literature is summarised in Hanushek and Woessmann (2008), and appears quite conclusive. This suggests that the socio-economic implications of this neglected educational phenomenon – private tutoring – could be potentially dramatic. Further work needs to investigate many of the broad ideas briefly touched upon in this study.

Notes

[1] This is based on both gross domestic product (GDP) per capita rankings of the states as well as the literacy rankings from latest figures available.

[2] To render the Pakistan and India samples comparable, the yearly expenditure on private tuition reported in the India data are rendered into monthly expenditures by dividing by nine. This was done with the view that children may not take tuition over the entire 12-month period.

[3] As on 17 June 2011 (www.xe.com)

[4] http://data.worldbank.org/indicator/SI.POV.2DAY

[5] UNICEF/UNESCO Institute for Statistics.

References

Alderman, H., Orazem, P.F. & Paterno, E.M. (2001) School Quality, School Cost, and the Public/Private School Choices of Low-Income Households in Pakistan, *Journal of Human Resources*, 36 (Spring), 304326.

Altonji, J.E., Elder, T.E. & Taber, C.R. (2005) Selection on Observed and Unobserved Variables: assessing the effectiveness of Catholic schools, *Journal of Political Economy*, 113(1), 151-184.

Andrabi, T., Das, J. & Khwaja, A. (2002) *The Rise of Private Schooling in Pakistan: catering to the urban elite or educating the rural poor?* Washington, DC: World Bank and Harvard University.

ASER (2010) *Annual Status of Education Report*, Pakistan. http://www.aserpakistan.org

Aslam, M. & Kingdon, G. (2008) Gender and Household Education Expenditure in Pakistan: Engel Curve evidence, *Applied Economics,* 40(20), 2573-2591.

Appleton, S., Atherton, P. & Bleaney, M. (2011) Growth Regressions and Data Revisions in Penn World Tables, *Journal of Economic Studies*, 38(3), 301-312.

Aslam, M. (2009) The Relative Effectiveness of Government and Private Schools in Pakistan: are girls worse off?, *Education Economics*, 17(3), 329-353.

Aslam, M. & Atherton, P. (2013) Private Tutoring and Student Learning: a cross-country analysis. Mimeo, Institute of Education, University of London.

Aslam, M., Kingdon, G. & Rawal, S. (2011) Teacher Quality in South Asia. Mimeo, University of Oxford and Institute of Education, University of London.

Betts, J.R. (1996) Is There a Link between School Inputs and Earnings? Fresh Scrutiny of an Old Literature, in G Burtless (Ed.) *Does Money Matter? The Effect of School Resources on Student Achievement and Adult Success*, pp. 141-191. Washington, DC: Brookings.

Bray, M. (2007) *The Shadow Education System: private tutoring and its implications for planners*, 2nd edn. Paris: UNESCO.

Bray, M. (2009) *Confronting the Shadow Education System: what government policies for what private tutoring?* Paris: UNESCO Publishing, IIEP Policy Forum, International Institute for Educational Planning.

Card, D. & Krueger, A.B. (1996) School Resources and Student Outcomes: an overview of the literature and new evidence from North and South Carolina, *Journal of Economic Perspectives*, 10(4), 31-50.

Chudgar, A. & Quin, E. (2012) Relationship between Private Schooling and Achievement: results from rural and urban India, *Economics of Education Review*, 31(4), 376-390.

Dang, H. & Rogers, F.H. (2008) The Growing Phenomenon of Private Tutoring: does it deepen human capital, widen inequalities or waste resources?, *The World Bank Research Observer*, advanced access published 18 April 2008. https://openknowledge.worldbank.org/bitstream/handle/10986/6587/wps45 30.pdf?sequence=1

Evans, W.N. & Schwab, R.M. (1995) Finishing High School and Starting College: do Catholic schools make a difference?, *Quarterly Journal of Economics*, 110(4), 941-974.

Figlio, D.N. & Stone, J.A. (1999) Are Private Schools Really Better?, in S. Polachek (Ed.) *Research in Labor Economics,* 18, pp. 115-140. Stamford, CT: JAI Press.

Filmer, D. & Pritchett, L. (1999) What Education Production Functions Really Show: a positive theory of education expenditures, *Economics of Education Review*, 18(2), 223-239.

Glewwe, P., Kremer, M. & Moulin, S. (2007) *Many Children Left Behind? Textbooks and Test Scores in Kenya.* Nairobi: NBER Working Papers 13300, National Bureau of Economic Research.

Glewwe, P., Kremer, M., Moulin, S. & Zitzewitz, E. (2004) Retrospective vs. Prospective Analyses of School Inputs: the case of flip charts in Kenya, *Journal of Development Economics*, 74, 251-268.

Goldhaber, D.D. (1996) Public and Private High Schools: is school choice an answer to the productivity problem?, *Economics of Education Review*, 15(2), 93-109.

Hanushek, E.A. (1986) The Economics of Schooling: production and efficiency in public schools, *Journal of Economic Literature,* 24(3), 1141-1177.

Hanushek, E.A. (2003) The Failure of Input-Based Schooling Policies, *Economic Journal*, 113 (February), F64-F98.

Hanushek, E. & Woessmann, L. (2008) The Role of Cognitive Skills in Economic Development, *Journal of Economic Literature*, 46(3), 607-668.

Jacob, B.A. & Lefgren, L. (2004) Remedial Education and Student Achievement: a regression-discontinuity analysis, *Review of Economics and Statistics*, 86(1), 226-244.

Kingdon, G. (1996) The Quality and Efficiency of Public and Private Schools: a case study of urban India, *Oxford Bulletin of Economics and Statistics*, 58(1), 55-80.

Kingdon, G (2005) Where Has All the Bias Gone? Detecting Gender Bias in the Household Allocation of Educational Expenditure in India, *Economic Development and Cultural Change*, 53(2), 409-451.

Kingdon, G. (2007) The Progress of School Education in India, *Oxford Review of Economic Policy*, 23(2), 168-195.

Kingdon, G. (2010) The Impact of the Sixth Pay Commission on Teacher Salaries: assessing equity and efficiency effects, RECOUP Working Paper No. 29, May.

Kingdon, G. & Banerji, R. (2009) *School Functioning in Rural North India: evidence from School–TELLS Survey.* London: Institute of Education, University of London.

Krueger, A.B. (1999) Experimental Estimates of Educational Production Functions, *Quarterly Journal of Economics*, 114(2), 497-532.

Krueger, A.B. (2003) Economic Considerations and Class Size, *The Economic Journal*, 113 (February), F34-F63.

Lavy, V. & Schlosser, A. (2005) Targeted Remedial Education for Underperforming Teenagers: costs and benefits, *Journal of Labor Economics*, 23(4), 839-874.

Leuven, E., Lindahl, M., Oosterbeek, H. & Webbink, D. (2007) The Effect of Extra Funding for Disadvantaged Pupils on Achievement, *Review of Economics and Statistics,* 89(4), 721-736.

Neal, D. (1997) The Effects of Catholic Secondary Schooling on Educational Achievement, *Journal of Labor Economics*, 15(1), 98-123.

Open Society Institute (OSI) (2006) *Education in a Hidden Marketplace: monitoring of private tutoring. Overview and Country Reports.* New York: Open Society Institute, Education Support Program.

School TELLS (2008) Data set available from Geeta Kingdon.

Thapa, A. (2012) Public and Private School Performance in Nepal: an analysis using the SLC examination, *Education Economics*, 1-16.

CHAPTER 8

Ethical Dilemmas in the Education Marketplace: shadow education, political philosophy and social (in)justice in Cambodia

WILLIAM C. BREHM & IVETA SILOVA

> My child wanted to go to private tutoring. Although we did not have enough money, she still went to study [extra lessons] and owed her teacher for months. When I earned money, I paid off the debt. The teacher did not mind.

When the resources to educate students are scarce but the desire to be educated is great, students, teachers and parents find themselves facing ethical dilemmas such as the one described above by a parent of a secondary-school student in rural Cambodia.[1] This parent, like many others in Cambodia, finds herself paying for services in a marketplace of private tutoring services described broadly as 'shadow education' (Bray, 2007). It is 'hidden' because the Ministry of Education in Cambodia takes a *laissez faire* approach to regulation, which means education outside mainstream school hours is not under the government's purview.

Shadow education is a multi-faceted phenomenon that has been found worldwide (Bray, 2010, 2011; Bray & Lykins, 2012). Its geographical reach is as wide as its purposes are diverse. Shadow education has been used for expanding knowledge and interests for individuals (Bray, 2007), accumulating human capital for societies (Psacharopoulos & Patrinos, 2002), and providing new strategies for coping with rapid geopolitical transitions for a variety of education stakeholders (Silova, 2009; Silova & Brehm, 2013). Within such complexity and diversity, shadow education naturally embodies multiple perspectives on educational justice.

When a public-school teacher tutors his or her own students, as the quote from Cambodia implies, the situation could be interpreted in different ways. On the one hand, it may be thought that this teacher is somehow *forcing* the poor student of this family to attend private lessons on credit because examination preparation is often given during the extra lessons. Despite the 'trick' being played by the teacher (Dawson, 2009), this family has no choice but to go into debt in order to send their children to private-tutoring lessons where monthly examination questions are often reviewed or the answers handed out. On the other hand, the extra lessons might be essential for covering the national curriculum that is too difficult to complete during official school hours because of double-shift schooling, which reduces the school day in order to accommodate multiple shifts of students into a single school building. Since engaging in private tutoring limits a teacher's ability to hold a second job outside of school, which the vast majority of Cambodian teachers do (Benveniste et al, 2008, p. 68), the teacher must charge students for the extra instruction. Within this environment, households must find a way to justify, perhaps unwittingly, giving unwarranted power to teachers within a system of little accountability in order for their children to receive an education.

Whatever the decision by households, this particular situation raises issues related to educational justice. From the former perspective, which is based on the assumption that teachers force students to attend private tutoring, injustice is created in the very limitation of choice. Students have no choice but to attend the extra lessons in order to prepare for monthly examinations, which are graded by the teacher, receive the remainder of the national curriculum, or both. If they do not attend private tutoring, they are at a disadvantage compared to their peers who decided to pay for extra lessons. In this case, limiting choice is considered unjust because it harms a student's freedom to act autonomously and also unfairly burdens certain groups in society because of unchosen disadvantages like poverty, which may prevent them from attending extra lessons. Alternatively, the latter perspective contextualises the ethical dilemma to the circumstances of Cambodia, suggesting that justice may have actually been *served* because the teacher found ways of including poor students in the extra lessons that are typically populated by students from wealthy backgrounds. Through a progressive fee system, where costs are adjusted depending on households' economic situations or delayed until families have extra money, this teacher may be righting an injustice caused from an educational system that structurally disadvantages the poor. In both cases, distinct forms of social relations are constructed among teacher, student and parent that reflect particular understandings of educational justice, which in turn derive from different political philosophies. The former is within the tradition of liberalism, and based on the assumption that freedom, choice and fairness need to be upheld for a society to be considered just. The latter is within the tradition of egalitarianism, where justice is believed to derive from societal equality, which is mainly achieved through the redistribution of resources and opportunities.

The ethical dilemma is thus threefold. First, there is the ethical dilemma for the teachers who must decide on a daily basis whether or not to engage in private-tutoring activities. When choosing to provide private tutoring to their own students, teachers must weigh the consequences of providing more instructional time and earning extra money against the risk of undermining the teaching profession because such actions may be considered corrupt by the community, government or broader society. Second, households must decide whether to participate in a system of private tutoring that may improve their children's academic success at the risk of increasing socioeconomic inequities because private tutoring excludes students who cannot pay. Third, there is an ethical dilemma for researchers and policymakers. In their attempt to understand shadow education, researchers and policymakers often – and perhaps unknowingly – use particular definitions of social justice that ultimately make value judgments on the situation under investigation. Without critically reflecting on our own philosophical perspectives on social justice, researchers may universalise their beliefs to all contexts. Likewise, policymakers may design policies without fully considering the structural issues people within local communities actually face.

It is with these ethical dilemmas in mind that this chapter seeks to address the complicated terrain of educational justice within the education marketplace in Cambodia. Shadow education is a valuable point of entry for discussing educational justice because it raises 'foundational questions over the political philosophy and the political economy that frame the distribution of educational resources, as public goods, and the organisation of society more broadly' (Mazawi et al, 2013, p. 212). By contextualising the system(s) of shadow education inside six schools in Siem Reap, Cambodia, we aim to provide a nuanced understanding of educational justice situated within particular (mainly liberal) political philosophies.

Methodology

In this chapter we are concerned only with the type of shadow education where teachers tutor their own students. Notwithstanding the potential benefits of such tutoring for the learning of a child or its ability to 'compensate for qualitative shortcomings' of public education (Bray, 2012), it is nevertheless considered detrimental to the common good of public education (Mazawi et al, 2013). Such an argument is two-pronged: it can be detrimental by (re)producing social inequalities 'because rich households can invest more easily than poor ones' and/or it can 'undermine regular school systems' (Bray, 2012). The latter occurs because 'teachers who are also tutors may neglect their regular classes; and teachers who tutor their existing students may deliberately cut the curriculum in order to promote demand for private lessons' (Bray, 2012).

In this chapter we explore this argument in detail by examining the educational-justice issues that arise when teachers tutor their own students within one district in Cambodia. This chapter uses data collected between January and December 2011 within six schools in Siem Reap, Cambodia, including three schools in an urban location (i.e. areas where most families do not farm for subsistence and have brick/concrete homes and use motorbikes or cars) and three schools in a rural location (i.e. areas where subsistence farming, wooden homes and bicycles are common). Within each location, we worked with a 9th grade in a lower-secondary school. These schools were purposively selected out of the 13 lower-secondary schools in the district in order to represent different average hourly costs of private tutoring. We then worked backwards in each lower-secondary school, which corresponded to one urban (and a 'higher' cost for private tutoring) and one rural (and a 'lower' cost for private tutoring) school, to find two primary schools that fed into each lower-secondary school. Within the four primary schools that agreed to participate in this study, we worked with 6th-grade students and teachers. These grades were selected because the conclusion of the 6th grade signals the completion of primary school and the conclusion of the 9th grade culminates in a national examination, which is standardised and is not graded by a student's teacher, suggesting we would find higher rates of private tutoring. Within each school, we worked with students, parents and teachers, separately targeting 'private-tutoring' and 'non-private-tutoring' groups.

Over the 12-month period, we conducted focus groups, interviews and classroom observations, as well as grade and attendance tracking. A total of 21 focus groups were conducted, which included 118 students, parents and teachers. In these conversations, which lasted on average one hour, the participants discussed their various experiences with private tutoring and perceptions about the impact of private tutoring on education access and quality. In order to investigate some themes that emerged in the focus groups in more depth, we conducted a total of 21 informal interviews with parents, teachers, students and principals. In addition to the interviews and focus groups, a total of 28 classroom observations were conducted, including 14 in public-school classes and 14 in private-tutoring lessons. In the 6th grade, observations were conducted in classes that typically focused on mathematics and Khmer-language subjects. In the 9th grade, observations were conducted in Khmer Language, Mathematics, Physics and Chemistry classes. Data on academic achievement and attendance came from tracking a total of 444 students, including 162 6th graders and 282 9th graders. The goal of the tracking was to examine whether (and how) private tutoring impacted students' academic achievement in different subjects.

The research design consisted of three parts, including: (1) an examination of the state structures, policies and local practices that enable teachers to tutor their own students; (2) the differences in the quality of education provision between public schools and private tutoring; and (3) the equity implications for education and Cambodian society because of any quality differences and cost barriers to accessing private tutoring. In this chapter, we will focus on findings related to the issues of social justice.

Findings: multiple perspectives on educational justice

In Cambodia, the form of private tutoring where public-school teachers double as tutors and students double as customers is called *Rien Kuo* (extra study). It can also be referred to as *Rien Boban Porn* (supplemental study) or *Rien Chhnuol* (study for hire). This type of private tutoring focuses on covering the required school curriculum, which is not taught during school hours, but can also include national examination preparation. Such lessons are typically conducted in school buildings or a teacher's home.

It is precisely this situation that is considered detrimental to mainstream education as found, for example, in Bray's (1999) previous research, which revealed that teachers were purposefully 'slowing down' the delivery of curricular content to create a market for private tutoring (p. 55). Such a practice is generally discussed from the perspective of educational corruption because there 'is a thin line distinguishing an investment in learning and an investment in the result of that learning' (Heyneman, 2011, p. 185) when a teacher tutors her own students for a fee (see also Klitgaard, 1988; Chapman, 2002; Bray, 2003; Hallak & Poisson, 2007; Heyneman, 2009). When 'attendance at private tutorial classes is the only way of acquiring knowledge that is essential for passing examinations' (Hayden & Martin, 2011, p. 13), it is perceived as a form of social injustice that undermines the institution of public schooling.

This form of shadow education has been found in studies conducted in other low-income countries. Teachers who tutor their own students in such countries have been labelled 'monopoly suppliers' who have 'the full discretion in what they supply' (Biswal, 1999, p. 223). In this context, the teacher acts as 'a price discriminating monopolist' by charging a fee based on parents' income for the same tutoring effort, while also partially controlling the demand for tutoring through the supply of her effort in the public education system (Biswal, 1999, p. 59). Similarly, teachers have been referred to as 'monopoly suppliers' in some countries of the former socialist bloc, where the proportions of students tutored by their own schoolteachers reach 51% of students in Tajikistan, 40% in Kazakhstan and 39% in Kyrgyzstan and Mongolia (Silova et al, 2006). In Bulgaria, Croatia and Serbia, over 60% of surveyed university students 'knew of bribery for a grade or an exam among their faculty' (Heyneman et al, 2008, p. 5). In Moldova, it was reported as high as 80%. In all these cases, private tutoring has been understood and conceptualised as a form of corruption, which is detrimental to the public good of mainstream education.

In such situations, it is often structural deficiencies (i.e. limited funding, inadequate oversight, insufficient or dilapidated infrastructure, etc.) of the national education system that limit the supply of public education and thus create the need for private tutoring. In such situations, households often demand private tutoring from public-school teachers when the system of public education does not satisfy students' needs or desires to be educated. These structural issues, which contribute to the system of private tutoring, provide the context for understanding justice within the Cambodia system of education.

Structural Issues

The structural issues that affect the mainstream education system in Cambodia mainly centre on a curriculum perceived to be too long to complete during the official school day; limited educational expenditures that negatively impact teachers' salaries; and large class sizes that prohibit teachers form teaching effectively.

Private tutoring is partly needed because the national curriculum is perceived to be too long. Students and parents perceived private tutoring as a mechanism that enables teachers to properly teach the subjects included in the national curriculum. As one parent explained: 'There are many subjects in government school and teachers do not have time to teach them all.' In particular, many parents and teachers believe that there is simply not enough time in the school day or too many students in a mainstream classroom to cover the entire curriculum. This perceived lack of time leads to a perceived need for more instructional time simply to provide requisite coverage of the national curriculum. A teacher explained to us how she 'rushes' to finish the curriculum by saving some material for private-tutoring lessons:

> We rush to keep up with the curriculum. [During official school hours], we teach only theory and give only a few examples. If students go to private tutoring, they can practice [at the board] because there are fewer students ... We cannot get all students to practice [at the board] in government class. It requires a lot of time.

Low public educational expenditures also contribute to the demand for private tutoring. In countries financially unable to support public education adequately, private tutoring emerges as a mechanism to supplement low teacher salaries, provide smaller class sizes, and offer learning materials to students outside the national curriculum (Silova, et al, 2006; Silova, 2009; Bray, 2010; for the Cambodian case see Bray & Bunly, 2005; Brehm & Silova, 2014). The Cambodian government spends 2.3% of its Gross Domestic Product (GDP) on education, placing it among the lowest in Southeast Asia and below the world's average of 4.8% (European Commission, 2012). Although the budget allocation to the Ministry of Education, Youth and Sport (MoEYS) for recurrent expenditures increased starting in the 2000s, there has been a steady decrease since 2007 (see Figure 1). According to the European Commission (2012), there was a downward trend in budgeted recurrent expenditures between 2007 (19.2%) and 2012 (15.9%), which has disproportionately affected teacher wages (Benveniste et al, 2008, p. 74). Meanwhile, studies have found that households spend a larger amount on education per child than does the government: whereas the government spends on average US$50 per child per year (Ratcliff, 2009, p. 11), households spend between US$48 (rural areas) to US$157 (urban areas) per child per year (NGO Education Partnership [NEP], 2007, p. 18). Of household education expenditures, approximately 38% goes to education fees, which includes the cost of private tutoring (NEP, 2007).

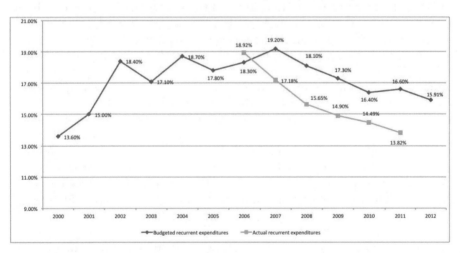

Figure 1. MoEYS budgeted and actual recurrent expenditures.
Source: European Commission (2012)

Consequently, the lack of educational resources disproportionately impact teacher wages. In Cambodia, there has been a broad consensus among educators, union leaders, administrators and society in general that teacher salaries are insufficient to cover living expenses (Benveniste et al, 2008). In 2007, for example, a primary teacher's base salary was US$44 per month, which made it difficult (if not impossible) for many teachers to afford the basic necessities of food, housing and health care, as well as support any children or elderly family members (Benveniste et al, 2008, 59). Notwithstanding the recent increases in teacher salary, private tutoring has helped underpaid teachers generate additional income. For example, a common second occupation among Cambodian teachers, especially in urban primary schools, is private tutoring (41.5% of urban teachers identified tutoring as out-of-school work; [Benveniste et al, 2008, p. 69]). Earnings from private tutoring can represent approximately two thirds of the monthly average base salary with basic allowances (Benveniste et al, 2008, p. 38). Similar to teachers in other geographic areas (such as the Southeast/Central Europe and the former Soviet Union), many Cambodian teachers have adopted the logic of 'service provision', using private tutoring as a key income-generation activity (Silova & Bray, 2006).

Making matters worse, there is often a delay in the allocation of funds. In Cambodia, both teacher salaries and Programme-Based Budgeting (unallocated money intended for individual schools, which used to be called the Priority Action Programme, or PAP) are routinely distributed late. Teachers have claimed that the distribution of wages is typically delayed (VSO, 2008). For example, salary disbursement in January 2012 had not been allocated to teachers in seven provinces by the end of the month (Denn Ayuthyea, 2012). A second issue with delayed funds is the leakage that occurs between the Ministry of Economy and Finance (the ministry responsible for releasing money to the MoEYS) and when it reaches teachers. As money is passed from the Economy and Finance Ministry to the MoEYS, which is then sent to the Provincial and District Offices of Education and then finally received by the schools, money is lost at each stage. One common complaint from teachers is that their salaries are never the correct amount. Combined, low wages – made even lower by leakage – require teachers to hold second jobs, which nearly 70% claim to have (Benveniste et al, 2008, p. 68). Conducting private tutoring is often the second job for teachers of subjects in demand by students (mainly, but not always, Khmer, Physics, Chemistry and Mathematics).

As a result of these structural deficiencies in the mainstream education system, private tutoring has become commonplace in many schools. In our study, education stakeholders commonly understood that a child's education requires *both* government and private-tutoring classes. As one parent said: 'You learn 50 percent in a government school and 50 percent in private tutoring.' Both are inseparable parts of one system necessary to receive a complete education. For this reason we conceptualised the education system as a 'public-private hybrid' (Brehm et al, 2012), because mainstream schooling relies on private tutoring to complement what is defined as adequate schooling.

Students in the schools in this study heavily demanded the hybrid system of education. 'Private tutoring helps the children a lot,' a parent told us, 'because government school is not enough.' Within our study, 68.4% (193 out of 282) of 9th graders attended at least one private-tutoring lesson each month data was collected (see Table I for attendance rates by subject). In the 6th grade, although attendance was lower than the 9th grade, 41.3% of all tracked students (67 out of 162) still attended a private-tutoring lesson, which mainly focused on mathematics and/or Khmer Language. We found that during the day, students seamlessly moved between spaces of public and private educational provision. Often times the only distinguishing characteristic between the two spaces were student uniforms, worn in mainstream schooling but not required in private tutoring. Students typically attended one shift (four or five hours) of government school and then, returning to school (or teacher's home), attended another shift of private-tutoring classes (one to four hours, depending on the student) each day, sometimes including Sundays, public holidays and summer vacation, which costs roughly 300-1000 Riel (US$0.08-0.25) per hour.

	Students in government class	Students in private tutoring	% of students in private tutoring
Mathematics			
Urban	58	35	60.34
Rural	113	63	55.75
Total	171	98	57.31
Chemistry			
Urban	95	58	61.05
Rural	113	19	16.81
Total	208	77	37.02
Khmer Language			
Urban	90	47	52.22
Rural	113	64	56.64
Total	203	111	54.68

Table I. Intensity of private tutoring by subject, grade 9.

Since the lines between the public and private provision were often blurred, we found many continuities between private tutoring and mainstream schooling. Data collected from classroom observations and confirmed in the interviews and focus groups suggest that private tutoring is in many respects a continuation of government school in terms of teaching methodology and curriculum content (see Table II). For example, teachers assigned homework and even presented new material in private-tutoring lessons. Likewise, students appeared to be involved in similar activities in both government classes and private-tutoring lessons, including answering multiple-choice questions and responding to teachers who give examples to the whole class.

However, there were some differences between private tutoring and mainstream classes. Not only were there fewer students in private-tutoring classes and teachers were able to offer examples outside the national curriculum, but teachers were also able to employ pedagogies tailored to individual students. In private-tutoring classes, we often observed teachers circling the room to help students complete individual practice examples, whereas in mainstream school students often worked on problems in groups. Although group work may be a preferable classroom-management technique (and recommended as part of the Child Friendly School modalities) in classes with many students compared to ones with fewer, it was not found to be an 'enjoyable' (a common word used during the focus groups) technique by students and teachers alike. One teacher explained: 'It takes students too much time to work in groups. It is not easy ... It is not like fetching water with a dipper. It is fine if we just asked them to raise their hand and answer our questions.'

Teacher pedagogy	Government school $n = 14$ % of classes observed (number of classes observed)	Private tutoring $n = 14$ % of classes observed (number of classes observed)
High-ability students work with low-ability students	28.6 (4)	14.3 (2)
High-ability students help teach whole class	71.4 (10)	50.0 (7)
Call on weak students to answer questions	50.0 (7)	42.9 (6)
Students answer multiple-choice questions	14.3 (2)	14.3 (2)
Students answer questions at board	100.0 (14)	71.4 (10)
Teacher assigns homework	64.3 (9)	42.9 (6)
Teacher presents new material	78.6 (11)	35.7 (5)
Teacher provides whole-class instruction	100.0 (14)	85.7 (12)
Students answer in chorus	71.4 (10)	64.3 (9)
Teacher gives example to whole class	78.6 (11)	78.6 (11)

Table II. Similarities between government-school and private-tutoring classes.

The Multiple Meanings of Educational Justice

Within a context of limited educational finances, classrooms too full for effective teaching, and a curriculum too long to compete in double-shift schooling situations, what issues of (in)justice arise from situations where teachers tutor their own students? We attempt here to unpack the various perspectives on educational justice in the context of teachers tutoring their own students. We will discuss the findings in relation to the most common argument that teachers who tutor their own students engage in and/or contribute to a form of educational corruption because it either reproduces social inequalities (i.e. rich students attend more private tutoring than poor students) or is detrimental to the institution of public school (i.e. causes teachers to act maliciously in order to manufacture demand for private tutoring). In both instances, when private tutoring is considered educational corruption, our study produces evidence for *and* against this claim.

A Reproduction of Social Inequalities?

Our findings reveal that rich students are perceived to attend private-tutoring lessons more often than poor students. Students who go to private tutoring are generally perceived to come from the upper-middle or upper classes of society, whereas those who do not attend tutoring come from lower-middle or lower classes. A primary-school student who does not attend private tutoring stated: '[Those students using private tutoring] are rich and have a medium-level living condition; very few are poor, [and] all have a budget and time [for extra classes].' This is obviously related to the costs of private tutoring, which was one of the main reasons cited why students did not attend private tutoring. One student who does not go to private tutoring observed: 'Students who go to private tutoring are the students from fairly rich families.' Agreeing with this student, another participant added: 'The students who go to private tutoring are the children from the families which do not have many members, are able to earn enough money to spend on food and education for their children.' Beyond the cost of tutoring, the amount of time students could devote to their education differed between groups of students. Students who did not attend private-tutoring lessons often had to work for their families after mainstream school had finished. Such work often includes farming, looking after siblings or participating in the informal economy through activities like weaving baskets. If and when students had the time and money, they would attend private-tutoring lessons.

The injustice arising from a system of private tutoring where only rich students can attend is precisely in the reproduction of inequalities along class lines, which manifests inside school. One teacher observed: 'Rich students hang out with rich students only.' Another example offered by a teacher of the self-segregation along class lines was when a poor student asked a rich student to borrow a pencil. The teacher explained that the rich student in her class did not lend the poor student the pencil because of the class difference. A student reiterated this point by saying: 'The literate play with the literate; the illiterate play with the illiterate.' This theme resonates with the historical separation of people who are rich (*neak mean*) from those who are poor (*neak kro*) in Cambodia (see Brehm & Silova, 2014), and suggests schooling – and therefore private tutoring – both creates and reinforces the gap between the different socio-economic groups in Cambodia.

However, many teachers we worked with said they allow poor students to attend private tutoring for free or reduced fees. Among the teachers, students and parents interviewed, we routinely heard that students who cannot pay the fees for private tutoring are sometimes allowed to attend for free and, in some cases, owe their teacher for the private-tutoring lessons. One teacher told us she always announces to her class that private tutoring is available for all students even those who cannot pay. The teacher gave an example of what she tells her class each year: 'I want to conduct private tutoring. Whoever wants to use private tutoring, please go to my home. Whoever cannot pay can also attend.' Students also echoed this point. One student who did not attend private tutoring recalled a conversation she had with a friend who did: 'A private tutoring student asked me to go to private tutoring and I said I don't have money. She said it was fine because the teacher said if you have money, you could give it to him. But if you don't have money, there is no need to pay.'

A Detriment to Public School?

The main impact private tutoring has on mainstream schooling is the delivery of national-curricular content for a fee and the differences in academic achievement that result from some students receiving more curricular content. As mentioned earlier, the national curriculum is often continued in private-tutoring lessons, meaning that those students who cannot attend both mainstream schooling and private-tutoring lessons miss some of the required content. Consequently, students who attended private tutoring in our sample performed better on monthly examinations than those students who did not attend private-tutoring lessons. The grade tracking of 282 9th graders and 162 6th graders revealed that in general students who attended at least one private tutoring lesson during the month of May scored at least one grade higher than students who did not. The ability to attend private-tutoring lessons, therefore, had a negative impact on some students' scores in mainstream schooling as compared to others.

However, the notion that teachers were maliciously manufacturing demand was rare and only occurred in urban schools. Many urban parents told us that teachers who tutor their own students do it because of their desire to profit as much as possible off the structural problems plaguing the national system of education. An urban 6th-grade teacher confirmed this belief when she proudly told us she takes 'money from students because of ... [her low] living conditions'. She went on to warn: 'The government dare not blame [us for this].' Indeed, urban centres are more expensive than rural areas, thus making a second income or a partner who also works a necessity to survive. Moreover, in urban settings where teachers do not necessarily live in the same communities as their students, there is less of a conflict of interest to tutor their own students than in rural locations where teachers have to live in the same, small communities as their students. Although these perspectives echo the idea that teachers may be forcing students into extra classes purely for a financial gain, they are contextualised in the structural deficiencies of the public-school system.

In contrast, many rural parents found the extra lessons to be very useful to their children and community because they provided additional instruction time. In nearly all of our focus groups and interviews, parents and students believed private tutoring to be a positive experience because it increased the knowledge of the students. Even students who did not attend private tutoring framed it within the notion of increased knowledge: '[It] helps us be more knowledgeable [and] provide assistance for understanding.'

In the rural schools, it was often the community that pressured and convinced teachers to hold extra lessons. One teacher recalled a question from a concerned parent: 'Teacher, don't you conduct private tutoring?' The same teacher went on to explain: 'Those who use private tutoring are those whose parents want them to do so, [for] those whose parents did not want them to use private tutoring, we don't force them.' Another teacher raised a similar example of a primary school where parents hired a teacher to teach their children at home by paying US$30 each per month. In case after case, we discovered the demand for private tutoring was not being manufactured by teachers but rather by households. Although the rural teachers did profit from such classes, the motivation for holding them derived from the belief of community members that a teacher – through the means of private tutoring – could correct structural problems such as low teacher salaries or a short school day.

Discussion: liberal views of justice in private tutoring

How then do we understand educational justice in Cambodia *vis-à-vis* private tutoring? Since the type of private tutoring of interest here is often conceptualised as a form of corruption, it is worthwhile to understand from where this viewpoint derives. When a teacher tutors her own students it is considered corrupt because it is a 'conflict of interest ... contrary to the professional standards of educators and should be punished with a fine and/or loss of teaching license (Heyneman, 2011, p. 186). In other words, the teacher who also tutors is corrupting the ideal form of a 'teacher', thus causing injustice. This line of reasoning is based on the political philosophy of liberalism because such a teacher corrodes an individual's capacity to make decisions freely and live life as he or she chooses.

Broadly speaking, liberalism suggests that individuals must respect: a person's 'freedom to develop and exercise those capacities that are considered essential or important to being a person'; the good life, however defined, by 'protection from coercive interference'; and 'citizens' capacity for reason as well as their sense of reasonableness or fairness' (Shapiro, 1993, pp. 180-181). From the liberal perspective, then, justice in the context of private tutoring must be understood in terms of 'the extent to which parents from diverse social and economic backgrounds can effectively pursue their *choices* without being marginalised or excluded' (Mazawi et al, 2013, p. 212, emphasis added). In this understanding, social justice is essentially an idea based on the freedom of choice and the fair protection of groups who may be disadvantaged. Exactly how 'marginalised or excluded' groups are given choice is a question that generates divergent opinions within liberalism.

Liberalism contains two main, contemporary branches of thought: libertarianism and liberal egalitarianism. The former is based on thinking that sees free markets as the only way to achieve freedom and therefore justice. Libertarianism 'favour[s...] "procedural" theories of justice which emphasise individuals' entitlement to keep whatever resources/advantages they earn or inherit, passing this on to their children as they see fit with no right for state or society to intervene' (Exley, 2010). From this perspective, private tutoring is considered just if students are free to choose educational services without interference and are entitled to the benefits they may gain from such lessons. When it comes to excluded groups, the best remedy is government protection of the free market of educational services. Liberal egalitarians, by contrast, take a more active approach in protecting choice within society through a redistribution of resources in cases where unchosen inequalities or disadvantages are found to be the limiting factors of choice (called a 'patterned' theory of distributive justice; see Shapiro, 1993, p. 173). From this perspective, private tutoring is considered just only if everyone has an equal opportunity to attend extra classes and if students' intentions to attend these lessons are derived from a moral duty and not from self-interest.

Liberal egalitarianism stems partly from a Kantian notion of justice, which is based on the assumption that actions in the self-interest of an individual go against his or her moral duty. If the motive to achieve some end derives from self-interest, then the moral worthiness of such an action is not achieved. For Kant (1785/1964), actions considered morally worthy are categorical and not hypothetical:

> If the action would be good solely as a means to something else, the imperative is hypothetical. If the action is presented as good in itself, and therefore as necessary for a will which of itself accords with reason, then the imperative is categorical. (p. 414)

Categorical imperatives are defined by two 'maxims'. First, for actions to be considered moral, individuals must be willing to turn that action into a universal law. That is to say, people 'should act only on principles that [they] could universalize without contradiction' (Sandel, 2011, p. 120). What is good for one, for example, must be good for all. Second, actions are moral only if they treat humanity as an end and not a means. Such thinking is the basis for notions of the universal declaration of human rights. These maxims taken together provided a way for Kant to determine whether actions freely taken by an individual could be considered moral and therefore just. This was a way to think about *social* justice because it embraces all of humanity unlike contemporary libertarianism, which is mainly concerned with *individual* justice.

More recently, John Rawls (1971) elaborated on the notion of moral duty *vis-à-vis* justice and freedom. He believed that freedom is best understood in an original position of equality. If we can put a 'veil of ignorance' over society, everyone would define the principles of 'moral duty' in a way that does not exclude one person if he or she is born into a poor family or lower class than another, but also does not limit someone if he or she is born with particular natural talents. The 'veil of ignorance' is another way of meeting both of Kant's categorical imperatives because through it a social contract can be agreed upon where 'no one would have a superior bargaining position, [so therefore] the principals [society] would agree to would be just' (Sandel, 2011, p. 141). From such a starting point, societal institutions like public education can be just by protecting freedom and choice through the equal opportunity granted to all members in society to use such institutions while limiting the negative aspects of a totally free-market society, which may result in some members *using* society as a means to gain a financial or other end. When unchosen disadvantages are present, it is considered just for a government to intervene to redistribute resources or opportunities accordingly.

Since there is a 'surprisingly thin line between strict egalitarianism and libertarianism' (Cappelen & Tungodden, 2004, p. 4), it is common to find mixtures of the liberal theories of justice. The notions of educational social justice found in the six schools under investigation offer an example of this. Within the notion of libertarianism, we found self-interest present and accepted in many communities; for example, private tutoring was considered just for a student who can afford and was interested in attending private tutoring. Within the notion of liberal egalitarianism, there were cases of redistributive measures designed to include disadvantaged students into private-tutoring classes. Thus, the moral duty of teachers to act in ways that are good for all of humanity (Kant's second categorical imperative) was also present, particularly in rural communities where private tutoring was perceived to be righting a wrong. In addition, there were hints of utilitarianism when some people believed that the greater number of 'knowledgeable' people was good for society even if that meant excluding poor students from private-tutoring lessons. In the end, we found that the collective interests for society to provide education to all students were recognised, but ultimately displaced by the individual interests of households that could afford the extra lessons.

Conclusions: educational justice in an era of privatisation

In an attempt to overcome our natural proclivities towards a liberal theory of justice and acknowledge the complexity of shadow education, the case of teachers tutoring their own students in Cambodia was examined to show different theories of social justice within a context structural deficiencies. What we found was similar to Johnson's (2011) emphasis on context rather than corruption in his study of private tutoring in Kyrgyzstan, where 'students blame the context, not the culprits [i.e., teachers]' for corruption (p. 254), because 'workers perceived to be contributing to the greater good of society ... [are allowed to] deviate from the law' (p. 253). Our goal in this chapter was to overcome 'the immediate difficulty one confronts when examining the idea of social justice' by not thinking there is 'a single essential meaning' of social justice but rather see it as 'embedded within discourses that are historically constituted and that are sites of conflicting and divergent political endeavours' (Rizvi, 1998, p. 47).

The perspectives from teachers, students and parents in Cambodia made visible different perspectives on educational justice within private tutoring. This is apropos in today's climate of privatisation of public education, where 'private tutoring operates in relation to the larger field of private education' (Mazawi et al, 2013, p. 210). In this context, systems of mainstream education are like 'enterprises' that function as 'a self-maximizing productive unit ... in a market of performances' (Ball, 2012, p. 31). This system changes 'who we are and how we think about what we do' (Ball, 2012, p. 37). In other words, when the 'private sector is the model to be emulated' in schools (Ball, 2012, p. 30), the very social relations between people change, educational justice takes on new meanings, and political philosophies shift. Even the government's role in education has been 'reconstitut[ed...] from that of service delivery to a combination of regulation, performance monitoring, contracting and the facilitation of new providers of public services' (Ball, 2012, p. 36). As this chapter has illustrated, this is clearly the case in the sites under investigation where the demand for private tutoring looks similar to the demand for education within the knowledge economy, which is 'driven by the production, distribution, and consumption of knowledge' (Kenway et al, 2006, p. 4).

In such a climate, the ethical dilemmas described in this chapter – teachers who may be perceived to degrade their profession, households who may exacerbate inequality and researchers/policymakers who may universalise their perspectives on shadow education – become profoundly important to future directions of public education in a society. That the meaning of social justice results in diverse understandings between urban and rural communities, between wealthy and poor families, is an expected outcome in a hybrid system of education. As choice and self-interest dominate conversations about education, it is important for teachers, households and researchers/policymakers to step back and ask: 'What virtues come from education that society should honor?' Such an Aristotelian question asking society to articulate a *telos* of education demands these diverse opinions about educational social justice to come into dialogue with each other.

Notes

[1] This quote was obtained during a yearlong 2011 study of private tutoring in Cambodia as part of the project entitled *The Hidden Privatization of Public Education in Cambodia: quality and equity implications of private tutoring* led by the authors in collaboration with Tout Mono and funded by the Open Society Institute Education Support Program.

References

Ball, S.J. (2012) *Global Education Inc.: new policy networks and the neo-liberal imaginary*. New York: Routledge.

Benveniste, L., Marshall, J. & Araujo, M. C. (2008) *Teaching in Cambodia*. Washington, DC: World Bank.

Biswal, B.P. (1999) Private Tutoring and Public Corruption: a cost-effective education system for developing countries, *The Developing Economies*, 37(2), 222-240.

Bray, M. (1999) *The Private Costs of Public Schooling: household and community financing of primary education in Cambodia*. Paris: UNESCO International Institute for Educational Planning (IIEP).

Bray, M. (2003) *Adverse Effects of Private Supplementary Tutoring: dimensions, implications, and government responses.* Paris: International Institute for Educational Planning (IIEP).

Bray, M. (2007) *The Shadow Education System: private tutoring and its implications for planners,* 2nd ed. Paris: UNESCO International Institute for Educational Planning (IIEP).

Bray, M. (2010) Blurring Boundaries: the growing visibility, evolving forms and complex implications of private supplementary tutoring, *Orbis Scholae,* 4(2), 61-73.

Bray, M. (2011) *The Challenge of Shadow Education: private tutoring and its implications for policy makers in the European Union.* Brussels: European Commission.

Bray, M. (2012) How Shadow Education can Undermine the EFA Goals: the expansion and implications of private tutoring. http://norrag.wordpress.com/2012/11/05/how-shadow-education-can-undermine-the-efa-goals-the-expansion-and-implications-of-private-tutoring/

Bray, M. & Bunly, S. (2005) *Balancing the Books: household financing of basic education in Cambodia.* Hong Kong: Comparative Education Research Centre, The University of Hong Kong.

Bray, M. & Lykins, C. (2012) *Shadow Education: private supplementary tutoring and its implications for policy makers in Asia.* Manila: Asian Development Bank and Comparative Education Research Center, The University of Hong Kong.

Brehm, W.C. & Silova, I. (2014) Hidden Privatization of Public Education in Cambodia: equity implications of private tutoring, *Journal of Education Research Online,* 6(1), 94-116.

Brehm, W.C., Silova, I. & Tuot, M. (2012) *The Public-Private Education System in Cambodia: the impact and implications of complementary tutoring.* London: Open Society Institute.

Cappelen, A.W. & Tungodden, B. (2004) The Liberal Egalitarian Paradox. http://www.nhh.no/Files/Filer/institutter/sam/Discussion%20papers/2004/08.pdf

Chapman, D. (2002) *Corruption and Education.* Washington, DC: Management Systems International and United States Agency for International Development.

Dawson, W. (2009) The Tricks of the Teacher: shadow education and corruption in Cambodia, in S.P. Heyneman (Ed.) *Buying your Way into Heaven: education and corruption in international perspective,* pp. 51-74. Rotterdam: Sense.

Denn Ayuthyea (2012). Teachers in Seven Provinces haven't Received January Salary. *Voice of America,* Phnom Penh, Cambodia, 22 Feb. http://www.rfa.org/khmer/indepth/teachers_complain_about_late_salary-02222012051916.html (In Khmer.)

European Commission (2012) Analysis of the Continuous Decline of MoEYS Recurrent Budget Share in Recent Years. Presentation at the EDUCAM meeting, 10 February 2012. Phnom Penh, Cambodia.

Exley, S. (2010) *A Note on Social Justice and Education.* Royal Society for the Encouragement of Arts, Manufactures and Commerce Online. http://www.thersa.org/action-research-centre/learning,-cognition-and-creativity/education/social-justice/a-note-on-social-justice-and-education

Hallak, J. & Poisson, M. (2007) *Corrupt Schools, Corrupt Universities: what can be done?* Paris: UNESCO, International Institute for Educational Planning.

Hayden, M. & Martin, R. (2011) The Education System in Cambodia: making progress under difficult circumstance, in C. Brock & L.P. Symaco (Eds) *Education in South-East Asia,* pp. 31-51. Oxford: Symposium Books.

Heyneman, S.P. (Ed.) (2009) *Buying Your Way into Heaven: education and corruption in international perspective.* Rotterdam: Sense.

Heyneman, S.P. (2011) Private Tutoring and Social Cohesion, *Peabody Journal of Education,* 86(2), 183-188.

Heyneman, S.P., Anderson, K.H. & Nuraliyeva, N. (2008) The Cost of Corruption in Higher Education, *Comparative Education Review,* 52(1), pp. 1-25.

Johnson, E. (2011) Blaming the Context not the Culprit: limitations on student control of teacher corruption in post-Soviet Kyrgyzstan, in I. Silova (Ed.) *Globalization on the Margins: education and postsocialist transformations in Central Asia,* pp. 233-258. Charlotte: Information Age Publishing.

Kant, I. (1785/1964) *Groundwork for the Metaphysics of Morals,* trans. H.J. Paton. New York: Harper Torchbooks.

Kenway, J., Bullen, E., Fahey, J. & Robb, S. (2006) *Haunting the Knowledge Economy.* New York: Routledge.

Klitgaard, R. (1988) *Controlling Corruption.* Berkeley: University of California Press.

Mazawi, A.E., Sultana, R.G. & Bray, M. (2013) Beyond Shadows: equity, diversity, and private tutoring, in M. Bray, A.E. Mazawi & R.G. Sultana (Eds) *Private Tutoring across the Mediterranean,* pp. 205-216. Rotterdam: Sense.

NGO Education Partnership (2007) *The Impact of Informal School Fees on Family Expenditures.* Philippines: Asia South Pacific Association for Basic and Adult Education.

Psacharopoulos, G. & Patrinos, H.A. (2002) *Returns to Investment in Education: a further update.* Policy Research Working Paper 2881. Washington, DC: World Bank.

Ratcliffe, M. (2009) *Study on Governance Challenges for Education in Fragile Situations: Cambodia Country Report.* Brussels: European Commission.

Rawls, J. (1971) *A Theory of Justice.* Cambridge, MA: The Belknap Press of Harvard University Press.

Rizvi, F. (1998) Some Thoughts on Contemporary Theories of Social Justice, in B. Atweh, S. Kemmis & P. Weeks (Eds) *Action Research in Practice: partnerships for social justice in education,* pp. 47-56. London: Routledge.

Sandel, M.J. (2011) *Justice: what's the right thing to do?* New York: Farrar, Straus & Giroux.

Shapiro, D. (1993) Liberal Egalitarianism, Basic Rights, and Free Market Capitalism, *Reason Papers,* 18.

Silova, I. (Ed.) (2009) *Private Supplementary Tutoring in Central Asia: new opportunities and burdens.* Paris: UNESCO International Institute for Educational Planning (IIEP).

Silova, I. & Bray, M. (2006) The Context: societies and education in the post-socialist transformation, in I. Silova, V. Budiene & M. Bray (Eds), *Education in a Hidden Marketplace: monitoring of private tutoring*, pp. 41-60. Budapest: Education Support Program (ESP) of the Open Society Institute.

Silova, I. & Brehm, W.C. (2013) The Shifting Boundaries of Teacher Professionalism: education privatization(s) in the post-socialist education space, in T. Seddon, J. Ozga & J. Levin (Eds) *World Year Book of Education*, pp. 55-74. London: Routledge.

Silova, I., Budiene, V. & Bray, M. (Eds) (2006) *Education in a Hidden Marketplace: monitoring of private tutoring.* Budapest: Education Support Program of the Open Society Institute.

Voluntary Service Overseas (VSO) (2008) *Teaching Matters: a policy report on the motivation and morale of teachers in Cambodia.* England: VSO.

CHAPTER 9

Early Private-School Responses to India's Right to Education Act: implications for equity

PRACHI SRIVASTAVA & CLAIRE NORONHA

In August 2009, the Government of India passed the *Right of Children to Free and Compulsory Education Act, 2009* (RTE Act), effective April 2010, changing the landscape for education in the country. This chapter reports school-level findings from a larger study on the early phase of implementation of the RTE Act in Delhi focusing on one slum, Karampur.[1] We report early private-school responses to the Act regarding the implementation and mediation of its provisions. At the time of data collection, the validity of the Act was being challenged in the Supreme Court and a verdict had not been passed. A number of procedures, rules and regulations had also not been notified. As such, data presented here provide a rare glimpse into the earliest phase of implementation and the actual practices of a small number of private schools attended by the large majority of private-school children in our study site.

The RTE Act is the result of a long process of deliberation and public debate, causing much controversy. Since its enactment, the debate has been centred on the 25% free-seats provision. Section 12(1)(c) of the RTE Act compels all private unaided schools to allocate 25% of their places in Class 1 (or pre-primary as applicable) for free to 'children belonging to weaker section[s] and disadvantaged group[s]' to be retained until they complete elementary education (Class 8) (Government of India, 2009). Economically weaker sections (EWS) are defined as children with a parent or guardian whose annual income is lower than the minimum limit specified by the appropriate Government (Section 2(e), Government of India, 2009). In Delhi, as in most states, this is procedurally interpreted as those with annual incomes below Rs. 100,000 as stipulated by the Ministry of Finance. Disadvantaged groups are defined in the Act as children belonging to scheduled castes, scheduled tribes, 'socially and educationally backward' classes or disadvantaged by gender, social, cultural, economic, geographic or linguistic factors (Section 2(d), Government of India, 2009).

These students are meant to be admitted via a 'freeship', randomly allocated through a lottery. Private schools are to be reimbursed for each child enrolled under the 25% free-seats provision at the level of state expenditure per child or the tuition fee charged at the school, whichever is less (Section 12(2), Government of India, 2009). In Delhi, this amounted to a maximum of Rs. 1190/child/month for the 2011-12 school year (Government of NCT of Delhi, 2012).

Powerful private-school lobbies contested the Act, arguing that it impinged on their right to run their schools without undue government interference, and was thus unconstitutional. In April 2012, a Supreme Court verdict was passed upholding the Act and the 25% free-seats provision after a long and contentious hearing. Additionally, in Delhi, unaided schools allotted land at concessional rates from the Delhi Development Authority were already meant to be instituting a similar 25% quota, and were barred from increasing tuition fees without approval from the Delhi Directorate of Education (Juneja, 2005). This was difficult to institute as most land-allotted schools were high-fee, elite schools with influence (Juneja, 2005).

In 2004, a Supreme Court judgement instructed the Director of Education to examine whether conditions of the allotment were being met, and to take action against schools found not to comply. However, according to interviewees in our study, only a minority of unaided allotted schools made an effort to institute the allotment quota, and strict action against errant schools was not taken. The feeling was that this was because of a general laissez-faire attitude towards the expansion of the private sector in view of more pressing *Sarva Shiksha Abhiyan* (the Government of India's Education for All programme) goals since the early 2000s, as well as the considerable political clout that many of these older, more established, elite schools had. In many ways, the quota instituted by the land-allotment contract in Delhi, the 2004 Supreme Court judgment, and the subsequent response of private schools, foreshadowed the RTE Act's 25% free-seats provision and the response to it by private schools. It is within this wider context that the RTE Act was born and is being implemented, and within which our study was conducted.

The broader debate surrounding the Act raises questions about the role that the private sector could and should play in expanding access to basic education for the most disadvantaged, and whether the 25% free-seats provision in particular is emblematic of further privatisation. Arguments in the public discourse are framed around two main issues, both raising equity concerns. The first is the increased privatisation and resulting hyper-segmentation of the education sector in India, particularly over the last two decades. Low-fee private schools at the lower-end of the cost spectrum have proliferated, and the numbers of middle-fee and high-fee schools have increased, all operating alongside the more established elite schools at the top of the spectrum. Research in India generally shows that access to private schooling is complicated by household ability to pay and factors such as gender, caste and location (De et al, 2002; Härmä, 2009; Siddhu, 2010; Woodhead et al, 2013).

The second is the state subsidisation of the private sector through the free-seats provision. Researchers and activists have long argued that such initiatives divert much-needed funds from the already under-resourced state sector, which the majority of children, particularly the poorest and most marginalised, actually access (Tilak, 2007; Kumar, 2008).

Nonetheless, proponents of the free-seats provision claim that it is an equity measure aimed at opening up a highly stratified school system to disadvantaged children. In the best case, it is meant to provide them with the chance to access the most desirable (i.e. high-fee/elite, private) schools. Proponents also claim that it is the only way to achieve universal elementary education because of insufficient state-sector capacity (Jain & Dholakia, 2010). Critics maintain that the provision marks the most explicit institutional legitimisation of the private sector in education without sufficient efforts to strengthen the decaying state sector (Ramachandran, 2009; Jha & Parvati, 2010). Results presented here question the ability of private schools in this study to redress education inequities in the earliest phase of implementation.

The chapter is organised as follows. First, we present the study design and detail methods for school-level data. This is followed by a presentation of school profiles. Next, we locate private unaided schools in the RTE Act, providing an analysis of relevant provisions. This is followed by findings on private-school implementation and mediation of the Act. We conclude by raising potential implications for the Act to address equity issues in light of preliminary findings.

Research Design

Fieldwork for the full study was conducted between June 2011 and January 2012. The bulk of the household- and school-level data were collected between June and September 2011, and documentary analysis was completed in April 2012. Data for the full study were collected through: a survey of 290 households in one resettlement block and adjacent squatter colony in Karampur; semi-structured interviews with 40 households drawn from this larger sample; semi-structured interviews with the seven most accessed local government and private schools by survey households; semi-structured interviews with policy officials and implementers; and documentary analysis of the RTE Act and rules and relevant documents. Here we present only the methods and design for data reported in this chapter.

The Study Site

Considerations for site selection included: a recognised slum area; access to both government and smaller local private schools; and our own familiarity with non-governmental organisations (NGOs) in the area that could facilitate access to local residents. With the help of key informants, Karampur was selected for school- and household-level data collection as it met these criteria. Additionally, compared to other potential sites, it had the advantage of having local NGOs that had worked on disseminating the RTE Act and assisting some parents with freeship admission. Thus, we assumed that there was greater likelihood of capturing freeship households and schools implementing the Act's provisions in the early phase of implementation.

Karampur is known as a 'resettlement colony'. During 1975-77 one of the largest ever relocations of slum clusters was carried out, resulting in around 26 new resettlement colonies (Government of NCT of Delhi, 2002), of which Karampur was one. More than 35 years later, Karampur comprises a number of blocks and is well developed with *pakka* houses and several public facilities. One block was chosen for the sample site because it was adjacent to a squatter ('*jhuggi*') colony, visibly poorer and much more congested. The squatter colony also formed part of the study site to capture a wider spectrum of households.

School-level Research Methods

A preliminary survey yielding data on 290 households was conducted to obtain socio-economic and education profiles of the study site, and from which to generate household and school sub-samples for semi-structured interviews. The survey was simultaneously conducted in the selected resettlement colony block and adjacent squatter *jhuggi* colony, though the latter was discontinued because of negligible access to private schools. The entire resettlement block was covered. Every household was surveyed, but since we were interested in school participation, only those with young people between 6 and 16 were selected. The survey also documented the names of all schools ever attended and school fees for anyone between 0 and 18 in the household. Finally, since our initial analysis showed only four households in the resettlement colony block and squatter colony accessing private schools through the 25% free-seats provision, an additional six households in an adjacent block were surveyed by snowballing.

The school sample for semi-structured interviews consisted of seven schools drawn from the most frequently accessed government and private schools by survey households. The school interview schedule consisted of questions in five parts for all schools, and a sixth for private schools only. Questions were on: school background (establishment, management, general policies and so on); household–school interaction; inclusion practices; perceptions, knowledge and understanding of the RTE Act and its provisions; experience of instituting the free-seats provision (private schools only); and school data (e.g. enrolment, numbers of teachers, numbers of classrooms, freeship students, caste breakdown and so on). Observations on infrastructure and teaching activities supplemented semi-structured interviews. In most cases, visits were unannounced. Interviews lasted approximately 45-60 minutes, and were conducted on school premises in Hindi. Interviews were recorded and transcribed, and coded in Atlas ti. The foci for analysis were policy interpretation and implementation by schools, and school perceptions of their role in the community.

Finally, official documents pertaining to the RTE Act, including draft versions of preceding RTE bills, the final Act, Central Government model rules, Delhi rules and associated government orders and notices were analysed involving critical discourse analysis (Fairclough, 2003). At the school level this was used to interrogate emerging insights from school interviews on how the Act was implemented/mediated in practice, and to match school understandings about the RTE Act against official articulations. Some of the relevant official rules and government orders/notices (e.g. Delhi RTE Rules and free-seats provision reimbursement procedures), did not exist at the time of fieldwork. These were analysed as and when they became notified. School-level analysis was not done retroactively but in accordance with the information that was known to schools at the time.

School Profiles and Access

Households accessed a variety of government and private schools, a total of some 44 schools. Schools were sorted by management type, fee level and numbers of children in the study attending (see Table I). As the data show, the majority of children (56.6%) attended Delhi Department of Education government secondary schools, almost all of which were integrated schools for the primary and secondary levels. At 28%, the private unaided sector claimed the second highest proportion of children, though freeship students comprised a very small minority of children overall. A sizeable number also accessed the local Municipal Corporation of Delhi (MCD) government primary schools (13.7%).

Our household survey revealed two categories of private schools accessed – one with an annual fee range of Rs. 3600-6000 at primary level (named Fee Level 1), and the second encompassing a larger variety of schools with a fee range higher than Rs. 10,000 per year (named Fee Level 2).[2] The most frequently accessed private schools were Fee Level 1 schools, and were usually within 0.5 km of the study area.

School type	Fee reported by households		Number of children attending	% of children attending
	Mean	*Median*		
Central school (Class 0-12)	3,699	3,340	8	1.3
Government senior secondary (Class 1-12; 6-10; 6-12)	259	240	358	56.6
MCD primary (Class 1-5)	104	150	87	13.7
Fee Level 1 private (Class 0-5; Class 0-8)	4,449	4,320	127	20.1
Fee Level 2 private (Class 0-8; 0-12)	17,127	13,200	38	6.0
Fee Level 2 private EWS freeship	0*	0*	12	1.9
Private aided school	2,340	2,100	3	0.5

Notes: Most private schools begin with one to two years of pre-school classes. This was sometimes found in government schools. Government primary schools are supposed to be fee-free.
*Freeship households reported no tuition fees. This is not the same as annual expenditure. Our data found substantial school expenditure by freeship households reported in Noronha & Srivastava (in press).

Table I. School participation and reported fees.
Source: Household Survey Field Data

Fee Level 2 private schools were situated outside the study site in more middle-class areas. The more commonly accessed Fee Level 2 schools had fees of around Rs. 10,000/year at the primary levels, and even though it was against the RTE rules, often demanded a donation for admission (capitation fee). Fees at the most expensive Fee Level 2 schools could range from Rs. 20,000-30,000 per year at a conservative estimate, and though highly desirable to parents, were largely unaffordable to households in our study. The small minority of children in our study that attended them had, with rare exceptions, been admitted into these prized schools under the freeship and did not pay tuition fees, though other expenses were incurred.

Table II presents a summary of general school characteristics of the seven schools in our study. Of these, four (Schools 1-4) were Fee Level 1 schools, and were the most frequently accessed private schools by survey households. Between them, they claimed 89% of all children attending Fee Level 1 schools in survey households. School 5 was an elite Fee

Level 2 school which offered freeships to 6 of the 12 (50%) freeship students in our sample. It was also the only Fee Level 2 school to consent to the research. It did not charge tuition fees to these students, although other expenses were incurred by freeship households. Schools 6 and 7 were government MCD primary schools, one of which was a girls' school (in the morning shift), and the other, a boys' school (in the afternoon shift), respectively.

Unfortunately, official permission to visit the integrated government secondary schools, the most accessed by the community overall, was denied. Furthermore, the private schools were reluctant to provide data on fee structure and salaries. Despite repeated visits and requests, these could only be collected in full for two Fee Level 1 schools, and partially for School 5. The latter provided data without specifying fee structure and salaries as required. Both government schools complied.

School ID no.	Management type	Year established	Year recognised	Level	Tuition fees (Rs./ year)	Enrolment	
						Boys	Girls
1	Private unaided	1995	2004	Primary	4,800-6,000	Missing	Missing
2	Private unaided	2000	2004	Primary	3,600-6,000	238	163
3	Private unaided	1998	2001	Primary	4,200-6,600	134	65
4	Private unaided	1984	1992	Primary and junior	3,600-6,600	320	197
5	Private unaided	1988	1991	All-through secondary	24,000 – nil for freeship students*	1,496	1,132
6	Local Gov't	1978	1978	Primary	Nil	-	643
7	Local Gov't	1976	1976	Primary	Nil	264	–

Note: *Though tuition fees were not charged, other expenses were reported by freeship households.

Table II. Profile of schools in study.
Source: School Field Data.

The community has long had exposure to government schooling. The two primary schools were set up in the 1970s along with the colony, and are situated within it. Schools 1-3 were all relatively new, and School 4 was about 1.5 km away in a slightly better-off area. School 5, the freeship school, was an all-through, elite school in an upscale middle-class neighbourhood around 3 km away. Among the private schools, Schools 4 and 5 were older.

Infrastructure-wise, all except School 5 had modest facilities. Classrooms were *pakka* and had desks and benches or chairs. All schools had separate toilets for girls and boys, lights, fans and drinking water. School 5 had extravagant infrastructure with a number of two- and three-storey buildings, accessed through guarded gates, a big garden, swimming pool, games facilities and spacious classrooms. It also had a large array of activity rooms and facilities for art, music, dance, theatre, computers and so on, libraries, and well-equipped science laboratories.

Unlike the buildings of the Fee Level 1 private schools which were situated on compact premises, government-school premises were sprawling and had a playground. Conversely, well-guarded premises were a feature of all five private schools, whereas government-school gates were not guarded. This had an important bearing on experienced school quality regarding security issues, which were reported as being particularly problematic in the boys' school.

Locating Private Unaided Schools in the RTE Act

Private schools under the Act fall in the category of 'recognised school' specified as 'an unaided school not receiving any kind of aid or grants to meet its expenses from the appropriate Government or the local authority' (Section 2(n)(iv), Government of India, 2009). These are commonly referred to as private unaided schools, and in reality, may function on recognised or unrecognised bases, or owing to the earlier practice in certain states of granting 'temporary recognition', somewhere in between (see De et al, 2002; Srivastava, 2008). Under the Act, unrecognised schools and recognised schools not meeting Schedule 1 norms, have up to three years to obtain recognition or to apply for 'upgradation' (as the case may be), or face school closure. This is also applicable to unaided schools in Delhi (Sections 14 and 15, Government of NCT of Delhi, 2011a).

Though all general provisions of the Act apply to private unaided schools, the most immediate in the early phase of implementation were found to be: the 25% free-seats provision (Section 12(1)(c)) and related conditions for reimbursement (Section 12(2)); prohibition on charging fees or instituting screening procedures of any kind for admission (Section 13(1)); conditions for recognition, withdrawal and associated sanctions for existing and new unaided schools (Sections 18 and 19); and operational standards including infrastructure and associated teacher qualifications and teaching expectations (Schedule 1).

A set of model rules was drafted by the Ministry of Human Resource Development (MHRD) providing further specification to direct action for implementing the Act's provisions. Since implementation is largely a concern of the states, the aim of the model rules was to provide a basis for states to develop their own rules, or alternatively, adopt the central rules. In Delhi (as in most states), there were bureaucratic delays in the official notification of rules and procedures.

The Government of the National Capital Territory (NCT) notified the *Delhi Right of Children to Free and Compulsory Education Rules, 2011* (Delhi RTE Rules) in November 2011, well into the 2011-12 school year. Furthermore, free-seat reimbursement procedures and amounts were only specified in March 2012, near the end of the year (Government of NCT of Delhi, 2012). Nonetheless, the *2011 Delhi Free Seats Order*, specifying the rules and procedures to institute the free-seats provision was issued in January 2011, in time for the 2011-12 school year. Also, despite the delay in notifying the Delhi Rules, principals mentioned receiving circulars and having had meetings with the Department of Education, specifically regarding the 25% free-seats provision before the beginning of the school year.

The overall delay, however, led to a climate of uncertainty and precariousness about the Act. In addition, the process was contested by education activists and private-school lobbyists alike. Education activists bemoaned the fact that it took nearly 18 months after the Act came into effect for the Delhi Government to notify rules, despite the fact that a commitment to do so had been made in 2009. Private-school lobbyists on the other hand, largely contested the 25% free-seats provision; the compulsion for all teachers to meet specified qualification norms; and processes of recognition and recognition withdrawal. They also felt that the rules would not be as stringently applied to government schools.

School-Level Implementation and Mediation of the RTE Act

The following describes how schools in the study understood and implemented provisions of the Act they deemed important, with special reference to the 25% provision, infrastructure and recognition norms, and curriculum issues. Nuances in interpretation by schools led to various school-level responses and mediation strategies. Variations in implementation may be due to incomplete and/or delayed information, conceptual errors in interpretation, lack of preparedness for implementation, or other institutional barriers that may indicate a degree of resistance. These may have results that were unintended by policymakers, specifically regarding the impact on disadvantaged groups.

General Entry Point Barriers

The RTE Act envisages removing barriers to schooling, whether at the point of entry or in the school itself. For example, affidavits specifying age for admission were earlier mandatory, but Section 14(2) of the Act bars schools from denying entry to a child lacking proof of age. The Act also extends the admission period to any time of the school year. Further, children are not meant to be struck off the rolls easily, even after long absences, and more easily reinstated when they return. These basic provisions are applicable to all schools under the Act.

Specific policies varied slightly across the private schools, with one demanding documentary proof of age, and another requiring forms to be submitted. Nonetheless, the Fee Level 1 schools noted that they already admitted children at any time during the year, and readmission was not a problem. This was noted as a challenge by the government schools. Similar to earlier research on low-fee private schooling (e.g. Srivastava, 2007; Härmä, 2009), flexibility in the private schools was a response to the challenge of maintaining adequate enrolment and securing revenue.

Mediating the 25% Free-Seats Provision

Research on resistance to the free-seats provision by private-school lobbies is emerging (Ohara, 2013), and is well documented in the media. As mentioned above, the resistance culminated in a Supreme Court case, which ultimately ruled that private unaided schools must comply with the 25% free-seats provision. However, RTE implementers in our study confirmed that they knew of a number of cases where private schools did not comply, or where the 25% free-seats provision was retroactively applied to select students already enrolled. In other instances, private schools enrolled children of domestic workers or support known to them, rather than expanding enrolment to neighbourhood children as stipulated in the Act.

One interviewee, a high-profile private school lobbyist in Delhi and private-school owner, spoke from knowledge of private-school practices in his association. He insisted that many freeship admissions were not given to students who fit eligibility criteria, but to those who had personal connections or sway with school owners, or who were relatively more advantaged. This is indicated in household-level data in our study reported elsewhere (Noronha & Srivastava, in press). Furthermore, despite the RTE Act's obligation, he refused to implement the provision in his own school as backlash against the government:

90% are fake admissions.

The ones admitted under EWS?

188

They are in [good economic] position.

Are there EWS children in your school?

I didn't even implement it ... I'll shut the school down but I won't implement it.

I see, so you just didn't implement it?

No, I didn't. I'll close down but I won't implement it.

I see.

I won't suffer this government bullying. I'd rather lock the school up, but I won't implement the EWS quota. I'm talking about those schools where parents have gotten admission. (Private School Lobbyist and Owner. Translated from the original in Hindi)

There was open and covert resistance by private schools in our study. Although they all claimed to have received government circulars, Fee Level 1 principals admitted that freeship admission in their schools was negligible overall. The rationale and mediation strategies ranged from non-compliance, to evasion, to reinvention of the Act and the provision. For example, School 1 insisted that the provision was expressly meant for schools other than lower-fee schools, since the latter's fees were already low, and such concessions would not be possible:

Of course, I think that the EWS quota is important. The stipulation is to give free education to 25% of your students. Earlier these people [higher-fee schools] did not comply but when the High Court order came [referring to the 2004 Supreme Court Order], they were forced to take in the 25%. It has to be 25% of the total number enrolled. If four children are admitted, one has to be in the EWS category. One seat out of the four has to be kept vacant.

Are you taking such students?

No, we don't do it. Other private schools are doing it. (Principal, School 1. Translated from the original in Hindi)

School 1's principal attributed the 25% free-seats provision to the earlier 2004 Supreme Court Order for schools allotted land in Delhi, and distanced his and other lower fee schools from its applicability under the RTE Act. Two of the other Fee Level 1 schools claimed to have received applications under the quota, though this could not be confirmed. The

189

fourth said that no new admissions had been made since households provided inadequate documentation. This latter school, thus, submitted the names of 10 children already enrolled and who fell below the poverty line, and forwarded them to the Department.

We must reiterate that while the 2011 Delhi Free Seats Order specifying the rules and procedures to institute the provision was issued in time for the school year, actual freeship reimbursement amount and procedures were not issued until March 2012. Thus, schools faced a legitimate lack of clarity on reimbursements aggravating implementation, particularly those schools with precarious financial viability. It is another question as to whether a reimbursement model with delayed pay-out is suitable for lower-fee schools. Given the precarious nature of their operations, they may not have the reserve funds to cover the up-front costs of admitting additional students via a freeship and simultaneously meet other provisions of the Act (i.e. hiring more and better qualified teachers, upgrading facilities, etc.).

On the other hand, the principal of School 5, the elite freeship school, showed a high degree of comfort with the free-seats provision. This school was allotted land at concessionary rates, and claimed to have been admitting children under the previous quota for a long time. The principal espoused the lottery system as a sound strategy, claiming it was one that he used. However, he proudly introduced another instructional strategy that he instituted claiming it to be much more successful, but which, in actuality, contravenes the RTE Act.

Children from disadvantaged groups were taught in a separate shift in the evening with separate staff but in the same facilities. This initiative was known as the 'slum area school project'. The principal claimed that children received free meals, uniforms and books, and did not pay fees. Anecdotal reports in other elite Delhi schools also cite examples of establishing separate shifts in response to the Act's requirements. However, instructing freeship children in separate shifts not only goes against the spirit of the Act, it contravenes it.

The Delhi Free Seats Order clearly states: 'No separate or exclusive class or shift shall be arranged for imparting education to the students admitted against free seats' (Section 3(b), Government of NCT of Delhi, 2011a). Further, the Delhi RTE Rules specify: 'The school ... shall ensure that children admitted in accordance with [the free-seats provision] shall not be segregated from other children in the classrooms nor shall their classes be held at places and timings different from the classes held for the other children' (Section 10(1), Government of NCT of Delhi, 2011b). This is in reference to Section 8(c) of the RTE Act specifying non-discrimination (Government of India, 2009).

While one freeship household accessing School 5 knew about the separate shift system, they claimed that their children were instructed as part of the regular school and that it was being phased out. The latter, was not, however, confirmed by the principal.

Operational and Recognition Norms

All schools must fulfil the infrastructure and other norms specified in Schedule 1. The children in our household survey patronised a staggering 44 schools, of which at least 50% were smaller private schools. Almost all of these could be traced to the MCD list of recognised schools. None of the private schools in our sub-sample or in the immediate vicinity of our site were unrecognised.

As intimated above, the four Fee Level 1 schools had basic infrastructure, while School 5's infrastructure was impressive. All private schools claimed complete compliance as recognised schools, but this was not necessarily accurate. All of them were reluctant to provide data on student enrolment, staff qualifications and salaries. Informal enquiries suggest that teaching staff was largely untrained. Most Fee Level 1 schools claimed that they were paying salaries as per government scales to their teachers, though this could not be verified. Despite these issues, none of the principals expressed any anxiety about Schedule 1 norms. Only longer-term research can show if, as in previous studies (Tooley & Dixon, 2005; Srivastava, 2008; Ohara, 2013), private unaided schools are successful in maintaining their recognition status by leveraging perverse incentives through administrative or political influence and bribery, or if they will be compelled to comply with the norms.

While the focus in the discussion has been on private schools, it was evident from the two government schools that there is much to be done in state schools to ensure minimum infrastructure mandated under the Act. While teachers in government schools in our study were trained and drew impressive salaries, the problem of adequately trained staff and teacher absenteeism in the state sector more generally, is acute. The well-known strategy of hiring contract 'para-teachers' at lower salaries, i.e. locally available personnel even if not adequately trained, was a stop-gap measure to expand access quickly but is no longer viable under the Act.

Child-friendly, Child-centred Education

The 'continuous comprehensive evaluation' (CCE) method mandated by the Act (Section 29, Government of India, 2009) envisions a system without high-stakes testing, favouring instead summative and formative continuous assessment. Furthermore, children are neither meant to be held back nor failed (Section 16), and board examinations are to be eliminated during the elementary school years (Section 30(1)) (Government of India, 2009).

During school visits, all Fee Level 1 schools were quiet, disciplined and functional, with obvious teaching activity. However, teachers used the chalk-and-talk method, and the stress was on homework, private tuition and tests. Interviews with principals of Fee Level 1 schools and researcher observation did not suggest any change in curriculum delivery or pedagogic practice as envisaged under the Act, though these seemed better incorporated in School 5, the elite freeship school.

During observations, the government girls' school had some level of teaching activity, but administrative tasks occupied teachers in the boys' school and no teaching was taking place. Nonetheless, the rhetoric of change required in classroom processes and pedagogic practice was used relatively more frequently in the government schools. For example, the girls' school principal praised the simple language of the general textbooks, but said teachers worried about the social science text because of the unavoidable use of technical words. She also said that children were not 'rote learning parrots', and that they needed to be engaged in order to learn.

However, there was less commitment to CCE principles in practice. In fact, the danger of a technicist interpretation of some of the provisions (e.g. policy of not failing or holding students back) without earnest measures to ensure student learning is meaningless, automatic promotion. For example, the boys' school interpreted these provisions as a compulsory order to promote and mark all children present whether or not they attended, providing even less incentive to change pedagogic practice:

> Principal: It's a problem for us when we have to declare results.

> *Actually, how do you assess?*

> Principal: Now that's the thing see ... we get orders from above that, 'Don't fail anyone, you're not allowed to mark anyone absent, don't do this, and their attendance should be a certain percentage'. Now they're saying that we have to pass them under any circumstances.

> Teacher: The students don't even come to sit for the exam. Even then we're getting orders from above to pass these children. So the child who hasn't even sat for the exam has to be passed. (Principal and Teacher Intervention, School 7)

Private- and government-school principals felt that prohibiting the possibility of failing did nothing but postpone the problem. However, there was little mention of focusing on new ways of ensuring that learning occurs. This is complicated by the fact that there was no official pedagogic framework in response to the new RTE compulsions and CCE approach, posing a serious and legitimate concern. However, CCE was purportedly implemented by the Central Board of Secondary Education, the board governing most elite schools, including School 5, and by secondary schools run by the Delhi Government.

School 5's principal claimed to have changed teaching practice in accordance with CCE principles, cancelling tests and claiming to prefer broad-based learning to develop a child's full potential:

> No test. I cancelled it. You see the beauty of this Act is I still don't believe that the child who has not taken 90%, 60% cannot do anything in life. Therefore, what is the harm if that child gets admission? If he does not pass Class 10 but through the education, through the other part of the education, through activities ... the confidence that child builds up – that will work.
>
> He will find his way, and it is happening. The children who are not strong academically, they are still doing wonderfully. They have gone on to some vocational streams. They have the confidence to move to the people and display their powers.
>
> Children should be given freedom. You see when CBSE [Central Board of Secondary Education] has introduced the CCE – excellent. The productivity has increased. Our basic duty is to expose the talent of the child. If the child has got talent beyond academics and certain activities then our duty is to encourage it. (Principal, School 5)

However, this optimism about a system that explores and develops the talents of every child disappeared when he considered the issue of integrating freeship students. There was little recognition of difficulties posed by differences in the language used at home and the medium of instruction (i.e. English), or the unaffordability of private tuition that middle-class counterparts relied on for specialised instruction as grade levels increased. In fact, School 5's principal felt that the integrative model espoused in the Act is pedagogically weak. He stressed that demanding the integration of disadvantaged children in the same classroom as more privileged students was harmful given the discrepancy in learning levels and background knowledge, and felt this was a source of worry for teachers and students:

> The child who is scoring 90% and the child who comes from a totally different background and does not even know his ABCD – at what level should a teacher teach? Even at average level, the children find it difficult to cope. Education is to build confidence in the child. It's not about providing marks. (Principal, School 5)

The principal contrasted this with his slum-school project, claiming it to be a 'successful experiment' since it 'came down to their level' and catered to the presumed different needs, social backgrounds and supposed habits of these students:

> I tell you they [slum school project students] are doing much, much better. They are confident ... the staff is very well equipped. You see these are Indians, so they know the conditions in the *jhuggi jhopdi* and slum area. They know ... how parents talk to their children in that area, what are their food habits, sanitation ... so they talk to them in their language only. They come down to that level. (Principal, School 5)

Thus, according to the elite freeship school principal and contrary to the spirit of the Act, presumed success rested not on redressing differences between groups through inclusionary principles, but on an approach based on distinct social groupings. In fact, the assumption was that segregation was doing the job much better:

> Integration does not come simply by making children sit together ... If I go to the billionaire and I sit there, what will I do? Is this integration? I must come at par with him so that I can talk with his tongue. So I first bring these children at par with the others and I find that their growth is better. I can produce IITans, doctors, engineers from that *jhuggi jhopdi* by this project.[3] These students will not ... there are students which I have taken under this 25% quota failing in their subjects. Though I do not feel like it, I promote every child but they are failing for the last four to five years. If I take them failing up to Class 10, where will they land? In the evening school I teach them, train them, rather, specially for eight years – and no child fails. (Principal, School 5)

Potential Implications

While the data provide a revealing glimpse into initial school-level implementation, the full implications of the RTE Act's provisions on private unaided schools are not obvious. This is due to a number of factors – not all procedures had been established as of April 2010 when the Act came into effect; this led to a lack of clarity for schools which was framed in a broader climate of contestation; and organisational responses to institutional change require a much longer time to accurately assess (North, 1990). Nonetheless, we highlight some important considerations for the implementation of the Act, raising questions about the role that the private sector may play in redressing inequities.

Although all principals in our study claimed to be well aware of the Act, there was a considerable gap between the official articulation of its provisions and its implementation in practice. Data from our study showed two sets of mediation strategies that emerged in the early phase of implementation.

The first is misinterpretation and/or evasion. For example, schools admitted existing students under the free-seats provision; operated separate shifts; narrowly interpreted the fee-free stipulation to cover tuition fees only (freeship students incurred significant costs uncovered in household data); or evaded its implementation altogether. The second strategy is a technicist interpretation of the Act so that the letter of the law of some provisions is followed, but not its spirit. A cogent example is how the 'no detention' policy of the Act was interpreted as compulsory promotion, without earnest efforts to ensure students achieved learning levels. This has serious implications in increasing disincentives to changing pedagogic practice.

There may or may not have been a deliberate attempt to usurp the official rules, but instituting appropriate responses envisioned in the Act were aggravated by a lack of clarity and timely information on key aspects. It may be that since the freeship reimbursement amounts and procedures are clearer, the scenario may change. Nonetheless, it is likely that responses by private schools occupying different tiers of the spectrum will remain differentiated.

For example, schools charging less than or close to the monthly reimbursement maximum may be inclined to institute the free-seats provision to a greater degree, as for the lowest-fee schools, it may help to secure a certain level of income which is otherwise precarious. Of course, the reimbursement model assumes that schools have the upfront capital to accommodate more students while meeting other norms (i.e. upgrading infrastructure, teacher qualifications, prescribed salaries, etc.). This may not be possible for the lowest-fee schools. Further, some private schools may enrol students on a freeship basis and take advantage of state reimbursement without meeting RTE norms, further aggravating the unevenness of provision by 'recognised' schools.

There is the converse possibility that private schools drawing their clients from more socio-economically advantaged pools will further increase their fees *en masse* in order to accommodate freeship students. In fact, media reports to this effect have already emerged. As state reimbursement norms are well below fees charged by higher-fee and elite schools, the effect may be to squeeze out households falling outside freeship eligibility criteria but who are also on margins of affording access to higher-tier private schools. In the worst case, these households may strategise to take advantage of social networks or pay extra under-the-table fees to access freeships, ultimately denying access to the most disadvantaged. This was evidenced by households successful in securing freeships in our study (Noronha & Srivastava, in press).

The RTE Act has *de facto* further institutionalised the participation of private unaided schools in expanding schooling to disadvantaged groups most concretely through the 25% free-seats provision. Ideally, it is envisaged that if the provision is fully instituted (particularly in the high-fee, elite sector), a proportion of the most disadvantaged children will have access to schools previously the preserve of the most privileged. However, the potential of the Act to redress equity issues seems to be compromised in different ways.

Private schools may not comply, disadvantaged parents may face procedural challenges like providing adequate documentation, more privileged parents may strategise and private schools may invent new ways of maintaining social closure. These were all evidenced in our study. A striking example comes from the elite private school which admitted the largest proportion of disadvantaged children under the 25% free-seats provision overall, but also employed the most segregationist pedagogic strategy. In all these ways, the exclusiveness and attractiveness of private schooling, particularly of the elite sector, is retained for the privileged.

Regarding the 25% free-seats provision, given the heterogeneity of the private unaided sector in India, with schools ranging from modest one-room operations in rural areas to elite upscale urban schools, some with facilities rivalling small colleges in Western contexts, it is unrealistic to assume that it will be able to level the playing field *en masse*. Even if all elite schools complied in spirit, freeships were only secured by the most disadvantaged, and these students, once admitted, were equitably treated, the number of such schools is not large enough to reorient the inequities of the system. Thus, even in the ideal scenario, the private sector will funnel a small number of disadvantaged children, diverting funds from the state sector without any real recuperative effect, and leaving the majority of children behind.

Notes

[1] Karampur is a pseudonym.

[2] While Fee Level 1 schools were relatively less expensive than Fee Level 2 schools, in the absence of an official definition of 'low-fee private' schools, they did not fall within Srivastava's (2008) operationalisation of low-fee private schools as private unaided schools charging a monthly fee equivalent to a maximum of one day's labour at the primary levels and two days' labour at the secondary levels. Also, while Fee Level 2 schools charged relatively higher fees, most of them would not be considered high-fee, elite schools.

[3] 'IIT' refers to the Indian Institute of Technology, a premier and highly competitive body of colleges for engineering and related fields.

References

De, A., Noronha, C. & Samson, M. (2002) Private Schools for Less Privileged: some insights from a case study, *Economic and Political Weekly*, 37(52), 5230-5236.

Fairclough, N. (2003) *Analysing Discourse: textual analysis for social researchers*. New York: Routledge.

Government of India (2009) *The Right of Children to Free and Compulsory Education Act, 2009*. No. 35 of 2009, 26th August 2009. New Delhi.

Government of National Capital Territory [NCT] of Delhi (2011a) *Delhi Right of Children to Free and Compulsory Rules, 2011*. No. DE.23(462)/Sch.Br./10/17-33. Delhi: Department of Education, Government of NCT of Delhi, 23 November 2011.

Government of National Capital Territory [NCT] of Delhi (2011b) *Delhi School Education (Free Seats for Students belonging to Economically Weaker Sections and Disadvantage Group) order, 2011*. No.15 (172)/DE/Act/2010/69. Delhi: Education Department, Government of NCT of Delhi, 7 January 2011.

Government of National Capital Territory [NCT] of Delhi (2012) Circular No. F.DE 18/11/27/2010/Plg. 2615-20. Delhi: Directorate of Education, Planning Branch, Government of NCT of Delhi.

Härmä, J. (2009) Can Choice Promote Education for All? Evidence from Growth in Private Primary Schooling in India, *Compare*, 39(2), 151-165.

Jain, P.S. & Dholakia, R.H. (2010) Right to Education Act: public private partnership, *Economic and Political Weekly*, 45(8), 78-80.

Jha, P. & Parvati, P. (2010) Forward. *Budget Track*. Special issue on Right to Education, 7(2/3), 1-3.

Juneja, N. (2005) Exclusive Schools in Delhi: their land and the law, *Economic and Political Weekly*, 33(13), 3685-3690.

Kumar, K. (2008) Partners in Education?, *Economic and Political Weekly*, 43(3), 8-11.

Noronha, C. & Srivastava, P. (In press) *India's Right to Education Act: household experiences and school responses*. Education Support Program Working Paper no. 53. Privatisation in Education Research Initiative, Open Society Foundations.

North, D.C. (1990) *Institutions, Institutional Change and Economic Performance*. Cambridge: Cambridge University Press.

Ohara, Y. (2013) The Regulation of Unrecognised Low-Fee Private Schools in Delhi and the Right to Education Act, in P. Srivastava (Ed.) *Low-Fee Private Schools: aggravating equity or mitigating disadvantage?* Oxford: Symposium Books.

Ramachandran, V. (2009) Right to Education Act: a comment, *Economic and Political Weekly*, 44(28), 155-157.

Siddhu, G. (2010) Can Families in Rural India bear the Additional Burden of Secondary Education? Investigating the Determinants of Transition. CREATE Pathways to Access Research Monograph Series 50. Brighton: Centre for International Education, University of Sussex. http://www.create-rpc.org/pdf_documents/PTΛ50.pdf

Srivastava, P. (2007) For Philanthropy or Profit?: the Management and Operation of Low-Fee Private Schools, in P. Srivastava & G. Walford (Eds) *Private Schooling in Less Economically Developed Countries: Asian and African perspectives*. Oxford: Symposium Books.

Srivastava, P. (2008) The Shadow Institutional Framework: towards a new institutional understanding of an emerging private school sector in India, *Research Papers in Education*, 23(4), 451-475.

Tilak, J.B.G. (2007) Inclusive Growth and Education: on the approach to the Eleventh Plan, *Economic and Political Weekly*, 42(38), 3872-3877.

Tooley, J. & Dixon, P. (2005) An Inspector Calls: the regulation of 'budget' private schools in Hyderabad, Andhra Pradesh, India, *International Journal of Educational Development*, 25(3), 269-285.

Woodhead, M., Frost, M. & James, Z. (2013) Does Growth in Private Schooling Contribute to Education for All? Evidence from a Longitudinal, Two Cohort Study in Andhra Pradesh, India, *International Journal of Educational Development*, 33(1), 65-73.

CHAPTER 10

Socialisation Policy and Access of the Rural Poor to Education in Vietnam

TA VAN TUAN

Introduction

Today, access to education is widely recognised as a basic human right both as an important end in itself and as a means to achieving the Millennium Development Goals (MDGs). Although states are committed to fulfilling the rights of children to access basic services, many developing countries face daunting challenges in service delivery. Public spending on services too often does not reach poor and marginalised children, who suffer from high rates of child mortality and low rates of school attendance (UNICEF, 2010).

Vietnam has achieved considerable improvement in some education-quality indicators, such as school enrollment and adult literacy rates, as well as the Human Development Index (HDI) (UNDP, 2009) improving from 0.62 in 1990 to 0.73 in 2007 ranking 116 out of 182 countries. Despite this progress, the education system in Vietnam has encountered persistent challenges in resource availability, quality and accountability. In response, the government adopted the 'socialisation' of education reforms (UNDP, 2009). Central to the socialisation policy is the shifting of costs for public-service provision from the state to society; thus the provison of social services is no longer purely an entitlement, but a shared responsibility.

Under the theme of 'socialisation', cost recovery has been implemented in all schools and at all levels of education in Vietnam. The term 'socialisation' is directly translated from the Vietnamese term *xã hội hoá*, which means to mobilise the whole society to make contributions to national education under state guidance. In most other countries this policy would be known as privatisation. Indeed, in no society, except for Vietnam, is 'socialisation' used to refer to a process whereby institutional responsibility is shifted from the state/public sector onto households (ActionAid, 2009).

Since the introduction of the fee-charging policy for lower- and upper-secondary education in 1990, household expenditure on education has significantly increased in Vietnam (Bray, 1996). In the early 1990s, individual households were responsible for 67% and 72% of the costs of lower- and upper-secondary education respectively, while household sources accounted for around 50% of the costs of primary education (Bray, 1996).

In more than 10 years of implementing the socialisation of public services under the government's Resolution No.90/CP, dated 21 August 1997, the structure of the education sector has changed significantly. In some aspects, the role of private schools in education has become more important than public schools. At pre-primary level, for example, 43% of the schools are now non-public, and these schools attract 45% of the total number of children attending pre-primary schools (Vu Hoang Linh, 2010). Primary and secondary schools and tertiary education centres are comparatively less privatised (non-public). At college and university level, some public institutions offer non-state-funded classes for those who were unable to acheve entry requirements into state-funded classes (UNICEF et al, 2008).

Remarkably, in 2003, the government granted financial and managerial autonomy to revenue-raising public-service entities, including government health facilities and schools.[1] The Decree on Financial Autonomy (Decree 10) grants sweeping powers to revenue-raising public agencies to manage financial and human resources, and to exploit alternative revenue sources. The decree has far-reaching implications for the delivery and financing of education services as it provides managers of public facilities with incentives similar to those of for-profit private facilities.

By 2009, non-public education institutions include three types, namely 'semi-public' (*bán công*), which refers to those owned by the state but managed by public authorities at various levels and operating on the cost of tuition fees; 'people-founded' (*dân lập*), which refers to institutions that are owned and managed by non-government organisations or private associations and operate on the cost of tuition fees; and 'private' (*tư lập*), which are institutions owned and managed by private individuals.

In addition, public concern has already emerged over the implications of this reform for the cost burden of publicly provided services and the accessibility of health services for the poor and vulnerable (UNDP, 2005). Without targeted support, children from poor households can also be denied access to education, as evidenced by the low participation rates among the poor, particularly at the pre-primary and secondary levels.

Concerns have also been raised regarding the potentially adverse effects of the reforms on quality of and access to education for the poorest families. Decreased government funding to schools can result in huge gaps between rich and poor communities, with the schools in rich communities able to levy higher user fees than the latter, to be spent on school facilities, supplies and other inputs.

Therefore, it is necessary to highlight issues of access to eduction service in rural areas in the context of socialisation policy in Vietnam. This includes analyses of user charges, resource mobiliation and the impact of the policy on the affordability of education services.

Study Objective

The general objectives of the study are to assess the impacts of the socialisation policy and its implementation on access of the poor to education services in selected rural areas.

In particular, the study assesses the benefits as well as the burdens that the socialisation of education policy brings to the public, including the poor, in order to assess its ability to encourage society's overarching values and missions while allowing for financial and organisational autonomy among service providers.

Research Design and Methods

The study was designed to cover two parts:

1. Review of policies and the legal framework on education socialisation and perspectives of local authorities on implementation of those policies;
2. Assessment of the impacts of socialisation on access of the poor to education services in selected areas.

In order to achieve these objectives, the analysis is primarily based on a survey conducted by the Public Aminstration Reform Initative in project areas in which the author is project coordinator. A variety of data-collection methods were used to ensure a comprehensive and diverse range of background information with which to conduct analysis and propose solutions. Such methods inluded desk reviews, in-depth interviews and structured questionnare surveys. The survey sample of this study included 215 households from three districts in Lai Chau, Ha Tinh and Dak Lak provinces. Data were collected by the project team and T&C Consultants from:

- Interviews with leaders (in the surveyed areas) at local-government level, about education socialisation;
- Surveys on the operation of public and non-public education institutions;

- Structured interviews on education socialisation and barriers of access to education with people, especially the poor, in the context of socialisation.

These sources were supplemented by data from the Department of Education and Training (DOET) that have implemented the socialisation policies. The paper is also informed by discussions with key stakeholders including government officials from the local authorities and People's Comittees.

Limitations of the Study

The greatest challenge encountered while conducting the study was collecting data from policymakers and government departments, which delayed the completion of the report. Some interviews with local officers were facilitated by partners and field offices of the project funded by DANIDA to ActionAid Vietnam in these areas.

Another limitation was that analysis of the impact of the socialisation reforms on access by the poor to education services was limited to indirect research on improvements in access over the past years.

Key Findings

Legal Framework and Implementation
of Socialisation Policies in Vietnam

The Resolution No. 90/CP dated 21 August 1997 was the first legal document on socialisation and set the policy foundation for subsequent socialisation reforms. It did not indicate the objectives of socialisation except to outline some principles on education and health socialisation. Under the resolution, socialisation is considered to be:

> Expanding investment resources; exploiting the potential of human, material and financial resources in society; developing and using effectively human resources; creating favourable conditions to support more rapid and quality development of education, health and culture; a long-term policy providing guidelines for implementing social policy of the Communist Party of Vietnam (CPV) and the state; these are not temporary methods with immediate means, because the State does not have sufficient budget for the activities ...

The socialisation policy is also considered to be a solution to social inequality in public services:

> Privatizing education, health, and culture is also an important method for achieving social equality in the socioeconomic

development strategy of the CPV and the State. Social equity is
not only about public service, but also about the contributions
of people to society based on the ability of each person, in
each locality.

Therefore, under socialisation, contributions towards public goods and
services are made by individuals, on a user-paid basis, based on their
circumstances and income – with the poor afforded a reduction or
exemption from such contributions. In this way, the socialisation policy
is ostensibly aimed at promoting equality by ensuring that those with a
greater ability to pay contribute more for the use of public services.

However, the objectives of the socialisation reforms were much
broader than that, as outlined in Resolution No. 05/2005/NQ-CP dated 18
April 2005 as follows:

Firstly, to promote the intellectual and physical potential of
society and to mobilize resources of society to enhance
education, health, culture and sports. This objective was
reiterated in the resolutions following that of the 6th CPV's
Congress-1986 of the CPV and State. Secondly, to create
conditions for the whole of society, especially those receiving
preferential treatment and the poor, to benefit increasingly
from education, health, culture and sports. This objective aims
at identifying socialisation and ensuring social equality, not
putting the poor outside.

In order to achieve the two objectives above, the resolution indicated that
the state should continue to renovate the management mechanism;
enhance the completion of the policy; increase investment resources;
innovate objectives, methods, structure and finance; focus on priority
objectives and national programmes on education, health, culture and
sports development; support remote areas and ethnic minorities; assist
beneficiaries of the preferential treatment policy and support the poor by
implementing exemption/reduction mechanisms and providing funding
directly to the beneficiaries.

Under Resolution 90/CP issued in 1997 by the government, the
socialisation of public services such as education must maintain or
improve education quality and social equality and limit any potential
negative outcomes such as the degradation of teaching and learning
standards, abuse or corruption of the spirit or law of the policy reform, or
inequality in access to education services.

In implementing socialisation, the state does not seek to reduce
overall funding to education services, but rather to prevent unsustainable
cost increases while seeking a redeployment of funding to 'where it is
needed most' and transferring a degree of responsibility for the financing
of education services to those who can afford to pay- including
households, social organisations and businesses.

Resolution No. 05/2005/NQ-CP provided a picture of how education services would be resourced under the socialisation-policy platform, including:

1. State resources, to be increased overall but be focused on: universalising education; investing in national target programmes; training personnel for major sectors and professions that are difficult to mobilise social resources; and investing in remote areas and ethnic minorities

2. Tuition fees and 'voluntary contributions'. In order to leverage public finances with extra resources from, and transfer a portion of responsibility for the improvement of education quality to society, the state has allowed for the extraction of tuition fees and contributions from households for education service delivery and school expenses. However, under Decision 241/1993/QD-TTg and Decision 70/1998/QD-TTg by the Prime Minister on tuitions and fees, the state is responsible for subsidising most educational expenditures.

The state has favoured the establishment of non-public education, training and vocational institutes; the pritivatisation of public institutions; the limiting of the establishment of more public institutions in developed areas; and the discontinuation of support for semi-public institutions or semi-public classes, as strategies for placing downward pressure on the public cost of education services. It also advocates cooperation and linkages with high-quality educational institutes around the world and encourages the opening of training institutes with up to 100% foreign-capital funding.

Under the policy on socialisation, education and training institutions can be divided into four main types:

- *Type1:* Public schools: state-owned education institutions. Socialisation aims to mobilise voluntary or consensus-based contributions from households to facilitate better investment in quality infrastructure as well as teaching and learning. Such contributions are often collected by parent associations rather than the school itself.
- *Type2:* Semi-public schools: heavily state-subidised education institutions that receive investment from the private sector for operation and improvements. Under socialisation and since 2009, semi-public schools have been abolished and converted into public, private or people-founded schools.
- *Type 3:* People-founded schools: Non-public education institutions founded by civil society, and operating on a non-profit basis. The main objective of these institutions is to increase access of pupils at all levels to education services.

- *Type 4:* Private schools: For-profit education institutions that are founded by the private sector and trade in education and/or training services.

Characteristics of four types of schools by 2010 under context of socialisation are presented in Table I.

	Public schools	Semi-public schools	People-founded schools	Private schools
Operational objectives of the institutions	Provides publicly funded education services as mandated by the State and the CPV.	Providing education services for students with poor performance.	Non-profit education institutions providing access to poor performance students.	Trading in education for profit.
Goals of socialisation	Socialisation in public schools aims to 'mobilise the State and people to work together' to improve study conditions for the students.	Abolished under socialisation and transformed into either public, people-founded or private schools.	Capital for building and operating school is contributed by civil society organisations and households or loaned from development assistance funds.	Invested by investors seeking a profit.
Characteristics of pupils and students	Universalised for primary and secondary school.	Recruited students who failed the entry examinations to public schools. School fees are much higher than public ones.	These schools provide access to education for low-income households in areas not serviced by public schools.	Students of these schools are from households with a greater capacity to pay.
Capacity for providing services	Have the highest capacity for providing quality and equitable education services. Usually have experienced managing boards and teachers.	Physical facilities, managing boards and teachers are similar to that of public schools.	Facilities are adequate and initial investments are sufficient without improvement.	High quality and high school fees

Service costs	Operating and investment costs are provided by the government, and tuition fees for households are lower than for private schools.	Service costs are higher than in public schools.	Service costs are higher than in public and semi-public schools.	Service costs are the highest of all schools.
Preferential policies for poor students	Public schools often apply policies on full fee exemptions and reductions for the children of poor households and ethnic minority families.	Similar to public schools.	None	None

Table I. Comparison of the main operational characteristics of the education institutions.

Perspectives of Local Government Leaders on Education Socialisation

The implementation of socialisation depends on the opinions and approaches of local government leaders. After interviewing the leaders of provincial departments and district divisions, the study team drew four main conclusions on the issue of socialisation.

First, local authorities agree with the general policy on socialisation in education, and they are implementing solutions to stimulate socialisation at the local level. Both provincial and district education departments in the three surveyed provinces are in general agreement over the necessity for socialisation reforms in a context of increasing demand for higher-quality education and limited budgets.

Each province has enacted policies promoting socialisation reforms at the micro-level, such as land grants and tax exemptions for private schools, as well as progressive reductions in government assistance to schools combined with the explicit or implicit authorisation of the collection of fees from households. While the principles of socialisation apply across all levels of education, socialisation has been integrated most strongly within the pre-primary and vocational secondary levels. In part, this is due to the continued extension of government support for primary and non-vocational secondary levels in line with universal education commitments. (Interview, Deputy Director of the Department of Education and Training in Ha Tinh).

Second, although much has said much about the benefits of socialisation and policies supporting socialisation, managerial officers of departments were not able to explain what they could do to ensure the quality of education and uphold State regulations for privatized education institutions. Most local managerial officers understand socialisation as mobiliSing social resources to provide public services. The roles of state management, such as orienting (forecasting, strategy, planning) or monitoring and evaluating, which are a key aspect of socialisation policy and necessary for ensuring that the quality of and equity of education services are maintained, have not been given sufficient focus. This poses potential problems in promoting the effectiveness of socialisation, especially in assisting the poor in accessing education services and guaranteeing that teaching and learning standards do not decline.

As an example, the Education Departments in Lai Chau and Dak Lak provinces entirely lack a planning framework for education, resulting in newly opened schools failing to meet the needs of local learners. In this case, the private sector is unable to fill the service gaps due to their limitations to operate in less commercially feasible environments i.e. where the concentration and ability of households to pay is lower than conditions present in Lai Chau and Dak Lak provinces.

In addition, education planners in those provinces have not been able to collect adequate statistics on the capacity, available capital and resource needs of schools and teachers that fall outside the publicly funded system, aside from tuition fees that have been collected. This deficiency in monitoring and evaluation can lead to abuse of the socialisation reforms in terms of fee collection or low-quality education service delivery. In either case, the poor are impacted most heavily.

Third, there are different experiences with socialisation at the local level. In local areas where income is relatively high, such as in Buon Ma Thuot City, Dak Lak province, departmental leaders are in strong support of education socialisation. However, there is markedly weaker support in poor areas such as Lai Chau, where education socialisation is considered to be less suitable for the local context and consequently features the least comprehensive implementation of the socialisation process. In the words of the Leader of the Department of Education in Lai Chau province:

> Socialisation of education is an appropriate policy of the Party
> and the State to attract the society to provide educational
> services for the children. However, there are differences in the
> execution of the policy in the delta and mountainous
> provinces because mountainous areas have a low development
> of economic conditions and knowledge. Presently, having

> public schools for the children to study in is a success of the
> organizations [and the] efforts of the schools and society.
> Many teachers are facing difficult life (both physical and spirit
> life) to transfer knowledge to pupils. They even have to go to
> each family to persuade the parents to send children to school.
> I think no individual or organization can provide education
> services to ethnic minority people except the State.

This implication here is that socialisation is most beneficial for those who can afford to pay for a high-quality education, and least beneficial for those who are unable.

Fourth, there are differences in opinions about socialisation between officials, private institutions owners and citizens. A leader of the Provincial DOET said: 'Socialisation means that people voluntarily contribute, so the poor will not be impacted. Socialisation does not create pressure for the poor because the poor are exempted from 50 percent of school fees in people-founded and private schools.'

However, when the study team interviewed two headmasters from non-public schools, it was found that no such policy was in place:

> Under regulations, school fees of private vocational schools
> can be 2 to 3 times higher than that of public schools.
> However, we do not exempt or reduce school fees for the poor
> students. There have been several dozen students dropping
> out of school because they did not have money for school fees.
> Most of the students are ethnic minority people. When the
> families suffer from natural disasters, they remove their
> children from the school. (Headmaster of a private vocational
> school)

> No, our school does not have a policy to exempt or reduce
> school fees for poor pupils. Whoever wants to send their
> children to our school, she has to lend one million to our
> school without interest for five years. The money will be used
> to pay for bank debt that the school loaned to invest in
> facilities for teaching and learning. (Headmaster of a high-
> quality people-founded primary school)

According to central managerial officials surveyed, this discrepancy is explained as follows: 'The managerial officials have their own perspective, the private institutions have their own views and people also have their viewpoints (which are often narrow because people are only concerned about what they gain and how much they have to pay).'

The study team found similar differences in knowledge and attitudes towards education socialisation among local authorities, Principal Investigators and the community throughout the study. This shows that both communication and awareness-raising for the policy changes needs to be undertaken more effectively, and in addition, that some gaps exist between education socialisation policy and practice.

Access of Poor Students in Four Types of School under Socialisation Context

First, in the three surveyed provinces, there were more poor students in people-founded and semi-public schools than in public schools. Although public schools are almost entirely subsidised by the government, and provide substantial learning support to the children of disadvantaged households, they remain difficult to access for such children due to their prohibitively stringent entry requirements – from which they are not exempt. Children from poor households often fail the entry examinations into public education-service providers (including primary and secondary schools, colleges and universities) and are forced to attend people-founded schools as a result. In fact, 95% of pupils of people-founded schools in Ha Tinh were children from disadvantaged farming families.

Private schools, on the other hand, attract students from higher-income households, but the number of private schools is low, and they are prohibitively expensive to attend. Private and people-founded schools do not focus on implementing policies to ensure access for poor students (such as providing exemptions or reductions on school fees, school building costs, textbooks, living costs and so on).

In this way, although education socialisation increases the number of service providers, ostensibly to increase access to education services for all who need it, the poor benefit the least from the reforms, with the most beneficial impacts of the reforms being that households are extended alternative (albeit user-paid) opportunities to access education if they fail the public-schooling entrance exams.

Second, people-founded schools in surveyed areas face significant problems in the quality of teaching and learning, particularly at higher levels of education. Although people-founded schools aim to provide high-quality services, the reality is that they attract less academically inclined pupils compared to public schools, and are staffed by teachers that are usually young and inexperienced. As a result of this combination, the quality of teaching and learning at such schools is generally lower than that of public education providers – even though the cost of attending people-founded schools is much higher for households than it is for public schools.

Third, the socialisation reforms have been used as an opportunity to extract heavy financial contributions from households, including those with a limited ability to pay. An officer of DOET said that most of the state-owned schools in the city are operating under the mode of finance self-control. The schools can still get money from the state education budget (30-60% of total expenses), while they also collect tuition from students to cover expenses. Therefore, the schools are not allowed to set overly high tuitions like privately run or people-founded schools. However, in Ha Tinh province, the state budget in 2009 may account for only 22% of the total budget, 80% of which will be used to pay to teachers. With education socialisation, the difference in tuition levels of schools proves to be unavoidable.

Interviewing education policymakers and practitioners at the district level, the study team learned of the abuse of the socialisation reforms by schools, as highlighted by the following comments of a district leader:

> Visiting the schools, I said directly that everyone knew you abused the Association of Students' Parents' regulation of grassroots democracy to rationalize needs of your schools.

In interviews on the implementation of the socialisation in education reforms in public schools, there were various opinions:

> The school said that they exempt school building costs for the poor, but in the meeting with the Association of Students' Parents, they still decided to collect extra costs to improve learning conditions. There are many costs we have to pay such as statue building costs. (A household member from Eakar district)

> We are the poor households, and we never head the Association of Students' Parents. In meetings, the head made all decisions, so we have to get loans for our children to pay school fees; if not, the children will be made ashamed to go to school. (Citizen of Ha Tinh province)

In this way, financial contributions are extracted from all households, even low-income households who attend public schools. The charges are disguised as 'voluntary contributions' or charges for items that were previously free, which speaks to the state of monitoring and evaluation processes within Vietnam's education system.

People's Perspectives in Rural Areas
on Socialisation and Access to Education

Expenditure on education and selection of service provision types. As a result of the socialisation in education policy reforms, the proportion of household expenditure on education has grown progressively higher. Of the surveyed households, 72.5% have to pay up to VND1.4 million (US$66) in financial contributions on top of standard tuitition fees per school year, per household. Education expenditure often equates to more than 30% of household income.

In contrast, only 34.6% of households benefit from policies on exemption and reduction of school fees or receive other support, the average value of which is VND0.82 million per household per school year.

The study found that average household income has little effect upon the selection of education-service type. Rather, the majority of respondents preferred sending their children to public schools, due to the free and high-quality education they offer, and would only pursue an alternative option if their first choice were not available. The education-service-provider preferences of households, in a scenario in which they were freely able to choose between public and non-public schooling, is presented in Table II.

Income ('000s)	Common		Households with poor-household card	
	Public schools (%)	Non-public schools (%)	Public schools (%)	Non-public schools (%)
Under VND1500	58.9	3.6	80.0	4.3
From VND1500 to VND3000	21.4	2.6	8.6	0.0
Over VND3000	12.5	1.0	7.1	0.0
Total	92.8	7.2	95.7	4.3

Table II. Household preferences for education-service providers.

Impacts of education socialisation on education accessibility. Five major barriers were identified with regards to accessibility of the poor to education services.

- *Tuition fees:* Fees paid by learners or learners' families to pay for formal education under the regulations of the government.
- *Extra fees:* Additional costs paid by the learners or their families, for maintainance, upkeep or investment into new infrastructure or improved teaching and learning strategies. These fees are allowed under the socialisation in education-policy platform – although there is insufficient clarity, and even less monitoring and evaluation, with regards to how these fees may be extracted, from whom, and on what they are spent.
- *Education quality:* Quality of educational services in specific localities, in terms of facilities, teaching methods, content and teachers' attitudes.

- *Distance*: Distance from the learners' houses to the schools they attended can pose barriers when schools are situated far from their home.
- *Relationships*: Specifically, relations between the school, teachers and the family, which is deemed necessary to ensure optimal studying conditions and learning outcomes.

In order to assess the relative importance of each of these barriers to households, they were assessed by way of a scorecard. Under this method, the lower the score (1 point minimum), the smaller barriers are, and the higher the scores (5 points maximum), the greater the barriers. The evaluation results of barriers to accessing education are shown in Tables III, IV and V. Across the whole survey sample, school fees, both official and unofficial, were ranked as the strongest barrier to accessing education services, followed by quality and distance, with the weakest barrier being relations between school and family. Compared with five years ago, barriers posed by school fees, extra fees and distance increased in importance, while those posed by quality decreased in importance, with relations between school and family remaining a minor barrier.

Barriers	2010				2005			
	Ha Tinh	Dak Lak	Lai Chau	Average	Ha Tinh	Dak Lak	Lai Chau	Average
School fees	4.0	3.8	2.5	3.6	4.0	3.3	2.7	3.5
Extra fees	4.0	3.8	2.7	3.7	3.8	3.3	2.8	3.5
Quality	2.4	3.2	2.1	2.5	2.7	3.0	2.3	2.7
Distance	2.8	2.9	2.3	2.7	2.8	2.4	2.0	2.5
Relations	1.8	2.1	1.9	1.9	1.9	2.0	2.0	1.9

Table III. Barriers to education in localities and whole-survey sample.
Source: Study survey.

Barriers	2010				2005			
	Ha Tinh	Dak Lak	Lai Chau	Average	Ha Tinh	Dak Lak	Lai Chau	Average
School fees	3.7	3.5	2.2	3.3	3.8	3.0	2.8	3.4
Extra fees	3.8	3.7	2.5	3.3	3.6	2.9	2.9	3.3
Quality	2.4	3.2	2.1	2.5	2.6	2.9	2.5	2.6
Distance	2.8	2.8	2.4	2.7	2.8	2.2	2.3	2.5
Relations	1.9	2.1	2.0	2.0	1.9	2.9	2.2	2.0

Table IV. Barriers to education for non-poor households in localities and whole-survey sample. *Source*: Study survey.

Barriers	2010				2005			
	Ha Tinh	Dak Lak	Lai Chau	Average	Ha Tinh	Dak Lak	Lai Chau	Average
School fees	4.5	4.0	2.9	4.0	4.8	3.5	2.5	3.7
Extra fees	4.4	4.0	3.2	4.1	4.3	3.7	2.8	3.8
Quality	2.3	3.2	1.9	2.5	2.8	3.2	2.0	2.8
Distance	2.8	3.1	1.9	2.7	2.8	2.5	1.6	2.4
Relations	1.5	2.1	1.7	1.7	1.7	2.1	1.6	1.8

Table V. Barriers to education for poor households in localities
and in whole-survey sample *Source*: Study survey.

Figures 1 and 2 illustrate the relative importance of these barriers within
poor and non-poor households. The figures illustrate that compared with
five years ago, non-poor households are not as strongly affected by the
costs of education services, whereas poor households have experienced a
greater negative impact from the cost of education services.

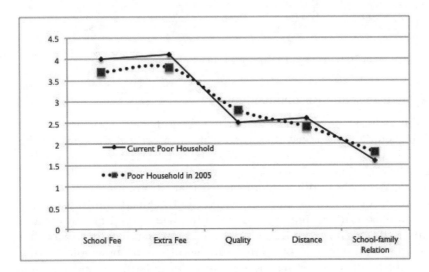

Figure 1. Changes in barriers for poor households.

Barriers to accessing education also differ according to locality. In Ha
Tinh province, barriers to accessing education, and in particular
education costs, were considered to be very strong. On the other hand,
they were considered to be significantly weaker in Lai Chau province.
Barriers to accessing education were perceived to be stronger for the poor
than they were for the non-poor (excluding the barriers of school and

family relations). It is noteworthy that the barriers of education costs are perceived to be weaker in Lai Chau, where educational institutions have not yet implemented socialisation and no privatised educational institutions have been established. Thus, since implementing education socialisation, the barriers to accessibility to education services for the poor have strengthened rather than weakened.

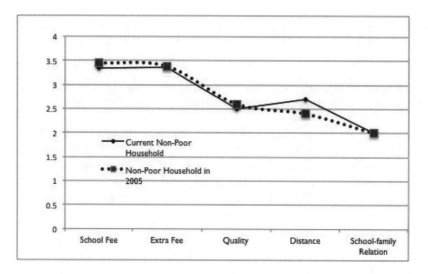

Figure 2. Changes in barriers for non-poor households.

Conclusions and Recommendations

Although efforts have been made to promulgate legal documents providing guidance on privatising education, a critical analysis of the socialisation in education reforms reveals issues related to inequality among households in accessing education services. The main shortcoming of the policy platform is that it emphasises resource mobilisation for providing public services, but neglects the transformed yet nonetheless critical role of the state in implementing the reforms and continuing to facilitate the delivery of education services in a way that ensures the maintainance of quality and equity. This new role for the state consists of orientating (forecasting, formulating strategies and planning), regulating (through policies) and monitoring operations of the transforming education sector. Current policies on socialisation in education provide insufficient guidance for authorities to undertake this role – leaving the reformed education sector and its beneficiaries at risk from corruption and abuse. The two main shortcomings of the socialisation in education policy are:

(a) *Shortcomings on the quality control of privatised education*: No criteria for assessing quality education or mechanisms with which to track it are in place. The framework for cooperation between education institutions is insufficient, resulting in problems in providing certification for the standardised recognition of educational achievement. Finally, there is no mechanism for the classification of private for-profit and non-profit institutions, which has lead to the commercialisation of education.

(b) Shortcomings on regulating the total costs for households of education services: There are no specific regulations or control mechanisms to prevent the financial abuse of socialisation, such as the collection of financial contributions for a variety of formerly central, but now 'ancillary', components of any given education service. In addition, insufficient focus has been given to ensuring access to education for the disadvantaged, including ethnic minorities, under the reformed education system.

From the survey results in the three provinces, the following conclusions can be drawn:

- Guidelines and policies on education socialisation are valued and supported by local authorities. Leaders have identified that socialisation is a good method for mobilising social resources, increasing resources and diversifying service provision in order to meet the increasing and varying needs of citizens. However, localities with under-developed economies face many difficulties in implementing the reforms because of limited investment and willingness on the part of households to contribute.
- In terms of state management in localities, the implementation of socialisation has proceeded in the absence of appropriate planning, regulation and supervision. This is one of the reasons that socialisation has not been as successful as expected: the quality of services have not been ensured, and some abuse in the extraction of fees has occurred. The poor are the primary victims of these limitations.
- Investigation in some education institutions has shown that the socialisation reforms have not addressed the disadvantages of the poor. Firstly, in practice, the policy on school-fee reduction is applied in only public schools, which many poor students are unable to access due to the prohibitive entry requirements. Therefore, they do not benefit from the policy. Moreover, the teaching and learning results in alternative schooling options, such as people-founded schools, are below those in public schools.
- Household-survey results demonstrate that the barriers to access to education are official and unofficial school fees, which have increased for the poor in the past five years in line with a certain degree of improvement in the quality of education.

215

Based on the survey results, the study team has the following recommendations:

- Education privatisation should be linked with changing the role of state management from providing service to macro-management. Thus, parallel with the implementation of socialisation, local authorities have to enhance roles of forecasting, planning, organising and regulating the development of localities, as well as monitoring and supervising the operation of institutions with various owners. At present, local authorities are not sufficiently concerned with the roles of management associated with socialisation. They focus only on the impact of growth (resource mobilisation) of socialisation.
- In terms of orientation, the provinces need to put in place development plans for educational institution systems in different localities, thereby devising and issuing policies to incentivise the establishement of educational institutions in remote areas, thus reducing the barrier of distance. In some cases, the state invests more in public schools in remote areas because in urban areas, more people-founded and private schools are being established, thus increasing the supply of educational services.
- It is necessary to pay more attention to monitoring and evaluating quality control and the implementation of policies on school fees and extra fees, to prevent misuse of finance or abuse of households.
- It is necessary to have policies to ensure that poor students are benefitting from school-fee reduction policies. One direction of research is assessing the effects of shifting from school-fee reduction to financial support that the poor can access, which means they could select any schools to attend. Another direction involves policies supporting poor students in people-founded schools (especially in secondary schools and higher levels), as these are the schools many poor students attend.

Notes

[1] Inter-Ministerial Circular no. 21/2003/TTLT-BTC&BGD-BNV provides guidelines for financial management of revenue-earning public-service delivery units in the sectors of public education and training. Decree no. 10/2002/ND-CP regulates financing of revenue-generating service-delivery agencies. Decree no. 25/2002/TT-BTC sets out guidelines for implementation of Decree no. 10/2002/ND-CP dated 16 January 2002 on the financial mechanism applicable to income-generating service units. Inter-Ministerial Circular no. 13/2004/TTLT-BYT-BNV provides guidelines for financial management of revenue-earning public-service delivery units in public health.

References

ActionAid Vietnam (2009) *Study Report on the Possible Impacts the Privatization Process Could Have on the Poor's Access to Public Services in Vietnam.* Hanoi: ActionAid: Hanoi.

Bray, M. (1996) *Counting the Full Cost: parental and community financing of education in East Asia.* Washington, DC: World Bank.

Resolution 05/2005/NQ-CP of the Government dated 18 April 2005 on stepping up socialization of educational, healthcare, cultural, physical training and sport activities.

Resolution 90/CP of the Government dated 21 August 1997 on the direction and policy of socialization of educational, medical, and cultural activities.

UNICEF East Asia and Pacific Regional Office (2010) Regional Analysis Report 2010. Bangkok: UNICEF.

UNICEF, MoET and UNESCO (2008) *The Transition of Ethnic Minority Girls from Primary to Secondary Education.* Hanoi: UNICEF and MoET.

United Nations Development Programme (UNDP) (2005) *User Fees, Financial Autonomy and Access to Social Services in Vietnam.* Hanoi: Office of the United Nations Resident Coordinator.

United Nations Development Programme (UNDP) (2009) *Human Development Report 2009.* Hanoi: UNDP.

Vu Hoang Linh (2010) Education Issues in Viet Nam in the New Millennium: access, disparities and financing. Working Paper. Hanoi: NHDR.

CHAPTER 11

Education Service Contracting in the Philippines: assessing benefits for marginalised users

CHONA S. SANDOVAL & CECILIA V. SORIANO

Education Access and Quality in the Philippines

Basic education provisioning in the Philippines is largely public. The 1987 Constitution of the Philippines mandates that: 'The State shall protect and promote the right of all citizens to quality education at all levels and shall take appropriate steps to make such education accessible to all' (Article XIV, Section 1). Further, the State shall '[e]stablish and maintain a system of free public education in the elementary and high school levels', where 'elementary education is compulsory for all children of school age.'

Clearly, the Constitutional Committee considered both access and quality of education as key to the country's democratisation and development. Section 2 of the same Article states that the State shall 'establish, maintain, support a complete, adequate and integrated system of education relevant to the needs of the people and society'. The Constitution promulgated after 'People Power' and guarding against going back to authoritarian rule reiterates that all education institutions shall include in the curricula respect for human rights, nationalism and citizenship.

Over the years, the government built schools, and aimed to have one in every village, at least at the elementary level. In 2011, the Department of Education (DepEd) reported a total of 40,763 elementary schools nationwide, 89% (36,234) of which were public schools and of which 11% (4529) were private schools. This number drastically narrowed at secondary level. There were only 7683 high schools nationwide; about 58% (4422) of these were government-run and the remaining 42% (3261) were privately owned (DepEd, 2011b).

When the K-12 education was signed into law early 2013, the state's education responsibilities broadened to cover Kindergarten, six years of elementary education (grades 1-6), three years of Junior High School (grades 7-9) and three years of Senior High School (grades 10-12).

Government efforts to realise the constitutional mandates and Education for All 2015 goals have been failing. The Functional Literacy and Education, Mass Media Survey (FLEMMS), a government survey conducted every five years, revealed in 2008 that one in every three Filipinos between the ages of 6 and 24 is not attending school. The number of out-of-school children and youth increased between 2003 and 2008 – from 11.4 million to 12.3 million (Education Watch – Philippines, 2007). In terms of the completion of basic education, data shows that only 30.4 million (38%) of the 80 million Filipinos (six years old and above) have completed formal secondary schooling.

FLEMMS 2008 further validates the concern about the quality of Philippine education. Among Filipinos who completed elementary education, about 20% were not functionally literate. More alarming is that about 10% of those who have reached high school were not functionally literate. This means that while Filipinos' average years of schooling has increased, literacy has improved only marginally if at all.

Consistently, the 'high cost of education' and 'looking for employment' were the top reasons for the low rates of participation in and completion of education (FLEMMS, 2008). The Education Watch (E-Net Philippines, 2007) confirms that even when public schools do not collect tuition, families are burdened with transportation expenses, especially at the secondary level, when schools are mostly in the *poblacion* or centres only. Parents also find it hard to finance school-related costs such as uniforms, school supplies, test papers and most especially, school contributions.

Even for those who have the means to send their children to school, parents opt to enrol their children in public schools to avail themselves of free education. Mass transfer of students from private schools to public schools was first experienced from 1987 to 1988, when the Free Public Secondary Education Act (Republic Act 6655) was passed into law. A second wave of public-school migration occurred in 1997 when the Asian financial crisis hit the country. This was repeated during the economic downturn of 2003. In 2006, the education expenditure of Filipino families further decreased from a low of 2.3% to an even lower 1.9% of the total family income (Family Income and Expenditure Survey, 2006), thus the migration to public schools. These shifts in enrolment resulted in overcrowded classrooms, which gave rise to the term 'aisle students', referring to students accommodated beyond the classroom's full capacity.

This increasing demand for public education, however, is not equally met with the public financing of education. The Philippines ranks among the lowest spenders on education in Asia and the rest of the world. The country's spending level of 2.9% of its Gross Domestic Product (GDP) is below the East Asian regional average of 3.6% of GDP and South Asia's average of 3.8%. When countries were classified into income categories, the education spending level of the Philippines, a middle-income country, was even lower than the median (3.9% of GDP) expenditure of countries belonging to the lowest income group. This is despite the latest report on the progress of the Millennium Development Goals (MDGs), where the government admitted that the education 'target of universal access to elementary education by 2015 is in great risk of not being achieved'.

For the fiscal year 2011, PHP207.27 billion (US$5.05 billion) was allocated to education. The amount is equivalent to 12.6% of the total national budget and 2.9% of the country's GDP. It is the highest allocation given to education in the last 20 years, but still below the international benchmark (Alternative Budget for Education Policy Brief, E-Net Philippines, 2012). In 2012, the education budget was PHP238.76 billion (US$5.8 billion), which is 15.2% higher than the previous year. From this amount, at least PHP5.8 billion (US$142 million) has been earmarked for service contracting. For 2012, the amount reached PHP 6.3 billion (US$154 million). Stakeholders, particularly the private sector, have been enjoined by the government to participate in ensuring that all children and youth are given access to quality education. While in 1987 the administration of the then President Corazon Aquino argued for public provisioning, the current President Benigno Aquino III has framed public–private partnership (PPP) as a necessary financing and governance strategy for education.

PPP in Education: focus on education service contracting

Public–private partnership in education has been practised by the Philippine government since the 1980s. Two factors have led to the application of this strategy. One is the need to accommodate the growing number of school-aged children. Second is the need to respond to the call for universal access to basic education. At present, the government partners with the business sector, non-government organisations, private enterprises, privately run education institutions, church-based organisations and community-based organisations in the financing and delivery of education. The Government Assistance to Students and Teachers in Private Education (GASTPE) law, Early Childhood Care and Development law, Governance of Basic Education Act, ALS Program, Adopt-a-School Program and Brigada Eskwela Program include provisions for government partnership with private institutions and organisations.

221

The research done by the Civil Society Network for Education Reforms (E-Net Philippines) with PERI on PPP in education in 2011-12 and reported in this chapter, focused on the Education Service Contracting (ESC), a major PPP under the GASTPE law.

Studies on the ESC component of GASTPE have been undertaken prior to the passage of RA 6655. In 1981, the Fund for Assistance to Private Education (FAPE) was commissioned by the Ministry of Education (MECS) to conduct a feasibility study on ESC. Pilot testing took place from 1982 to 1983. In 1986, a PHP5 million budget was earmarked by MECS for ESC's initial implementation. Positive gains accrued during its implementation eventually led to the passage of GASTPE in June 1989 (FAPE, 2011). The law was amended in February 1998.

A recent policy guideline (DepEd Order No. 8, s. 2011 [DepEd, 2011ba) on GASTPE states that its primary objective is to 'democratize and improve access to quality secondary education'. It seeks to achieve this by providing assistance to 'deserving elementary school graduates' who wish to pursue private schooling. In a separate document, FAPE (2011, p. 7) qualifies that support from GASTPE is extended to 'poor but deserving students'. This mechanism allows the public schools to reduce their class sizes to manageable levels and the recipient private schools to operate viably.

Programme components: There are currently three components of GASTPE: the Education Service Contracting Scheme (ESC); the Tuition Fee Supplement (TFS); and the Teacher Salary Subsidy (TSS). ESC is a programme that seeks to reduce class sizes in public high schools. The programme accomplishes this by 'contracting the excess capacities of private high schools' to accommodate students from low-income families who would have otherwise enrolled in the public high schools. TFS is a minimal tuition subsidy for students given in addition to ESC. The third component, TSS, was adopted during school year (SY) 2009-10 to encourage teachers in private schools to continue serving in the private-school system. The TFS and TSS components of GASTPE are not tackled in this study.

Programme management: ESC, together with the other components of GASTPE, is managed by FAPE. FAPE was established through an Executive Order in 1968 to support private education in the Philippines. The FAPE board consists of the Philippine Association of Colleges and Universities (PACU), the Catholic Education Association of the Philippines (CEAP) and the Association of Christian Schools, Colleges and Universities (ACSCU). The DepEd Secretary sits as chairperson of the board. FAPE operation is supported by a trust fund 'created by and between the Philippines and US governments under EO No. 156, s. 1986' (DepEd, 2011a). It receives an administrative service fee, currently pegged at PHP100 per student grantee, for the management of

GASTPE. FAPE's role in the implementation of ESC consists of: (1) certifying the participating private schools based on specified guidelines; (2) determining the allocation of ESC slots per school based on DepEd determined regional quotas; and (3) collating, reviewing and forwarding the billing statements submitted by the participating private schools to the DepEd Central Office. In addition to these functions, FAPE provides in-service training for teachers and principals. Together with DepEd representatives, they also monitor the implementation of the programme by the grant-recipient private school.

A Regional Project Management Committee (RPCom) manages ESC implementation at the local level. In most instances, the RPCom is lodged in private colleges and universities. It is composed of a chair, a coordinator and an information technology (IT) person. In most cases, the president of the university where the RPM is lodged sits as regional chair of FAPE (Porio, 2010). The RPM is responsible for directly coordinating with the grant-recipient private schools. They conduct the certification process and coordinate the school's submission of the billing statements to FAPE national office.

Programme scope and coverage: ESC is implemented across all regions in the country and covers all divisions under the Department of Education. The initial budget for ESC was close to PHP354.57 million (SY 1996-97), which covered 210,630 grantees across the country. As the years progressed, the budget amount and number of grantees steadily increased. By SY 2010-11, the ESC budget had broken the PHP3 billion mark. The amount covers 595,566 students in 3178 schools across the country. For SY 2011-12, budget allocation has been pegged at PHP5.8 billion. This was further increased to PHP6.3 billion for SY 2012-13. LaRocque and Lee (2011, p. 22) aver that GASTPE is 'one of the largest educational service-delivery programmes in the world'.

In 2011, budget allocation per student was pegged at PHP10,000 in the National Capital Region (NCR) and PHP5500 in all other regions in the country. All grants are given to first-year students. Financial support is provided until the students reach their 4th year of secondary school (grade 10), on condition that they enrol on a continuous basis (i.e. no dropping out). Grants are non-replaceable. Allocation per student is forfeited once the student drops out. No other student may take the place of the grantee. Budget allocation for the grantee is automatically cancelled once the grantee drops out of school.

Selection of recipient schools and targeting of student beneficiaries: Private schools are selected using a certification process. The RPM Committee coordinates and facilitates the process. In terms of targeting student beneficiaries, all graduating public elementary pupils are considered eligible for the programme. As of 2011, eligible students are instructed to register directly with the participating private schools.

A screening committee composed of parent and teacher representatives is created within the school. Applicants are profiled according to Family, Individual, Community and School (FISC) factors (DepEd, 2011a). Specific criteria for selecting students have not been identified. A World Bank (2011) study, however, cited that criteria for selection include: (1) the family's income level; (2) completion of six years of basic education; and (3) capacity of the student to complete four years of high school without dropping out. No grade ceiling is required as long as the student passes.

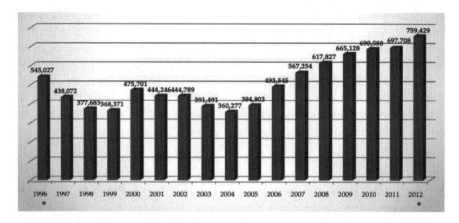

Figure 1. The number of ESC grantees has increased by 40% since SY 1996-97. *Source*: DepEd (2012).

Research Objectives and Problem Statement

The objective of E-Net Philippines' research was to review and assess the implementation of the Education Service Contracting (ESC). The Assessment was focused on the programmes' goal of increasing citizens' access to education, particularly the marginalised, excluded and vulnerable sectors of society. Criteria for assessment were efficiency, equity, social cohesion and sensitivity to ethnic, gender and socioeconomic status. Based on these criteria, the following research questions were formulated.

In terms of access to basic education of the marginalised, excluded and vulnerable sector (MEVS), does the ESC programme:

1. Promote *social cohesion* in terms of rationale, objectives and strategies?
2. Use government resources in an *efficient* manner?
3. Address *equity* of access to education opportunities?
4. Promote *sensitivity* to ethnic, gender and socioeconomic class?

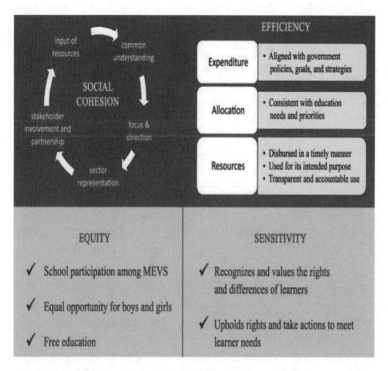

Figure 2. Criteria for assessing ESC (E-Net Philippines, 2011)
(Belfield & Levin, 2002).

To address the research objectives identified, a case-study approach was utilised. Five provinces across the country were chosen. Representation of the three main island groups – i.e. Luzon, Visayas and Mindanao – and the three sectoral groups – i.e. Muslim, Christians and Indigenous Peoples – were considered in the selection of communities. Because the study is primarily interested in the impact of the programme on access to education of the marginalised, excluded and vulnerable sectors (MEVs), municipalities chosen were limited to 3rd- and 4th-year classes. The classes refer to the average annual income of the municipality during the last three calendar years. Third-class municipalities have an annual income range of PHP30 million to PHP40 million, and 4th-class municipalities have an annual income range of PHP20 million to PHP30 million.

Four provinces were included in the final study. These were Masbate province in Luzon; Northern Samar in the Visayas; Compostela Valley in Southern Mindanao; and Maguindanao in the Autonomous Region of Muslim Mindanao (ARMM). Masbate and Northern Samar are largely Christian communities. Compostela Valley is home to indigenous

225

cultural communities. Maguindanao province is populated mostly by Muslims, but indigenous groups are also present.

Six municipalities in the five selected provinces were chosen as the focus of the study. Masbate City in Masbate province has a poverty incidence of 62.8%. The province's long history of political conflicts is said to have contributed to the continued poverty of its residents. The fishing community of Mondragon in Northern Samar is located on the eastern edge of the Philippine archipelago. It is prone to typhoons and storm surges. Mawab and Maco are agricultural communities in Compostela Valley. Mining is also considered a key industry. Pockets of armed conflict and tribal wars occur in these areas. Basic services rarely reach remote settlements. In Maguindanao, North Upi and Datu Piang were the two municipalities selected. Maguindanao, being the centre of long-term armed conflict, has a poverty incidence of 55.1%. Table I shows the six municipalities indicating their class (economic-income levels) and the education programmes selected for each municipality.

Region	Luzon	Visayas	Mindanao	
Province	Masbate	Northern Samar	Compostela Valley	Maguindanao
Municipality class	4th class	4th class	3rd class	3rd class
Private secondary schools	Masbate City (two schools)	Mondragon (one school)	Mawab (one school) Maco (one school)	Datu Piang (one school) North Upi (one school)

Table I. Representation by regions and municipalities of the education programmes.

Seven private secondary schools were identified in the six municipalities selected. There are two schools located in Masbate City and one school each for the municipalities of Mondragon, Mawab, Maco, North Upi and Datu Piang. In terms of sector representation, three schools cater to Christians, three to Indigenous Peoples (IPs) and one to Muslims.

Research Design

A mixed method was used in data gathering. For qualitative data, Key Informant Interviews were conducted with DepEd officials at the national, regional and divisional levels who are directly involved in the implementation of the programme. The FAPE national director, representatives of the regional project-management committees and school administrators were also interviewed. Focused group discussions with the teachers, parents and students of private schools were conducted. Stratified sampling was used for the schools. Representatives from different year levels were gathered for the students' and parents' group. For the teachers, subject areas, year level taught and the number of teaching years in the school were used as the basis for sampling. For quantitative data, a survey was administered to the total population of ESC grantees in the seven schools. Table II provides a summary of the number of survey respondents by year level.

Schools	1st year	2nd year	3rd year	4th year	Total no. of respondents
Seminary (S1)	18	18	11	13	60
Masbate City (S2)	52	42	41	43	178
Mondragon (S3)	101	88	80	76	345
Mawab (S4)	55	50	57	61	223
Maco (S5)	41	34	37	19	131
Datu Piang (S6)	85	86	51	49	271
Upi School (S7)	51	49	49	58	207
Total	403	367	326	319	1415

Table II. Number of survey respondents by school and year level.

The four assessment criteria of social cohesion, efficiency, equity and sensitivity were subjected to a construct validity test. Twenty-seven experts were asked to define the four concepts in the context of education in the Philippines. Based on the outcome of the validation, the following indicators were used to operationalise the assessment criteria.

1. Social Cohesion

- There is a common understanding of the objectives and implementing mechanisms of ESC.
- The ESC programme provides focus and direction for the stakeholders.
- There is sector representation.
- There is involvement and partnership among stakeholders.
- The programme promotes input of resources by stakeholders.

2. Efficient Use of Government Resources

- Resources are allocated in a way consistent with the country's education needs and priorities and aligned with education policies, goals and strategies.
- Resources are disbursed in a timely manner.
- Resources are used for their intended purpose within the target time frame.

- There is transparency and accountability in the allocation, disbursement and use of resources.

3. Equity of Access to Education Opportunities

- The programme focuses on marginalised, excluded and vulnerable sectors.
- The programme provides free education.

4. Sensitivity to Ethnic, Gender and Socioeconomic Class

- The programme recognises and values the rights and differences of learners.
- The programme upholds rights and takes action to meet learner needs.
- There is pro-action towards the mainstreaming/inclusion of marginalised learners.

The Focus Group Discussions and Key Informant Interviews that were conducted focused on social cohesion and efficient use of government resources. Questions dealt with understanding the programme objectives, as well as the clarity and efficiency of the implementation and funding mechanisms. The school heads and service providers took care of identifying the participants for the focus-group discussions. The basis of or guidelines for selection were provided by the researchers. The survey instrument administered assessed equity of access and sensitivity to gender, ethnicity and socioeconomic class. The survey instrument is a 45-item questionnaire consisting of three parts. The first part assessed school-aged children's access to education. Part 2 is a four-point Likert scale focused on sensitivity to gender and ethnicity. Part 3 deals with demographics and the socioeconomic profile of the respondents.

Findings and Analysis

The analysis is based on the four assessment criteria of efficiency, equity, sensitivity and social cohesion.

1. Equity of Access to Education Opportunities

The ESC programme is focused primarily on increasing access to quality education. Although the funds are directed to private schools, the poor are targeted as beneficiaries. This study seeks to determine whether equity in access is achieved by giving priority to the marginalised, excluded and vulnerable sectors (MEVs).

School choice and accessibility. The Survey outcomes revealed that a significant number of beneficiaries (43.7%) choose to enrol in their respective schools because they are privately operated schools. This may be indicative of the students' perception that private schools provide the kind of education they seek. This would refer to the quality of learning and the presence of spiritual and moral education, which were also identified as reasons for enrolling in a particular school.

Accessibility (33.6%) of a school was another significant deciding factor that emerged.

When asked why students decided to study in the school, 33.6% said that accessibility of the school is one of the key reasons. Based on the survey data, about 44% of the students walk to school. For the majority of them, the relative proximity of the school to their homes allows them to reach their school within 15 minutes. Although there are still some students who have to walk close to an hour to get to school, these cases are few.

Gender and ethnicity. Male and female access to the scholarship programme differs across schools. Except for the seminary school, it appears that there are more female beneficiaries in the surveyed schools compared to males. Children of Muslim and indigenous origins also benefit from the programme. Particularly noteworthy is the higher number of female ESC grantees in Maguindanao. Residents of this province are mostly of Muslim origin and it is one of the provinces in the country where access to education for girls is relatively low.

To further improve equity in access, the programme needs to provide clearer policies and mechanisms on gender and ethnicity, consistent with the country's national policy framework.

School	Male beneficiaries	Female beneficiaries
Seminary (S1)	100	0
Masbate City (S2)	52	48
Mondragon (S3)	41	59
Mawab (S4)	45	55
Maco (S5)	52	48
Datu Piang (S6)	31	69
Upi School (S7)	37	63
Average across schools	44	56

Table III. Percentage of male and female beneficiaries by school.

Application and selection mechanism. Using a three-point scale, with 1 being the highest, respondents were asked to rate the manner and process of acquiring scholarships in terms of their satisfaction with the following:

Process 1: Number of requirements
Process 2: Type of requirements
Process 3: Number of days spent applying for scholarship

Process 4: Manner of choosing beneficiaries
Process 5: Number of beneficiaries accepted

	Process 1	Process 2	Process 3	Process 4	Process 5
Seminary (S1)	2.35	2.48	2.33	2.36	2.40
Masbate City (S2)	2.30	2.43	2.47	2.60	2.65
Mondragon (S3)	2.28	2.33	2.33	2.34	2.51
Mawab (S4)	1.45	1.57	1.63	1.38	1.42
Maco (S5)	1.57	1.70	1.83	1.49	1.51
Datu Piang (S6)	2.16	2.35	2.18	2.42	2.43
Upi School (S7)	2.28	2.45	2.31	2.59	2.70

Note: 1= satisfied; 2 = median; 3 = not satisfied

Table IV. Satisfaction rating by school on ESC application process.

Comparing the seven schools (see Table IV), beneficiaries coming from Mawab (m = 1.49) and Maco (m = 1.62) appear to be more satisfied with the application process as compared to the other schools. Beneficiaries from Masbate City (m = 2.49) and Upi (m = 2.47) seem to be the least satisfied. Across all the schools, the beneficiaries were neutral in their satisfaction rating of the ESC application process, with total mean scores ranging from 2.06 (number of requirements) to 2.23 (number of beneficiaries accepted).

In terms of ethnicity, schools located in areas that are predominantly indigenous or Muslim tend to cater to those groups. However, this does not prevent them from accepting students coming from different sectors or cultural and religious affiliations. Results of the survey show a healthy mix of student grantees with regard to ethnicity.

Access of marginalised learners. As has already been stated, the programme provides only partial education subsidies to students. This has raised arguments about the issue of free basic education and equity in terms of targeting beneficiaries. The nature of the programme has kept the poorest of the poor from participating, and it has also prevented those who have limited financial means from accessing scholarships. Parents need to pay the differential between the ESC grant and the school tuition, books that are otherwise free in public schools and many miscellaneous costs related to student projects and contributions to schools. As reflected in the socioeconomic status of the grantees, there are current grantees who may not necessarily be poor. It is interesting to note that a very small percentage of the ESC grantees surveyed identified scholarship or access to ESC grants as a key reason for enrolling in their respective schools. In the presentation of the ESC study findings and validation workshop with DepEd and FAPE, the Directors of both institutions admitted the disconnect between the programmes' objectives and how the programme is being implemented. They however noted that a review of policies is being done to address this situation (E-Net Phil PPP Policy Forum, January 2011).

Socioeconomic status of grantees. The presence of siblings in the same school further confirms that the family is capable of supporting the education of two or more children in a private school. Although it may be said that the siblings are subsidised under the ESC programme, the family still shoulders a portion of the education cost.

In terms of livelihood/incomes, the beneficiaries in the Masbate schools have fathers whose livelihood is generally associated with stable and mid- to high-income sources. Close to 80% of the beneficiaries in the seminary and close to 60% of the grantees in the Christian school in Masbate have fathers who are businessmen, professionals, government employees, white-collar workers and overseas workers. In contrast, most of the beneficiaries in the IP community of Mawab and Datu Piang have fathers whose livelihood is generally associated with unstable and/or low-income sources. More than 50% of the grantees' fathers are farmers and fishermen, vendors, construction workers and manual labourers. In Upi (45%) and Datu Piang (58%), the majority of the fathers are farmers and fishermen.

The mothers generally have the same sources of livelihood as the fathers. The majority of the beneficiaries in the Masbate schools (85% for the seminary and 48% for the Christian school) have mothers who are businesspeople, professionals and government workers. In contrast, the mothers of ESC grantees in Maguindanao (50% for Datu Piang; 71% for Upi) and Compostela Valley (83% for Mawab; 60% for Maco) are mostly homemakers, farmers and non-skilled workers. Figure 2 provides a summary of livelihood sources.

The study shows that the majority of the grantees' families live in houses made of strong or predominantly strong materials. Most of them have access to basic needs such as decent toilets, water (although only very few have access to running water inside their homes) and electricity (60% have direct connections). A significant percentage (36%) of families own four-wheeled vehicles and 47% have motorcycles and tricycles.

This information seems to suggest the presence of relatively well-off grantees, particularly in the seminary school in Masbate. Less financially able grantees seem to be more prevalent in Compostela Valley and Maguindanao.

Concern around grantee profiles has also been raised by the World Bank study on GASTPE in 2011. It has been suggested that a more effective monitoring of the beneficiary-selection mechanism should be put in place. From a long-term perspective, solutions for effectively providing free education to all should be developed by the government. Such solutions would ultimately respond to the issues of equity and social cohesion.

From another perspective, DepEd argues that although the poorest are not able to access the ESC programme, the decongestion of the public schools as a result of the programme allows them to provide better-quality education for the most marginalised. In effect, the programme is able to address equity on two fronts: first, increased equity between children of affluent families and ESC beneficiaries who are now studying in private schools; and second, increased equity between the public- and private-school students as quality of education is improved in the public schools.

2. Social Cohesion and Governance

Local coordination. As stated in the policy guidelines of DepEd and the document released by FAPE in 2011, ESC is intended for students who are poor and deserving. Consequently, the schools are directed to recruit public-school elementary graduates and to consider in their selection those children who are at risk of dropping out. The schools are also instructed to form school committees that will be responsible for the profiling of students. The committee is supervised by the DepEd Education Supervisor and may be assisted by the Barangay Council. These local coordination mechanisms, however, were not in existence in the seven schools. At most, ESC schools coordinated with the Barangay chair on school issues.

Selection of marginalised. Consistent with the guidelines, results of the study revealed that most stakeholders perceive the programme as intended for the poor and deserving students, along with other concomitant objectives (i.e. support for private schools and teachers). However, the process for targeting and selecting beneficiaries varies across schools. Not all beneficiaries come from public elementary schools, and the identification of 'deserving' students as a criterion for selection seems to conflict with other factors that need to be considered when targeting the poor, who cannot afford the top-up fees. Providing only partial subsidies constrains the poorest of the poor from participating in the programme. They are left with no choice but to stay in the public schools.

'Competition' and lack of coordination between public and private schools. Allocation of ESC slots is based on the number of 'aisle students' in the public schools (DepEd Order No. 8 s. 2011 [DepEd, 2011b]). However, the process of identifying 'aisle students' appears to be problematic. This is because, as shared by an interviewee, there are cases when public schools prefer to hold on to their 'aisle' students in order to increase their operating budget, referred to as the maintenance operations and other expenditures (MOOE). Because the private schools are not provided by the public schools with a list of the aisle students, they are left with the dilemma of identifying ESC beneficiaries.

The DepEd Order of 2011 responded to this concern by allowing public-school elementary graduates to enrol directly in the ESC-accredited private schools. Still, public and private schools are required to coordinate with each other to ensure that all ESC slots are properly filled up. At present, this selection and coordination mechanism has yet to be implemented consistently across participating schools.

Sector representation and involvement. One positive result of ESC is the involvement of various sectors such as private schools and universities, education end-users, FAPE, DepEd and Barangay officials. FAPE's participation is crucial in that they provide a more efficient implementation of the programme. However, DepEd's role in the programme's implementation still needs to be maximised or used to its fullest. Apart from coordinating with the private schools and DepEd national office, FAPE should also effectively coordinate with DepEd at the regional and division level. This will allow better alignment and understanding of programme objectives and create a more cohesive and standardised implementation of policies and guidelines.

The private schools included in the case study are non-profit in nature. They express their commitment to providing quality education and most are focused on servicing the poor and marginalised. Helping these schools through ESC benefits them, the government and the students they support.

3. Efficient Use of Government Resources

A pertinent question is whether ESC funds are used for their intended purpose, are released in a timely manner and are managed in a transparent and accountable way.

The ESC funds under the GASTPE programme are directly disbursed by the Department of Budget and Management to the private-school recipients. Private schools are given sufficient autonomy to decide how and where to use the funds. Given that there have been no concerns raised by the school representatives with regard to fund leakage and other finance issues, it appears that direct fund disbursement is an efficient system employed by the government.

The concern raised by the recipient schools has to do with the schedule of the release of funds, which occurs between the months of October and January. The school year in the Philippines starts in June and ends in April and the government fiscal year is from January to December. The time frame for the budget release is considered to be within the parameters of efficient fund disbursement on the side of the government. However, private schools do not seem to see it that way.

The recipient schools included in the study are heavily dependent on GASTPE for financial support. As such, there are schools that are financially constrained during the first half of the school year when the budget has not yet been released. Because of this, some of the schools are forced to take out loans from outside institutions or advance money from their students in order to finance their operations.

In some schools, the teachers acknowledged that they share in this burden by accepting lower than minimum wages and less benefits. The inadequacy and delay in funds affect deeply teachers' welfare, and the reasons why teachers are motivated to continue teaching are: (1) their dream of excelling in their work so that they land a job in the public school; and (2) that they are able to continue serving the community. Scaled up nationwide, the impact of ESC on teachers' rights and welfare need to be evaluated. Public-school teachers are protected by the Magna Carta of Teachers. Private-school teachers do not have the same Magna Carta; their rights are protected through the Labor Office instead.

Transparency in the allocation, disbursement and use of resources. Based on the programme policy, mechanisms are provided at the national, regional and school levels to inform stakeholders about the financial, or budgetary, aspect of ESC. Despite this, there still seems to be a lack of stakeholder knowledge on this aspect. It is interesting to note, however, that parents and students don't seem bothered or apprehensive about the limited information. They appear to be content with the knowledge that they are being supported by the government and the private schools.

Based on the data gathered, the lack of transparency may be attributed to the apparent disinterest of the parents as well as the lack of reporting and monitoring mechanisms for schools and at different levels in the ESC programme with regard to reporting of expenditures.

Policy Recommendations

The research conclusions and recommendations were presented to DepEd and FAPE and enriched by a validation process with the schools.

1. GASTPE aims to decongest the public education system. With decreased class sizes, it is hoped that public schools will be able to reach out to more students and provide better-quality education. However, an enabling situation where administrators of both public and private schools work on the decongestion process is absent.

The national DepEd Planning Office allocates the number of ESC grantees per region but it does not have a monitoring system to verify whether private schools that were given ESC grantees are indeed near red-coded public schools: those that do not have enough classrooms and teachers to effectively meet the needs of the student population. Similarly, there is no tracking mechanism to monitor whether ESC grantees are indeed 'aisle students' from congested public schools. The RPCom is envisaged to perform this monitoring function. However, with the absence of specific guidelines and monitoring schemes, targeting of schools and students depends on the functionality of the RPCom and its capacity to manage the DepEd regional office. This makes governance of GASTPE uneven across regions.

A study on the effectiveness of the ESC in decongesting the public schools should be conducted. This can only be done by establishing an information-monitoring system that will provide quantitative data on congestion and qualitative data on the impact of decongestion on public-school students' access to and quality of learning.

Further, efforts to decongest the public schools should not result in dividing students from low-income families from those from high-income families, where the former remain in public schools and the latter are moved out to publicly supported private schools.

2. Private schools with different financial statures are given education service contracts. Some are mission or secular schools operating in remote areas; others are schools that collect relatively high tuition. For the latter schools, the ESC grant may comprise only one third or one fourth of the total tuition fee. Therefore, parents have to pay for the remainder. A major question is whether these schools should be included in the GATSPE programme. These schools may pass the criteria within a framework of decongestion but do not fit the access-to-education framework. The DepEd should review its aims for ESC, the framework and the selection criteria for schools.

3. The ESC has not been able to reach out to the poorest of the poor, as was envisaged. Indeed, the DepEd and FAPE confirmed that there is disconnect between this articulated objective and the implementation of the ESC. The additional costs for parents – tuition fees to augment the ESC subsidy provided per student, textbooks, school uniforms and other materials – are beyond the reach of families with meagre incomes. In addition, in private schools, students are more compelled to submit projects and participate in school activities compared to students in public schools, where such activities may be optional.

There is no support system instituted for poor students who may want to study in private school through ESC and whose parents may not have the resources to pay top-up fees. In the validation forums, ESC schools said that the DepEd has introduced a new requirement, which is the submission of income tax returns or a certification from the local government unit on capacity to pay, to ensure that ESC grantees are really in need of a subsidy (and who would otherwise attend a public school if there were no ESC). While this requirement is a start in addressing the needs of the poor, the main obstacle is that poor ESC grantees still need to shoulder additional costs.

4. DepEd argued that ESC is a cost-efficient way of providing education to a large student population, but the study found that different stakeholders bear the burden of this 'efficiency'. Parents pay for tuition and miscellaneous fees and purchase textbooks and other

materials that are provided free in public schools. Private schools take the risk of operating under extreme financial constraints, often incurring debts before the release of their grants. Teachers contribute immensely by agreeing to lower than minimum wages despite their teaching loads and the multiple tasks they perform. In summary, the government passes on to parents and private schools/teachers the costs of educating a secondary-school student that cannot be covered by the ESC grant.

GASTPE has witnessed radical budget increases in the past three years. The DepEd should study the impact of passing on the education costs to parents and private schools. The notion of GASTPE as a cost-efficient strategy should be investigated. Also, a study is needed on the long-term cost efficiency of increasing ESC compared to building its own high schools and hiring its own teachers.

5. The protection of the rights and welfare of teachers is an urgent issue that should be addressed within the GASTPE. Private schools, especially those that are 80% to 90% dependent on ESC grants, find it difficult to afford the teachers' salary mandated by law. Teachers are also not covered by insurance and health benefits. Although some of them are not licensed, ESC schools have stated that they are still able to perform their duties well. And because of the constraints in budget, schools are not able to attract many licensed teachers who will agree to the low pay. Licensed teachers prefer to apply to public schools or work abroad. Given this situation, the DepEd should be able to: (1) ensure the protection of teachers; and (2) facilitate the professional development of current ESC teachers and provide guidelines to those who have yet to pursue their licensure examination.

6. FAPE performs quality assurance through: (1) certification processes; (2) school monitoring; (3) training for teachers; and (4) conducting and/or supporting research designed to evaluate the effectiveness of the ESC programme.

These inputs to quality should be validated by impact studies. For example, ESC students in the survey argued that the small class size and better interaction between teachers and students are key to their motivation to learn and the quality of learning. A survey with students as well as time-series analysis of learning outcomes could do well to validate quality of learning through ESC schools.

7. Social cohesion and partnerships are weak in the ESC, and these should be strengthened in terms of programme transparency and accountability as well as to enhance collaboration. There is a need for localised monitoring of implementation and use of funds involving stakeholders at the school, at both divisional and regional levels. Localised capability building and partnerships among stakeholders in the private and public sector and all stakeholders would assist in achieving education for all (EFA). Mechanisms for dialogue and consultations between public and private schools should be put in place.

8. GASTPE is a public–private partnership (PPP) strategy that dates back to the 1970s, before the term PPP was being used. Historically, textbooks have been produced by private entities. Since 2005, alternative education programmes have been delivered by non-government organisations in partnership with DepEd. The DepEd has also embarked on a recent PPP strategy for school building/classroom construction.

Given these varied PPPs, the DepEd needs to articulate its overall PPP framework and strategies beyond its banner call for 'Education for All, All for Education'. Education is a right as mandated by the 1987 Constitution, and access to it by all Filipinos should not be compromised. Public–private partnerships should be crafted within this framework. The GASTPE in particular should be evaluated in terms of its long-term impact in either promoting or hindering the right to education.

As education is a public good, different stakeholders must be consulted on the PPP framework and strategies and how they can better serve EFA.

Private and social stakeholders should be made to account for the funds they receive from DepEd by instituting transparency and accountability guidelines and mechanisms. There should also be enough safeguards in place to ensure that all PPPs serve the interest of the people's right to a public good such as education and not the commercial interest of private entities.

Acknowledgements

This research is a collaborative work done by E-Net Philippines with the following researchers: Alve Berdan, Joelyn Biag, Chris Jerome Magpusao, Rene Raya, Luz Anigan and Maribella Tanag.

References

ASPBAE & E-Net Philippines (2007) Education-Watch Philippines Summary Report: Mapping Out Disadvantaged Groups in Education.

Belfield, C.R. & Levin, H.M. (2002) *Education Privatization: causes, consequences and planning implications*. Paris: IIEP-UNESCO.

Department of Education (DepEd) (2011a) Order 8. s. 2011 *Policies and Guidelines on the Implementation of the Government Assistance to Students and Teachers in Private Education (GASTPE) Effective SY 2011-2012.* January. Pasig City: Department of Education.

Department of Education (DepEd) (2011b) *Facts and Figures.* www.deped.gov.ph

Department of Education (DepED) (2012) National Budget Presentation to Congress.

E-Net Philippines Policy Forum on PPP in Education (January 2011).

Functional Literacy, Education and Mass Media Survey (FLEMMS) (2008) http://www.census.gov.ph/people/education-mass-media

Fund for Assistance to Private Education (FAPE) (2011) Education Service Contracting. Available from FAPE, 7/F Concorde Condominium, Benavidez Street, Makati, Metro Manila.

LaRocque, N. & Lee, S. (2011) Non-State Providers and Public-Private Partnerships in Education for the Poor. Written for the Joint ADB-UNICEF Workshop on the Role of -State Providers in Delivering Basic Services for Children, April 2010. http://www.unicef.org/eapro/Non_State_Provider_revised_25_apr2011.pdf (accessed 1 July 2011).

National Statistics Office (2006) Family Income and Expenditure Survey 2006.

Porio, C. (2010) Personal interview.

World Bank (2011) *Philippines Private Provision, Public Purpose: a review of the government's education service contracting program.* Washington, DC: The International Bank for Reconstruction and Development/World Bank.

CHAPTER 12

The Role of the World Bank in the Private Provision of Schooling in Pakistan

FRANCINE MENASHY, KAREN MUNDY & MOMINA AFRIDI

Introduction

The World Bank is the largest single provider of funds and expertise to education programmes in the world. With an education-sector lending portfolio of approximately US$9 billion as of January 2013, the Bank's education-sector operations, technical assistance and research spans tertiary, vocational, early childhood and K-12 (World Bank, 1999a, 2005, 2009b, 2013; Mundy, 2002; Jones, 2007). Over the past decade, educational programming at the Bank has expanded to its private-sector arm, the International Finance Corporation (IFC), which established a Health and Education Unit in 2000 (IFC, 2001). Although there exists a wide literature deconstructing the Bank's formal policy statements, many of which critique its rhetorical support of privatisation (see Klees et al, 2012), there are relatively few recent analyses of its lending operations and little is tangibly known concerning its country-level practices involving non-state school providers.

This chapter addresses this gap. In it we first provide a summary of an initial research project that looked at the Bank's education-sector lending portfolio and its research and technical activities in education, to better understand whether and how the Bank supports the privatisation of educational-service delivery. In the second part of the paper we use the Bank's education-sector activities in Pakistan – a country we propose has uniquely embraced many of the Bank's policy suggestions concerning private provision of education. This chapter concludes by offering a preliminary analysis that will inform future field research in five countries on the World Bank's role in supporting privatisation in K-12 education services.

A Global View of the Bank and its Support for Private Engagement in the Delivery of K-12 Education: a mixed story

This chapter builds upon and responds to lingering questions concerning the findings of a PERI (Privatisation in Education Research Initiative)-funded study, completed in 2012, into the World Bank's support to private provision of schooling worldwide. This study, entitled *The World Bank and the Private Provision of K-12 Education: history, policies, practices* (Mundy & Menashy, 2012), aimed to answer three main research questions: (1) Since 2000, how has the Bank's knowledge mobilisation and policy advocacy evolved on issues related to private-sector provision of K-12 education?; (2) To what degree has the Bank's role in policy advocacy for private involvement in education manifested at the country level in its operational practices?; (3) and What factors seem to determine Bank policies and practices in this area?

To answer these questions, we reviewed the Bank's formal policies on the inclusion of private-sector providers in education systems, as well as the Bank's role as a 'knowledge broker' through the analysis of several Bank-published knowledge products. We conducted a discursive review of the World Bank's education-sector strategies from 1995 to 2011. These policy documents were examined to determine positions advocated, evidence employed, citations and language used in relation to the engagement of the private sector in K-12 education. Frequency counts were conducted to determine use of recurrent terminology and keywords, as well as to identify changes in emphasis over time. To better understand the discursive arguments developed by the Bank in its knowledge products, we selected key documents (Patrinos et al, 2009; World Bank & IMF, 2009; Lewis & Patrinos, 2011) upon which to conduct a more detailed content analysis, using frame-analysis techniques (Campbell, 1998; Beland, 2005; Verger, 2011).

We then examined the Bank's K-12 education-project portfolio for a four-year span (approved between 2008 and 2012), coding projects for their inclusion of support for private service provision. To track broad trends in lending, a simple coding table was developed to provide descriptive data about 53 projects. In addition, we created a narrative coding for all 53 project documents, answering the following questions:

- Are private or non-state actors in the education sector mentioned, and how are the roles and contributions of these actors framed?
- Who are these actors (and is there a differentiation between for profit/non-profit)?
- What mechanisms (if any) are advocated to support private provision (subsidies, vouchers)?

- How is the government's role in relation to the private described?
- What household/community participation is advocated?
- How are teachers' unions or other non-business non-state actors treated?
- Is the IFC mentioned as a partner on this project?

Finally, we examined the work of the International Finance Corporation (IFC) – the private-sector arm of the World Bank Group – analysing its investments in K-12 education. Each component of the research project was accompanied by interviews with key stakeholders and staff members in the relevant divisions of the Bank.

Our study provided a mixed story about the Bank and its support for private service in K-12 education. The World Bank's approach to private-sector participation in education is characterised by several stark disjunctures between policy and practice. On the one hand, we found that over the past two decades there has been an evident push on the part of the Bank to expand the understanding of the role that the private sector can play to improve public education systems. In reference to private providers, World Bank education-sector strategy papers have all cited the efficiency and quality benefits of choice and competition, the equity benefits of voucher schemes, the need to increase community involvement, and the notion of the private as a partner. It is clear that at the level of policy, the Bank has advocated an increasing engagement with the private sector, and in support of this, a strengthened relationship with the International Finance Corporation (see World Bank, 1995a, 1999a, 2005, 2011). The World Bank has also taken an active and forceful approach to mobilising evidence about the advantages of private-sector provision of educational services, advocating via its knowledge products a variety of demand-side financing mechanisms to support the private sector (see, for instance, Barrera Osorio et al, 2009; Patrinos et al, 2009; Lewis & Patrinos, 2011).

Yet our study exposed a large gap between the Bank's above-described knowledge products and formal policy statements, and its actual project portfolio. Most notably, according to our analysis, surprisingly few Bank operations contain private-sector provision as an objective or component, despite a decade of rhetorical emphasis and research promoting private provision of K-12 educational services in developing countries. Our portfolio review found that only 17% of project documents analysed included any support of private provision, and all such projects were seen to be in contexts where a very large and engrained tradition of private-sector provision has existed for many years with government support.[1]

In only seven countries does the Bank have projects where private provision is directly aided: Bangladesh; Haiti; Indonesia; Nepal; Pakistan; India; and Uganda (see Table I).

Francine Menashy et al

Country	Year	Project name	Brief description of private engagement
Bangladesh	2009	Secondary Education Quality & Access Enhancement	The project supports a very dominant system of government-aided private schools, including both religious and secular schools.
Bangladesh	2010	The Reaching Out-of-School Children Project	With an allowance scheme, the project supports Learning Centres (LCs), non-formal schools that provide primary education and serve 8-10% of students, mainly from the poorest households.
Haiti	2010	Additional Financing for the 2007 Education for All Project	Provides per-student subsidy grants to accredited non-public schools. The project also aims to establish a National Education Partnership office as a PPP mechanism as well as a Department for Private Education and Partnership to be responsible for evaluating and accrediting non-public schools.
Haiti	2011	Second Phase of the Education for All Project	The objective of the Second Phase of the Education for All Project for Haiti is to support the strategy for rebuilding the education system through the implementation of sustainable programmes. The rationale for supporting private provision of education via tuition waivers is centred on the fact that, '90 percent of education establishments are private' (World Bank, 2009c, p. 2).
India	2012	Secondary Education Project	Offers school grants and technical assistance with the objective of 'improving secondary education services, provided by both government and private-aided schools (a form of public-private partnership)' (World Bank, 2012b, p. 3). Offers teacher training to those in private-aided schools.

242

Indonesia	2009	BOS (School Operational Assistance) Knowledge Improvement for Transparency and Accountability Project	The BOS programme disburses block grants to all schools throughout Indonesia based on a per-student formula, reaching all schools whether public, private or religious.
Nepal	2010	School Sector Reform Program	Continues per capita financing of community-based (co-financed) schools and matching-grant incentives. Project provides new funding to 'traditional' schools (e.g. private religious schools).
Pakistan	2009	Sindh Education Sector Project	Supports the introduction, rollout and impact evaluation of an innovative pilot public–private partnership programme, to be administered by the Sindh Education Foundation (SEF).
Pakistan	2009	Punjab Education Sector Project	Supports the introduction, rollout and impact evaluation of an innovative pilot public–private partnership programme, to be administered by the Punjab Education Foundation (PEF).
Pakistan	2012	Second Punjab Education Sector Project (PESP II)	Offers tuition-replacement vouchers to children from disadvantaged households in poor urban areas to promote access to and participation in low-cost private schools subject to a rigorous quality-assurance system.
Uganda	2009	Post Primary Education & Training APL-1	The project supports the existing private secondary sector via such measures as capitation grants. The private sector is seen as contributing to efficiency and equity. Private schools should be regulated and inspected by the government.

Table I. World Bank projects engaging the private sector in educational provision (since 2008).

Various forms of private provision are supported, some including only religious providers (Nepal), both religious and secular private schools (Bangladesh, Indonesia), 'Learning Centres' (Bangladesh) and for-profit schools (Haiti, Uganda, Pakistan). In these projects the private sector is financed via a variety of mechanisms. For instance, seven Project Appraisal Documents (PADs) (13%) indicated the support of 'subsidies' or 'stipends' for private schools (Bangladesh 2009; Pakistan 2009 [Punjab]; Pakistan, 2009 [Sindh]; Haiti 2010; Haiti 2011; Uganda 2009; Pakistan 2012), while fewer recommended voucher schemes or conditional cash transfers.

In our interviews with World Bank staff we aimed to gain a better understanding of this policy/practice divide, where few projects operationalise the Bank's forceful advocacy of public–private partnerships. Interviewees drew our attention to the fact that financing decisions are shaped at the country level by governments who often have limited interest in borrowing to support private provision, and are led by World Bank country-level staff frustrated in their efforts to pitch private provision or doubting its efficacy (Interview #4, World Bank; Interview #5, World Bank, Interview #7, World Bank). Thus the Bank's knowledge-mobilisation and policy-advocacy efforts in this area do not appear to have been a key factor in the development of country-level reform programmes supported by the Bank.

Beyond the operational policy/practice divide, we noted disjunctures involving the IFC's work in private education. An expansive rhetoric regarding a role for the IFC in addressing poverty via investments in private education is belied by the modest volume of IFC funding for education, its geographic concentration in middle-income and higher income countries, as well as its concentration (in K-12 education) on elite private schools (see Mundy & Menashy, 2014). As well, while the importance of IFC and Bank collaboration in education is highlighted in all recent Bank education-sector strategies, such collaboration has failed to develop over a 10-year period, according to our project analyses and interviews. Again, policy rhetoric relating to support to private providers has not translated into operational practice at the country level.

Our study concluded that Bank policy advocacy on the issue of private-sector participation has not manifested to any great extent in financial support for privatisation reforms at the country level. Many researchers have suggested that World Bank policies and actions are the often contradictory and inconsistent result of demands placed upon the Bank by different stakeholders: economists and their epistemic communities inside the Bank; rich country member governments; and external critics and lobby groups (Wade, 1996; Goldman, 2005; Weaver & Leiteritz, 2005; Weaver, 2008). Our research adds to this picture by showing how the World Bank's formal statements about the advantages of public–private partnership are quite different from its actual financial support to education. Advocacy for private provision as a policy choice has been crafted and driven by a small epistemic community anchored in its Economics of Education group, and are found frequently in the Bank's high-level policy statements on education, which target donor governments. But it does not appear that Bank policy advocacy is reliably influential at country level.

This begs a key question not explored fully in our previous study: What, indeed, does happen at the country level?

A Country-Level Snapshot

In order to understand the Bank's position and influence on the issue of private provision of K-12 schooling, we have argued that it is necessary to study the uptake of the Bank's policies and projects within particular country contexts where governments both have and have not embraced the Bank's policy agenda on private provision. In this chapter we explore, through a desk-based study, one particular and unique case: that of Pakistan, which has arguably become the poster child for international donor initiatives to support private provision and the most significant exemplar of Bank support for privatisation in the K-12 sector.

In Pakistan, financing to private providers is administered via government-established and Bank-supported Foundations responsible for the disbursement and monitoring of funds, making it one of the few countries where the Bank has overtly supported public financing to private for-profit schooling. Of our sample, Pakistan has hosted the largest number of Bank projects supporting the private sector (three). Furthermore, the most recent project in Pakistan exhibits the only instance of Bank support to a voucher system. Our rationale for focusing on Pakistan therefore rests on our speculation that a unique condition must exist within the country that has made it receptive to Bank advocacy of privatisation. We propose that in order to truly appreciate the Bank's role in the privatisation of education, it is necessary to better understand the country context where the Bank has gained a remarkable foothold in supporting private education providers.

What follows is an account of World Bank activities in Pakistan. Based on preliminary desk-based research that will lay the foundation for in-country fieldwork, we examine the unique history and current context of the country's education system and associated challenges, paying particular attention to the role of the non-state sector. From an analysis of World Bank Project Appraisal Documents, we explore the Bank's historical and recent support to private providers, the forms of financing mechanisms the Bank employs, and the justifications invoked by the Bank to support the private sector in Pakistan.

245

History and Context

Prior to the nationalisation of education in 1972 in Pakistan, private institutions were abundant in Pakistan, governing their own establishment and managing their own funds with very occasional financial assistance from the government, as grant-in-aid (Ahmad & Mirza, 1975). However, a sentiment grew against private education and the 1969 policy viewed private schools more as a problem rather than an alternative (Ali, 2012). It noted exorbitant school fees, underpaid teachers and administrative irregularities; it recommended the adoption of legislation by the government to streamline these issues and indicated that private education needed greater governmental oversight, supervision and regulation. After a decade of criticism concerning private institutions in policy documents, the 1972 policy nationalised the entire educational system except madrasas. Aly (2007, p. 81) notes that this marked the beginning of an era of public-sector education expansion and overlordship of the Ministry of Education. During this era it was observed that the state took a very negative stance towards privatisation of education as not only the creation and management of schools but also textbook production were invested in the functions of the state (Ali, 2012).

However, in the subsequent *National Education Policy* (1979), the government acknowledged its inability to make universal education a reality due to lack of resources and capability. Not only did the government reverse the 1972 policy but also viewed privatisation as a viable policy prescription for changing the direction of education in Pakistan. Since 1979, all Pakistani education polices have acknowledged the private sector and encouraged it to play an important role in education. The private sector has increasingly been involved in the financing, management and delivery of education services. The 1990s also witnessed an 'incentives programme' for the private sector inclusive of: tax-exemptions; concessional land; domestic tariff rates; Educational Foundations; and concessional financing (Aly, 2007). A substantial expansion of the private sector was justified to shoulder the efforts towards achieving education for all (EFA) and Millennium Development Goals (MDG) targets; the growth in enrolment in non-government institutions between 1990 and 1996/97 was 61% for boys and 131% for girls (Government of Pakistan, 1998, p. 23). This boom in private schools was different from that in the previous decades; while previously the private sector was monopolised by metropolitan elite schools and missionary institutions (Aly, 2006, p. 28), this time the increase was dominated by private provision in both the rural and urban areas (Andrabi et al, 2008). However, as Jamil and others (2012) argue, the final thrust to privatisation in Pakistan was spurred by the Musharraf government (1999-2008), seeking to implement the existing National Education Policy 1998-2010, operationalised through the Education

Sector Reform (ESR) Action Plan 2001-2005/6. The ESR Action Plan formally relegated the government's role from a provider to a facilitator and financier of the delivery of educational services with multiple partners (Ministry of Education, 2004).

The EFA Forum at Dakar in 2000 strengthened Pakistan's commitment to universal education provision and public–private partnerships (PPPs). PPPs were formally declared to be central to the plan of achieving the goals set for 2015. A document of the Ministry of Education echoed the same: 'An anchor area of the Education Sector Reforms Action Plan 2001-2005 has been the promotion of public private partnerships to address access and quality targets at all levels of the education spectrum' (MoE, 2004, p. 2). At the time of writing the education strategy paper in 2001 all key donors in the education sector – the World Bank, the Asian Development Bank, the UK Department for International Development (DFID), USAID, the United Nation agencies, the Japanese government, the Norwegian Agency for Development Cooperation (NORAD) and the European Union (EU) (Ministry of Education, 2004) – actively supported the idea of PPPs (Bano, 2008). This undertaking was assisted by the devolution plan put in place by the Musharraf government in 2001. The devolution and decentralisation plan entailed major changes in the education sector for evolving the mechanism of transferring responsibilities for recruitment, salaries and management of teachers and administrators from the province to district level (Shah, 2003, p. 21). The decentralisation efforts also included the setting up of Village Councils (VCs), Citizen Community Boards (CCBs), School Management Committees (SMC) and Parent Teacher Associations (PTAs) with the aim of involving the communities in the planning, management, monitoring and evaluation of service-delivery interventions at the grass-roots level. External actors strongly supported the ongoing decentralisation and devolution policy. The Bank and other donors, bringing to bear their experience from other countries, became very supportive, supplying technical and analytical assistance, as well as incorporating devolution elements into their projects (Boissiere et al, 2007, p. 25). Despite these efforts, Shah (2003) argues that there have been a number of persistent challenges during the implementation of these efforts at various levels, mostly due to the lack of capacity of the provincial and local governments to implement such programmes. Moreover, community participation remains very limited; even though school management committees (SMCs) and parent–teacher associations (PTAs) were established in many schools, most of these bodies have remained disorganised and ineffective (UNESCO, 2012, p. 9).

It is important to note that the *National Education Policy* (NEP) 2009, despite recognising the importance of PPPs, shifted the main responsibility back to the state, committing that the government ought to allocate 7% of gross domestic product (GDP) to education by 2015, rather than the current 2.7% (Ministry of Education, 2009, p. 20). Article 25 A of the 18th constitutional amendment of Pakistan (2010) further establishes that it is solely the state's responsibility to provide free and compulsory education to all children aged 5-16. Despite this declaration, however, state spending on education remains dismally low. Pakistan's education expenditure as percentage of GDP has ranged between 1.7% and 2.5% during the years 2003-12, but even with these small amounts, the utilisation rates have remained at an average of 90% (Government of Pakistan, 2013). According to recent data [2] 72% of educational institutions are public while 28% are in the private sector. The private sector serves 34% of students while 66% of students are served by the public sector.

At present there is a spectrum of private education providers in the country that covers low-cost private schools, community schools supported by community-based organisations and non-governmental organisations (NGOs), religious schools, madrasas, convent schools and elite private schools. There is also a bustling private-tutoring industry due to a rising trend in private supplementary programmes after school hours. According to the Annual Status of Education Report (ASER) (2012), approximately 25% of primary school students and 26% of students living in rural areas receive paid after-school tutoring in Pakistan. The majority of students who take private tuition are not from the poorly performing public-school system but are rather from private schools. Evidence from the Learning Educational and Achievement in Punjab Schools (LEAPS) survey and ASER data shows that around 34% of private-school students in Punjab receive private tuition compared to only 11% of public students (ASER, 2012).

The World Bank and Education in Pakistan

The World Bank has been one of the largest education donors in Pakistan, dispensing loans and grants since the 1960s, and, as discussed below, has introduced several projects that support private educational providers (Malik, 2007). For instance, in the 1995 North-West Frontier Province Primary Education Program (NWFP-PEP) Project Appraisal Document, the Bank states that the private sector ought to be engaged: '[T]o reduce the burden on provincial finances and increase gross enrollment, the Government of NWFP is encouraging private sector involvement in primary education through the Frontier Education Foundation (FEF) and through an improved regulatory framework for the private sector. The FEF will be particularly active in areas where market failure exists, and where the private sector can operate with lower costs than the Government' (World Bank, 1995b, p. 4). The report rationalises this investment in the private sector in terms of providing access, equity and efficiency in education, involving the private in education sector through '(a) increasing private sector involvement in the delivery of primary education and (b) expansion of construction management capacity through private sector participation' (World Bank, 1995b, p. 14).

According to the project report, the key objective of government subsidies to the private sector was to assist or to encourage NGOs/entrepreneurs to establish schools catering for low-income groups in urban and rural areas where a profit cannot be made from tuition alone: 'The Frontier Education Foundation (FEF) will support a series of pilots and components, including: (a) loan and grants to establish new schools, with particular emphasis on rural areas; (b) distribution of financial assistance to facilitate access to private schools for low income urban pupils; (c) canvassing of and assistance to private donors willing to sponsor private schools; and (d) research and development with a view to improving private school quality' (World Bank, 1995b, p. 18). In addition to this, private-sector participation is also mentioned in school-construction management and in the training of teachers.

The Bank's 1997 Northern Education Project (NEP) aimed to address the main sector issues confronting elementary education in the Northern Areas and Azad Jammu Kashmir, including low educational quality, low access for girls, lack of management capacity and low levels of community mobilisation (World Bank, 1997, p. 5). The NEP sought to address some of these issues by strongly supporting community-based schools that were run by NGOs; namely the Agha Khan Foundation, which at that time was the largest NGO education provider in the region and had established many community-level schools (World Bank, 1997). The Bank later touted the project's major achievements, particularly with regard to increasing community participation, establishing SMCs, and NGO involvement as private-sector actors. As well, school buildings in Northern Areas were constructed by the communities, who showed a greater sense of ownership towards the schools (World Bank, 2004, p. 12).

The Balochistan Education Project of 2006 was designed to contribute to Pakistan's long-term objective of achieving the Millennium Development Goals through launching and testing public–private and community-partnership delivery models to increase primary enrolment and completion rates, as well as to reduce gender disparities in the poor province of Balochistan. Limited participation of the private sector is described as a major roadblock to achieving educational progress in Balochistan. As the Bank highlights: 'Private schools account for about 6% of enrollment in primary education in Balochistan, compared with 28% for the country as a whole. While the rest of Pakistan has experienced an expansion in low cost private schools, in Balochistan, private schools have only increased from around 250 schools in 1993-94 to around 1,300 in 2003-04, mainly operating in the urban and semi-urban areas. Private sector expansion into rural areas is limited by financial constraints on both the potential private school operators and the target population' (World Bank, 2006, p. 2).

The Bank rationalises the programme based on its previous experience in the province, arguing that the current project builds on experiences gained under Balochistan Primary Education Project (BPEP)'s most successful components: the Community Supported Schools and the Urban Fellowship Schools Support to Balochistan. The Bank argued that since the government of Balochistan (GOB) recognised the multiple challenges facing the public sector in delivering quality primary education, it was committed to test different small-scale models of public–private partnerships in the delivery of primary education which, if successful, could be taken to scale (p. 3). The project consists of three components to be implemented under partnership arrangements between the Balochistan Education Foundation (BEF) and three distinct types of implementation partners (IPS): (1) Community Schools Implementation Partners (CIPs), including NGOs; (2) Private School Implementation Partners (PIPS), including private-school operators; and (3) Technical Assistance Implementation Partners, (TIPS), including NGOs, consultants, government training institutes and private training institutes (World Bank, 2006, p. 4). Under the Balochistan Education Support Program (BESP), the private sector was involved in provision, management and governance of education.

The 2009 Sindh Education Sector Project (SEP) responded to rural poverty, gender gaps, low transition rates to secondary school and low performance in national achievement tests for the students of Sindh. The Bank cited several factors that hampered efficient public spending on education, reflecting weak or absent governance and accountability systems. These include: the low monitoring and supervision capacity of district and sub-district education management, including limited accountability for performance; limited parent and community oversight/participation in school-level management; implementation delays on demand-side programmes (i.e. stipends for girls); lack of teacher standards and quality assurance. According to the Bank, schoolteacher hiring in the region has historically been patronage-based, potentially compromising the quality of incoming teachers and their accountability (World Bank, 2009a, p. 2), and so the project supports merit-based hiring. Moreover, the lack of private mobilisation is cited as a problematic feature of the educational system in Sindh: 'Enrollment rates in private school are lower in Sindh relative to the rest of Pakistan; this is particularly true in rural areas, where the private primary school net enrolment rate (NER) in Sindh is roughly one-tenth the corresponding value in the rest of Pakistan. In addition, the growth in private primary school NER has lagged that of the rest of Pakistan, and particularly so in rural Sindh. While the promise of the private sector in achieving educational outcomes is high, the natural growth of the private sector in rural Sindh appears to be inhibited' (World Bank, 2009a, p. 26).

In response, the Bank supported the introduction, rollout and impact evaluation of an innovative pilot public–private partnership programme, administered by the Sindh Education Foundation (SEF), which uses public funds to leverage the provision of schooling by private entrepreneurs in targeted underserved rural communities. The programme offers a per student subsidy to private entrepreneurs, subject to the entrepreneurs meeting specified quality standards for school infrastructure, and after the first year of operation, a minimum level of student academic achievement. Receipt of public subsidies also requires the entrepreneur to provide free schooling (World Bank, 2009a, p. 7).

The rationale for implementing this PPP and supporting private schools is framed as increasing equity and access to education for poor girls. The Bank argues: 'Programs such as the distribution of free textbooks, regular stipends to secondary school girls, and the establishment of new free private schools in educationally-undeserved areas are likely to have a larger impact on the participation of children from poor households relative to those from richer households' (World Bank, 2009a, p. 15); as well as that 'interventions such as the public subsidy program for private schools and the differential stipends program, which offers a higher stipend amount to secondary school girls, target (by design) the worse-off rural communities in terms of key educational outcomes' (World Bank, 2009a, p. 18).

Similarly, the 2009 Punjab Education Sector Project supported interventions to reduce primary drop-out rates, improve completion and participation rates, and increase the transition from primary to secondary levels by: '(i) providing demand side interventions, such as on-time delivery of free textbooks in Grades 1-10, continuing textbook publishing and printing through open competition, and on-time stipends to eligible girls in Grades 6-10 in fifteen low literacy districts; (ii) implementing supply side improvements, including filling of teacher vacancies, reducing missing facilities in schools, and up-gradation of schools from primary to middle, and middle to secondary levels according to criteria that favor girls and rural areas; and (iii) providing greater support to the private sector to establish schools in areas with low enrollments through the Punjab Education Foundation (PEF). EEPs under this subcomponent are: Girls Stipend Program and Public-Private Partnership Program' (World Bank, 2009b, p. 8). Investing in the private sector was argued to improve both the quality of education and to provide access, where the programme supported the private sector to reach the less privileged groups and female students (p. 18). The Bank and the government both recognise the contribution of the large low-cost private sector as a means to filling the access gap in education in the context of Punjab (p. 2).

The objective of the Bank's current (2012a) Second Punjab Education Sector Project (PESP II) is to support the education-sector reform programme of the government of Punjab to increase child school participation (at multiple levels) as well as student achievement, and supports the same objectives as PESP. The Bank applauds the growing privatisation of education, in particular the increase in low-cost private schools in Punjab. The PAD

discusses the growth of the private sector as overwhelmingly positive: 'One of the more significant positive developments in education in the province has been the dramatic growth in the private school system as reflected by the number of institutions. In addition, responding to the broad demand for greater access and better quality, the system has evolved in character, increasingly reaching low-income and rural households. This has produced a sizeable and rapidly expanding low-cost private-schooling system which serves as an alternative to the government school system for low-income and rural households (the main clientele for government schools)' (World Bank, 2012a, p. 2).

The report highlights that teacher quality and student learning are key concerns that need to be addressed in Punjab and continues to make a strong case for private-sector schools by arguing that they produce more learning (World Bank, 2012a, pp. 2-3). Actively promoting low-cost private schools, the report states that the current project aims to promote the retention of students in schools and school participation of new children. A key strategy for supporting the private is through targeted vouchers. Examples of such targeting include: '(1) attendance-tied cash transfers to girls who attend secondary schools in rural areas in districts with the poorest participation rates for secondary school-aged girls, (2) field-based teaching advisory support to teachers in achievement-poor schools, (3) cash bonuses tied to achievement gains to teachers in achievement-poor schools and districts, and (4) private school vouchers to children from disadvantaged households in poor urban neighbourhoods' (World Bank, 2012a, p. 17).

Moreover, the project supports increased community and household participation in governance at the school level, where the 'PESRP II promotes local demand-side accountability by communities and parents through multiple, mutually-enhancing actions' (World Bank, 2012a, p. 19).

Given the trajectory of Bank support in the country, and in particular the current project, it is evident that the World Bank and the government of Pakistan strongly advocate PPPs and private provision in education as inherently desirable mechanisms, and that via subsidies, voucher programmes and other demand-side mechanisms, more students can benefit from the better education of low-cost private schools.

Conclusions

The above case study of the World Bank's support to non-state education actors in Pakistan was prompted by questions that persisted following our study, which ostensibly concluded that the Bank does not readily support private providers in its K-12 projects – despite policy pronouncements and rhetoric otherwise. Pakistan, however, presented us with a unique case, where we speculate that the World Bank has gained a foothold in implementing a privatisation agenda.

Our above documentary research of the Bank's history of involvement in Pakistan exposed in detail the nature of Bank operations. For instance, in its current education project in Pakistan (2012a), the Bank supports for-profit low-cost private-school providers via such financing mechanisms as vouchers, conditional cash transfers, targeted scholarships and per student subsidies – essentially all the demand-side mechanisms advocated in the Bank's abundant publications on the topic of public–private partnerships in education (Patrinos et al, 2009; Lewis & Patrinos, 2011; World Bank, 2011). The Pakistani government's limited role is described primarily in terms of financing (via 'Foundations'), policy development and oversight. Arguments are provided that rationalise support to the private sector based on increased autonomy, quality and access. Again, the project documents echo the advocacy of privatisation displayed in Bank key knowledge products. The Pakistan case seemingly epitomises an instance of Bank 'success' in promoting private service provision.

However, this case is rather unique, and we continue to ask why in Pakistan yet not in most other countries?

Several of our interviewees suggested a possible answer. As mentioned, we were reminded that the World Bank's main lending arms, the International Bank for Reconstruction and Development (IBRD) and International Development Association (IDA), can only work directly with governments. Therefore, if the government does not wish to strengthen private participation, the Bank cannot force such a policy measure. By and large, governments will prefer to use Bank loans to expand their own organisational footprint (rather than fund alternative providers). As described by one World Bank staff member: 'We engage with the government, we don't engage with the private sector ... It's very difficult to engage the private sector in an operation' (Interview #5, World Bank). According to one staffer, when asked how Bank representatives react when a country government states that it does not wish to engage the private sector in its education system: 'It's a non-starter. And given that the Bank, the World Bank financing is through the ministries of finance, sector ministries, there has to be a lot of interest for this to work ... in some countries you know that's never going to happen' (Interview #4, World Bank).

As the historical context we provided above suggests, the Pakistani government has long supported private providers in education. And so perhaps a rather unique condition has existed in Pakistan, presenting one of the few occasions where 'a lot of interest' on the part of a government has met with the Bank's education operations. To verify this, however, we intend to conduct in-country field research on the Bank's work in Pakistan.

This brief overview of the Bank's education-sector activities in Pakistan extends the global-level analysis provided in our first PERI study. Our intention is to deepen this understanding of the World Bank's influence on governments' decision-making concerning the private sector by completing a full process-tracing study of the Bank's role in educational reform in five borrowing countries: Nepal; India; Pakistan; Ethiopia; and Indonesia. From discussions with World Bank project staff, government officials and policymakers, we aim to better appreciate what occurs at the country level when Bank projects are introduced and implemented, as well as to determine to what degree privatisation measures are Bank-driven at the country level.

Notes

[1] These findings vary slightly from our initial study published in 2012, which we have now updated to include an additional year in our sample.

[2] Data source: *Pakistan Education Statistics 2010-11* (National Education Management Information System, 2012).

References

Ahmad, Z. & Mirza, M. (1975) *The Financing of Privately Managed Schools in the Punjab.* IIEP Report 1. Paris: International Institute For Educational Planning.

Ali, S. (2012) Education Policy Borrowing in Pakistan: public-private partnerships, in G. Donn & Y.A. Manthri (Eds) *Education in the Broader Middle East: borrowing a baroque arsenal,* pp. 23-40. Oxford: Symposium Books.

Aly, J.H. (2006) *Education in Pakistan: a white paper.* National Education Policy Review Team. Islamabad: Ministry of Education, Government of Pakistan.

Aly, J.H. (2007) *Education in Pakistan: a white paper (Revised).* Documentation to Debate and Finalize the National Education Policy. Islamabad: Government of Pakistan, National Education Policy Review Team.

Andrabi, T., Das, J. & Khawaja, A.I. (2008) A Dime a Day: the possibilities and limits of private schooling in Pakistan, *Comparative Education Review*, 52(3), 329-355.

Annual Status of Education Report (ASER) (2012) Lahore, Pakistan. Facilitated by South Asian Foundation for Educational Development.

http://www.aserpakistan.safedafed.org/document/aser/2011/ASERPakistan2 0 11.pdf

Bano, M. (2008) Public Private Partnerships as 'Anchor' of Educational Reforms: lessons from Pakistan. Paper commissioned for the *EFA Global Monitoring Report 2009, Overcoming Inequality: why governance matters.* http://unesdoc.unesco.org/images/0017/001780/178017e.pdf (accessed 9 February 2013)

Barrera-Osorio, F., Patrinos, H.A. & Wodon, Q. (Eds) (2009) *Emerging Evidence on Vouchers and Faith-Based Providers in Education: case studies from Africa, Latin America and Asia.* Washington, DC: World Bank.

Beland, D. (2005) Ideas and Social Policy: an institutionalist perspective, *Social Policy and Administration,* 39(1), 1-18.

Boissiere, M., Baig, S., Modi, M. & Zafar, F. (2007) *Evaluation of World Bank Assistance for Primary Education in Pakistan: a country case study.* Washington, DC: World Bank.

Campbell, J. (1998) Institutional Analysis and the Role of Ideas in Political Economy, *Theory and Society,* 27, 377-409.

Goldman, M. (2005) *Imperial Nature: the World Bank and struggles for social justice in the age of globalization.* New Haven: Yale University Press.

Government of Pakistan (1998) *National Education Policy: 1998-2010.* Islamabad: Ministry of Education.

Government of Pakistan (2013) *Country Report of Pakistan Regarding: accelerating Millennium Development Goals 2013-15.* April 2013. Islamabad: Ministry of Education and Training.

International Finance Corporation (IFC) (2001) *Investing in Private Education: IFC's strategic directions.* Washington, DC: International Finance Corporation.

Jamil, B., Javaid, K. & Rangaraju, B. (2012) Investigating Dimensions of Privatization of Public Education in South Asia. PERI. Study presented at the Conference on Globalization, Regionalization and Privatisation in and of Education in Asia 28-29 September 2012, Kathmandu, Nepal. http://www.periglobal.org/role-state/document/document-investigatingdimensions-privatisation-public-education-south-asia (accessed February 2013).

Jones, P.W. (2007) *World Bank Financing of Education: lending, learning and development,* 2nd edn. London: Routledge.

Klees, S., Samoff, J. & Stromquist, N. (Eds) (2012) *The World Bank and Education: critiques and alternatives.* Rotterdam: Sense.

Lewis, L. & Patrinos, H. (2011) *Framework for Engaging the Private Sector in Education.* SABER. Washington, D.: World Bank.

Malik, R. (2007) *Aid Effectiveness and the Role of Donor Intervention in the Education Sector in Pakistan. A Review of Issues and Literature.* Working Paper no. 6. Research Consortium on Educational Outcomes and Poverty.

Ministry of Education (2004) *Public Private Partnerships in the Education Sector: Education Sector Reforms Action Plan 2001-2005. Policy, Options, Incentive*

Package and Recommendations. Islamabad: Ministry of Education, Government of Pakistan.

Ministry of Education (2009) *National Education Policy 2009.* Islamabad: Ministry of Education, Government of Pakistan.

Mundy, K. (2002) Retrospect and Prospect: education in a reforming World Bank, *International Journal of Educational Development*, 22, 483-508.

Mundy, K. & Menashy, F. (2012) *World Bank and the Private Provision of K-12 Education: history, policies, practices.* Sponsored Research Report for the Open Society Institute/Soros Foundation Education Support Programme. London: OSF.

Mundy, K. & Menashy, F. (2014) Investing in Private Education for Poverty Alleviation: the case of the World Bank's International Finance Corporation, *International Journal of Educational Development*, 35(1-2), 16-24.

National Education Management Information System (2012) *An Analysis of Educational Indicators of Pakistan – 2011.* AEPAM Publication 244. Islamabad: NEMIS-AEPAM.

Patrinos, H., Barrera-Osorio, F. & Guaqueta, J. (2009) *The Role and Impact of Public-Private Partnerships in Education.* Washington, DC: World Bank.

Shah, D. (2003) *Country Report on Decentralization in the Education System of Pakistan: policies and strategies.* Islamabad: Academy of Educational Planning and Management Ministry of Education, Government of Pakistan.

UNESCO (2012) *Situation Analysis of the Education Sector.* Islamabad: UNESCO.

Verger, A. (2011) Framing and Selling Global Education Policy: the promotion of public-private partnerships for education in low-income contexts, *Journal of Education Policy,* 27(1), 109-130.

Wade, R.H. (1996) Japan, the World Bank, and the Art of Paradigm Maintenance: the East Asian miracle in political perspective, *New Left Review,* 217, 3-36.

Weaver, C.E. (2008) *Hypocrisy Trap: the World Bank and the poverty of reform.* Princeton: Princeton University Press.

Weaver, C. & Leiteritz, R. (2005) 'Our Poverty is a World Full of Dreams': reforming the World Bank, *Global Governance,* 11(3), 367-388.

World Bank (1995a) *Priorities and Strategies for Education: a World Bank review.* Washington, DC: World Bank.

World Bank (1995b) *North-West Frontier Province Primary Education Program* (NWFP-PEP), Project Document.

World Bank (1997) *Northern Education Project,* Project Document.

World Bank (1999a) *Education Sector Strategy.* Washington, DC: World Bank.

World Bank (2004) *Implementation Completion Report,* Northern Education Project. Washington, DC: World Bank.

World Bank (2005) *Education Sector Strategy Update.* Washington, DC: World Bank.

World Bank (2006) Balochistan Education Project. Project Appraisal Document. Washington, DC: World Bank.

World Bank (2009a) Sindh Education Sector Project. Project Appraisal Document. Washington, DC: World Bank.

World Bank (2009b) Punjab Education Sector Project. Project Appraisal Document. Washington, DC: World Bank.

World Bank. (2009c) *Haiti Country Assistance Strategy.* Washington, DC: World Bank.

World Bank (2011) *Education Sector Strategy 2020 Learning for All: investing in people's knowledge and skills to promote development.* Washington, DC: World Bank.

World Bank (2012a) Second Punjab Education Sector Project. Project Appraisal Document. Washington, DC: World Bank.

World Bank (2012b) *India: Secondary Education Project Appraisal Document.* Washington, DC: World Bank.

World Bank (2013) Education: Overview. http://web.worldbank.org/WBSITE/EXTERNAL/TOPICS/EXTEDUCATION/0 ,,contentMDK:20575742~menuPK:282393~pagePK:210058~piPK:210062~the SitePK:282386,00.html (accessed 9 September 2013).

World Bank & International Monetary Fund (IMF) (2009) *Global Monitoring Report 2009: a development emergency.* Washington, DC: World Bank.

CHAPTER 13

Omega Schools Franchise in Ghana: 'affordable' private education for the poor or for-profiteering?

CURTIS B. RIEP

Introduction

Fee-paying for-profit private schools are on the rise. As governments of the global South continue to fall short of their efforts to provide 'Education For All', private corporations have increasingly become legitimate actors in educational programmes, partnerships and provision (Tooley, 2004; Bhanji, 2008). Private companies have set up schools to serve low-income communities in emerging markets such as India, China, Kenya, Ghana and Bangladesh. These low-fee private schools are an example of other forms of non-state provision that are receiving a heightened level of international policy focus as the necessary resources for education continue to diminish and new actors and modes of governance continue to reshape the sector (see Srivastava & Walford, 2007; Härmä & Rose, 2012; Robertson et al, 2012). However, the underlying motivations that drive private companies to participate in the education sector remain largely unknown – as do the quality, costs and implications of low-fee private schools. This chapter focuses on Omega Schools Franchise in Ghana, one of the fastest-growing chains of low-fee private schools in the world.

Omega Schools Franchise was co-founded in 2009 by James Tooley and Ken Donkoh. Tooley is a Professor of Education Policy at Newcastle University in the United Kingdom and Donkoh is a Ghanaian entrepreneur who previously worked for Oxfam and USAID.

> The Omega Schools chain has grown to 20 schools and 11,000 students in 3 years, creating a 'school-in-a-box' model that it is now ready to replicate more widely. Reaching financial break-even in 2011 was made possible through, in part, ultra-low

overheads and the innovative all-inclusive daily-fee model, which has proven highly attractive to parents: within 10 days of opening, a new Omega School is typically at capacity, with 500 students, and hence fully sustainable. (Omega website)[1]

In an interview at the company's head office on the outskirts of Accra, the capital city of Ghana, Donkoh stated:

We build a school and the same week we open the school it becomes sustainable because it fills up with students. With 500 fee-paying students it's able to cover the costs: the teacher salaries, the costs of running the school and it turns up a profit. This means that each school is self-sustainable and can contribute a surplus to the head of the company, which can then pool the money together and build new schools.

To reach the largest number of students at the lowest possible cost Omega Schools Franchise intends to scale up its chain through a 'school-in-a-box' model. Omega's 'school-in-a-box' approach involves the basic construction of a 12-classroom building, along with the initial materials and resources needed to run the private storefront school, at a start-up cost of approximately US$60,000. New schools in the chain are then financed and produce revenues through the daily-fee – or 'pay-as-you-learn' – payment system, which requires each student to pay 1.50 Cedis (the equivalent of US$0.75) per day to attend class. Omega Schools have thus 'successfully proven a viable model for starting new schools which are profitable and sustainable on opening' (Omega website).

This chapter aims to answer the following questions: what is the nature and motivation of Omega Schools' educational franchise? How did it come to rise? Are these schools 'affordable' for the poorest and can they be expected to expand rates of access to education in Ghana? Understanding the nature, scope and implications of Omega Schools is important because it represents a paradigmatic case to explore the rise of privately held chains of schools that are advancing new markets for low-fee educational services in less economically developed countries.

This chapter is divided into three main parts. Firstly, Omega Schools is outlined in relation to James Tooley and Pearson Education. Together, these actors represent the transnational corporate activity, networks of influence, ideas and private capital that have culminated in the rise of Omega Schools. The second section of this chapter provides an analytics of the teaching, learning and business model(s) of Omega Schools. It will be argued that Omega's model is based on: (1) efficiency (serving the largest amount of students at the lowest possible cost); (2) the standardisation of services; (3) brand reliability (as a form of quality control); and (4) consumerism ('pay-as-you-learn' and the commodification of basic educational services). Finally, the third part of this chapter will investigate the implications of Omega Schools Franchise in relation to access, equity and affordability.

Throughout this chapter the methodology relies on primary data collected through in-country field research in the Greater Accra region of Ghana between January and March of 2013. Over the course of this period semi-structured interviews were conducted with 9 schoolteachers and 'School Managers' from 6 different Omega Schools, as well as 20 students and 16 parents/guardians of Omega School students. The co-founder of Omega Schools, Ken Donkoh, was interviewed on two occasions. Six interviews were also conducted with ministerial officials from Ghana Education Service. The data here also draws from secondary sources of various kinds found on-line, such as Omega Schools' website, media releases, webcasts, interviews and reports which involve key players, as well as secondary research on the topic.

James Tooley, Pearson and the Rise of Omega Schools: a joint venture to develop a market for low-fee private education

This section aims to connect Omega Schools with the transnational corporate actors, networks of influence, ideas and private capital that have facilitated the growth of the Franchise (as well as the low-fee private-school sector more generally). Here the focus is on James Tooley and Pearson Education. Tooley is the chairman and co-founder of Omega Schools. He also occupies a variety of influential spaces and roles as an academic, businessman, 'policy entrepreneur' and 'thought-leader' in the low-fee private-school sector. Pearson on the other hand is the world's largest multinational education corporation, which recently established the Pearson Affordable Learning Fund (PALF); a global financial-investment fund intended to invest in, partner with and help grow private companies operating in the low-fee private-school sector. Pearson's Affordable Learning Fund made its first investment into Omega Schools Franchise. This section will triangulate between the ideational, institutional and material powers that have given rise to Omega Schools. It will map the transnational corporate activities of James Tooley and Pearson Education and their joint venture to develop a global market for low-fee private education.

As a Professor of Education Policy at Newcastle University, James Tooley's research over the last decade has aimed to show that private companies can help solve the educational challenges faced by low-income countries. One of Tooley's underlying arguments is that low-cost educational services provided by private entities on a profitable basis can improve the quality of and extend access to basic education for the world's poor. Tooley began to develop his theory while conducting research on low-cost education in India where his 'study revealed a huge private sector serving poor families in the slums' and that 'given the

261

burgeoning of the sector, it was found that running schools, even for low-income families, was potentially a profitable undertaking' (Tooley & Dixon, 2003, p. 5).

> [Tooley] argues that private schools were making profit and if invested in or supported financially, for instance, with low-cost innovative technology, they would be a potential area for business expansion. Altogether, for-profit schools aimed at poor communities are presented as the solution to India's problem of access to and quality of education and as a lucrative business opportunity. (Ball, 2012, p. 44)

Tooley claims that: 'The key relevant finding of the research is that the vast majority of private schools in the poor areas are *businesses*, not charities, dependent more or less entirely on fee income and, very importantly, making a reasonable profit' (Tooley, 2009, p. 252).

'Pro-market' think tanks, advocacy groups and other organisations working in the field of business and 'development' have been keen to support Tooley and his research on low-cost private schools for the poor. With financial backing from 'pro-market' foundations such as the John Templeton Foundation, CATO Institute and the Institute of Economic Affairs, Tooley has expanded his initial research in India to include studies in China, Kenya, Ghana, Nigeria and elsewhere. Tooley was the director of a global study on investment opportunities for private education in 'developing' countries fittingly titled: *The Global Education Industry* (Tooley, 1999). The 'findings' of such studies all definitively point to the need to advance a low-fee private-school industry to expand the educational franchise to more of the world's poor, whereby the redistribution of basic educational services takes place through quasi-market-oriented systems.

Tooley is a key actor in a transnational advocacy network that pushes the idea that low-cost private schools will universalise access to basic education. Through publications in academic journals, keynote speeches at international conferences, high-ranking consultancy and directorial positions, BBC and PBS documentary appearances and media reports and lectures to parliamentarians and policymakers in the United States, the United Kingdom and India, Tooley has emerged as a leading voice in the global business of education and 'development'. Tooley 'operates on a number of levels, to give legitimacy to neo-liberal solutions through research, to persuade and co-opt governments and philanthropists, to construct and animate infrastructures of financial and discursive relations, and to put ideas into practice through start-up enterprises' (Ball, 2012, p. 143).

Tooley capitalised on an opportunity to put his ideas into practice through a start-up enterprise when he came into contact with low-cost innovator Ken Donkoh. While completing his MBA at the University of

Cape Coast in Ghana, Donkoh came across Tooley's research on low-fee private education: 'I read Professor Tooley's research in business school and I decided to develop a business plan out of it, so I sent a copy of the business plan to him asking if we could create a business out of it and he really believed in it.' By the time Donkoh had made his pitch to Tooley in 2008, Tooley had already surveyed the viability for private start-up enterprises in Ghanaian education. Funded by the John Templeton Foundation, Tooley led a study which consisted of a school census and survey in the Ga District of Ghana between 2003 and 2005. The report found that fee-paying private school provision was 'mushrooming' in the Ga District of Ghana (Tooley et al, 2007). 'Of the total of 779 primary and junior secondary schools in Ga, 75% were private. There were almost as many unregistered private as government schools (23% compared to 25%)', reported Tooley and his colleagues (2007, p. 409).

In the business of private for-profit education, viable markets exist where the regulatory environment is more 'open' to private-sector influence, which is indicated in Ghana by both the high number of registered and unregistered private schools found by Tooley. Referring to the Indian market, Tooley claims that 'the regulatory environment is a big problem there. In the business of education, always, the regulatory environment matters. In India it's not conducive to for-profit education. And that's why were focusing for now in Africa where it's much easier to do business' (BBC, 2013).

Neoliberal calculations identify optimizing spaces and populations in relation to global market opportunities' (Ong, 2007, p. 6) In Ghana, Tooley found a business partner in Donkoh as well as a geo-political landscape that offered a viable market to carry out his business venture in for-profit private-school provision. However, the financial capital needed to kick-start and scale up Omega Schools was still missing.

In 2007 Tooley published his essay, 'Educating Amaretch: private schools for the poor and the new frontier for investors', which won first prize in the International Finance Corporation (IFC) and *Financial Times'* first annual essay competition entitled 'Business and Development: private path to prosperity'. In his essay Tooley argues that: 'Crucially, because the private schools serving the poor are businesses, making a reasonable profit, they provide a pioneering way forward for investors to get involved too' and that 'investing in a chain of schools – either through a dedicated education investment fund or through joint ventures with educational entrepreneurs – could help solve the information problem for poor parents' (Tooley, 2007, p. 42). Pearson – the world's largest multinational education corporation – bought into the idea sold by Tooley and created a large-scale investment fund that would make its first-ever investment into Omega Schools.

In 2012 Pearson established the Pearson Affordable Learning Fund (PALF) to invest in and grow for-profit companies working in the low-fee private-school sector.

> Pearson will invest an initial $15 million into the Fund, which will invest in private companies committed to innovative approaches, sustainable business models and improving learning outcomes, as well as its own projects. It will provide investment in private enterprise to meet the Millennium Development Goals. The Fund's launch underlines Pearson's commitment to experimentation to tackle access to and effectiveness of education where it is now absent. (Pearson website)[3]

Pearson invested in Omega Schools, at an undisclosed amount, with the purpose of creating 'a sustainable large chain of branded low-cost private schools in Ghana' (Omega website). Pearson's investments 'will help Omega expand from ten schools in greater Accra serving about 6,000 students to a full-service school chain serving tens of thousands of students throughout Ghana' (Pearson website). Ken Donkoh, of Omega Schools, explained that:

> Pearson's investments helped us to grow more rapidly. We got up to ten schools and with Pearson's investments we could then add another ten schools, which brought us to twenty. Now we will be adding twenty more schools, sending us to forty. Then we can add on and on, year after year.

While PALF is advertised as a seemingly 'to do good' venture intended to work toward Millennium Development Goals and bring 'education where it is now absent', at its core it represents a long-term business strategy to develop a market for low-cost educational services and create new sources of profitability for Pearson.

Michael Barber, chairman of the Pearson Affordable Learning Fund, explained in a *BBC HARDTalk* interview in 2012: 'To use economic jargon it's an immature market so there's lots of one or two school little family companies and we think we can find some, take them to scale, get large chains of schools that are consistent that are higher quality and still very low-cost' (BBC, 2012). Barber would go on to state that: 'It's absolutely for-profit. But get this right – its important to demonstrate profit because we want other investors to come in.' In a new emerging market such as low-fee private schooling, more investment is considered necessary for the growth and development of the market. In large part, Pearson has established PALF and invested into Omega Schools for this reason.

Omega has developed an innovative business plan to expand its chain of low-fee private schools, which Pearson has endorsed. It is based on the idea that 500 fee-paying students in each school can cover the operational costs while also generating a surplus, which is then pooled together with the total revenues accumulated from other schools in the franchise, which can then be used to build and expand the chain of profit-making schools. This is directly in line with PALF's purpose, which aims to tackle 'the educational needs of the world's poorest regions, to experiment with new approaches to low cost learning, and to demonstrate to how a for-profit approach can scale and solve education in developing countries' (PALF website).[2]

The nature and motivation of the joint venture between Omega Schools and Pearson is further reflected in the following statement made by Donkoh:

> I think [Pearson decided to invest in Omega Schools] for a couple of reasons. Obviously, it's a very interesting space – the low-fee education space is quite interesting. It's a huge market. It's getting more and more interesting. It's also a way that Pearson can really make an impact by helping the poor and helping low-income communities also get a better education. Previously, Pearson's investments have been in very mid-class to high-end schools and even with the government and all that. I think the low-fee sector has made a very strong statement – that yes, it is possible that the private sector can also educate the poor. I think that Pearson wants to be involved in these things. So I think that's the key thing. There's huge wealth at the 'bottom of the pyramid' as they put it. So who knows? Maybe in a few years to come it will be a very viable market. But I think for now they are driven by the fact that they want to be involved in this space, they want to support, they want to bring quality. In a way help achieve, if not even achieve, we get closer to the Millennium Development Goals.[...] I think that the reason why Pearson set up the Affordable Learning Fund, the Fund that invested in us, is not to make a short-term return, but instead to develop the market, develop the market to maturity, so perhaps one day the low-fee sector will become a viable and profitable market.

Donkoh's statement brings to light two key issues. Firstly, Pearson's investments in Omega are identified as a way to expand educational access in low-income communities and work toward Millennium Development Goals including 'Education For All'. However, as the findings from a survey across a sample of Omega Schools will demonstrate later on in this chapter, there is reason to seriously doubt that Omega Schools are in reality serving pupils who otherwise would not have been able to access basic educational services. Secondly, the

265

joint venture between Pearson and Omega Schools is a way to experiment in the low-fee private-school sector and develop a market intended to tap into the 'huge wealth at the bottom of the pyramid'. This corporate growth strategy has been referred to in the business literature as the 'fortune at the bottom of the pyramid' (Prahalad & Hart, 2002; Prahalad, 2005) and it considers the four billion people who earn less than US$2,000 a year as a huge source of potential revenue. 'Bottom of the pyramid' (BOP) strategies see the poor as a new source of profitability whereby multinational corporations can provide low-cost services on a massive scale, such as a large chain of low-fee private schools, which can become a highly lucrative business.

These are the transnational corporate actors, ideas, institutions and material capabilities that have given rise to the Omega Schools Franchise in Ghana. Tooley has supplied the intellectual leadership and international advocacy to legitimate the viability of a low-fee private-school sector for the poor, while Pearson and its Affordable Learning Fund has supplied the private capital for Tooley, Donkoh and the Omega Schools Franchise to further entrench their for-profit 'experimentation' in low-cost schooling.

Omega Schools and the 'McDonaldisation' of Education Model

This section investigates the interconnected teaching, learning and business model(s) developed by Omega Schools. Drawing inspiration from fast-food conglomerate McDonald's, 'where a consistent quality of hamburgers and French fries worldwide results from a deeply understood and standardized chemical process' (Prahalad, 2005, p. 37 cited in Tooley, 2007, p.42). James Tooley believes: 'There is, it seems, every reason to think that a similarly "deeply understood and standardised" learning process could become part of an equally successful model of private school provision, serving huge numbers of the poor' (Tooley, 2007, p. 42). This section will examine the model of Omega Schools Franchise and how it represents a re-conceptualised programme of educational-service delivery that can be understood as the 'McDonaldisation' of education (Ritzer, 1993). This is because large-scale chains of low-cost private-school franchises like Omega are based on market-oriented principles of: (1) efficiency (serving the largest amount of students at the lowest possible cost); (2) the standardisation of services; (3) brand reliability (as a form of quality control); and (4) consumerism ('pay-as-you-learn' and the commodification of basic educational services).

Efficiency

Omega Schools' model is based on the idea that a privately held chain of schools can provide mass access to basic education to low-income families 'at the lowest cost on an unprecedented scale' (Omega website). That is, to serve the largest number of students, or provide educational services to the highest number of fee-paying consumers, at the lowest possible cost. As James Tooley describes it:

> We try to be the lowest price because we see it a mass market.
> We're a very low-margin, high-volume business in a way.
> That's what we want to do. We want to serve as many children
> as we can, so we keep the costs down because our market are
> parents that wouldn't have previously been able to afford a
> low cost private school. (BBC, 2013)

High-volume, low-margin businesses such as Omega Schools can benefit from economies of scale, as they can produce a high volume of goods or services efficiently and at a low cost. In the 'McDonaldisation' of education, efficiency thus means that every aspect in the production of learning and outcomes are based on the minimisation of cost.

The critical point to be made here, in the case of Omega Schools and its model for low-cost schooling, is that the main source of cost saving has come as a result of the exploitation of teachers' labour. While teachers' salaries account for the bulk of educational costs, especially in low-income countries (Lewin, 2007), the Omega Schools Franchise has drastically reduced its costs by employing high-school graduates as teachers and paying them a fraction of what professionally trained and qualified teachers receive in the public sector. The monthly wage for an Omega School teacher ranges between 130 and 150 Cedis (equivalent to US$65 and US$75 per month or US$2.95 and US$3.40 per day): this is only 15-20% of what teachers in the public sector make in Ghana. Omega has cut costs by hiring non-unionised labour, and thus avoided public employment regulations and standards.

In addition to low teacher salaries, another way to minimise the per-unit cost of teaching while increasing margins has been to fill classrooms beyond the pupil–teacher ratio norm set by the Ghana Education Service at 35:1 and 25:1 for primary- and lower-secondary-school classrooms, respectively. This researcher has observed pupil–teacher classroom ratios in Omega Schools upwards of 50:1 in several instances. This combination of inadequately trained teachers and high pupil–teacher ratios brings up obvious questions related to the quality of Omega Schools.

With the dilution of available resources committed to education by international aid donors and governments, low-cost private-sector alternatives based on efficiency and the minimisation of expenditures have gained credence. Private-sector participation, including chains of low-cost private schools 'are being promoted as a cost-effective and fast solution to bring "Education for All" to developing contexts' (Verger, 2012, p. 125). For example, in its second global report, *The MDGs: everyone's business* (Gradl et al, 2010), research published by Tooley and Dixon (2005) is referenced, which emphasises the importance of private companies in the international effort to achieve universal access to primary education. Similarly, Omega claims its model is a cost-effective way to expand access because at its core it aims to provide a high volume of services at a minimal cost.

Standardisation of Services

Interconnected with efficiency (concerned with optimising educational access while minimising cost) Omega has developed a system of standardised services. This standardisation of services is based on the 'school-in-a-box' model: a franchising approach premised on uniformity throughout the chain of private storefront schools, involving the materials and resources that make up each institution. That is, from the construction of the school to student uniforms to curriculum, management and instructional methods, the 'school-in-a-box' technique is intended to guarantee uniformity in the production of standardised outcomes across the franchise, while also bringing down the per unit costs of production.

To optimise the teaching and learning throughout the chain of Omega Schools at minimal operating costs, the Franchise has developed its own uniform curriculum, hired unqualified teachers for minimum wage, and established a teacher-training programme to teach the 'teachers' how to deliver the lesson plans. As Ken Donkoh explains: 'Whatever research or whatever things we develop in terms of curriculum can be shared across a number of schools and that can drive down costs. So that's the second aspect of our model, we've developed our own proprietary curriculum and that ensures that even high school graduates can easily deliver the teaching and learning.' Donkoh further explains that the company has:

> developed lesson plans for the teachers because ideally it takes a very experienced teacher to be able to structure the lesson and design a lesson plan to be able to deliver the needed effect and we don't have that luxury. We can't get experienced quality teachers in the schools so what we've done is hired experienced teachers to write out those lesson plans at the head office and then give them to the schools so that our teachers can read them and just deliver them. These lesson plans come with complementary workbooks for the students.[...] We do this for all subjects, maths, English, science and social studies.

In the production of teaching and learning, the deskilling of teachers' labour has been replaced with standardised lesson plans that can easily be delivered by low-cost high-school graduates, who are supported by a two-week teacher-training programme to prepare unqualified teachers for their part in the production of uniform outcomes. This system has been a way to regiment the entire pedagogical process.

Thus, the 'McDonaldisation' model of education demonstrated by Omega Schools is related to the notion of 'predictability' (Ritzer, 1993), which is offered through uniform products (i.e. the standardisation of services), replication of settings (i.e. 'school-in-a-box') and scripting employee behaviours and interaction with customers (i.e. controlled pedagogical processes).

Brand Reliability

Another aspect of the commercialisation of education associated with Omega Schools' model is the importance placed on 'brand reliability'. This is most notably evident in the research carried out by James Tooley on for-profit education companies working in the low-fee school sector. Tooley explains:

> I was particularly surprised to find the importance of brand name – which many education companies were very keen to promote on billboards and in newspaper, radio and television advertising. From the study, brand name seemed to be particularly important because it helps parents and students overcome the 'information' problem. How do parents know whether they can trust the local entrepreneur who has set up the school? Because he or she is the franchisee for an established educational brand name whose quality control procedures are known and respected throughout the country. (Tooley, 1999, p. 28)

Thus, Tooley sees the recognition of brand name in the business of education as a measure of quality control. That is, a brand name resolves the issue of market 'information' for poor households caught up in the dilemma of which school to choose. Just as billboards, advertisements and other forms of marketing inform consumers about the availability and leading assumptions about their products, brand-name recognition provides a similar form of 'quality assurance' for educational consumers. As Tooley notes in his research: 'With the larger education companies it is clear that the brand name works as it does for other consumer goods and services, reassuring parents and students that high quality is being offered and maintained' (1999, p. 40). Tooley adds that for education companies that intend to increase their profitability they should spend roughly 10% of their income on advertising and promoting its brand name (Tooley, 1999).

Pay-as-you-Learn

Since the commodification of basic educational services for the poor is the underlying premise of Omega's business plan, the company has developed an innovative daily-fee payment system to attract low-income households. Advertised by Omega as 'pay-as-you-learn', this 'innovative all-inclusive no hidden cost daily fee payment system, ensures that we rope in a lot more lower-income families who otherwise may not be able to afford bulk term fees' (Omega website). Within the 'pay-as-you-learn' system families pay a fee of 1.50 Cedis (equivalent to US$0.75) per day per child for classroom services. This amounts to 315 Cedis, or approximately US$160 in annual tuition expenses for a 210-day school year.

In a seminar at Newcastle University Ken Donkoh explained that Omega's 'pay-as-you-learn' business plan is modelled after 'pay-as-you-go' services, and specifically, multinational mobile-phone companies operating in sub-Saharan Africa that have developed low-cost services on a 'pay-as-you-*can-afford*' basis. Donkoh explained that if in a low-income country such as Ghana where roughly 20 million out of 24 million people have become mobile-phone users by purchasing small amounts of credit to gain temporary telecommunication services, before having to pay again, than a similar business model could apply to expand the educational franchise:

> We saw that the poor people usually earn on a daily basis so trying to save up money to pay for a [school] term fee can be difficult because by the time they go to pay the term fee maybe something else came up, maybe their child gets sick or something and they don't have insurance – they don't have any social protection. So if they try saving up for education they end up using it for other purposes. So we felt that since the poor earn on a daily basis we must develop a payment system that allows them to pay on a daily basis.

In turn however, if low-income families use up their daily wages on daily tuition fees because they can't afford to save up for bulk term fees, where will the savings be in times of unexpected health, lodging and emergency situations?

Nonetheless, the daily fee provides Omega students with in-class instruction as well as daily lunches and a scheduled mass deworming. Students are also granted 15 free school days to ensure attendance when households may not be able to pay the daily fee.

While the innovative 'pay-as-you-learn' model has been credited with much of the success and growth of the Omega Schools Franchise, it will undoubtedly also have less impressive consequences. For example, as the 'School Manager' of one Omega School put it: 'The pressure to pay daily fees is the main cause of absenteeism.' Several Omega School Mangers and teachers reported that on any given school day, up to 20% of the student body is absent. One Omega School student expressed her experiences with the 'pay-as-you-learn' model by stating: 'I sell water on the streets one day so I can go to school the next.' This is indicative of the commodification of social relations inherent in Omega Schools' system of education, whereby students are transformed into consumers and the opportunity to 'get an education' is dependent upon one's ability to pay.

Access, Affordability and Equity

Omega Schools Franchise in Ghana is a paradigmatic case to investigate some of the implications of fee-paying for-profit private schools. This section investigates whether or not Omega Schools may be considered 'affordable' for the poorest families in Ghana, or if it represents a case of profiteering. First, Omega Schools' impact on extending initial access to basic education for first-time school goers in Ghana will be discussed.

If Omega Schools plan is to help achieve universal basic education they will have to extend its reach to the 'last 10%' of students in Ghana who still remain excluded from basic schooling (Akyeampong et al, 2012). To determine if Omega Schools could be expected to significantly expand initial access to the 'last 10%' a sample was taken of 437 pupils across four different Omega schools. Each student was asked if Omega was the first school they attended, or if they had been enrolled at a different school prior to Omega. Only 1 out of 437 students questioned said that Omega was their first school. In full 436 out of 437 students had already been enrolled in classes at another school prior to Omega. (Those questioned were students in primary 1, 2 and 3 classes, as well as students in junior high school 1 and 2 classes).

This finding refutes any suggestion that Omega Schools are expanding access to basic education through its provision of low-fee private education. This is because fee-paying private schools like Omega are more an elective for those who can already afford to pay their way into public or private school, rather than be a system for expanding initial access to the most marginalised students who remain excluded from any type of schooling. Looking at tuition fees in relation to average household income further supports this point.

Currently, the 20 Omega Schools operating in Ghana are clustered in peri-urban localities in the Greater Accra and Central regions. The Greater Accra region has the highest annual household income in the country with an average of 1529 Cedis while the Central region has the third highest average of 1310 Cedis (GSS, 2008). The poorest 5% in Greater Accra and the poorest 7% in Ghana's Central region earn, on average, an annual household income of 728 Cedis (GSS, 2008). If we were to take an annual household income of 728 Cedis in relation to school costs of 1.50 Cedis per day x 210 schools days in a year, it would cost 315 Cedis or 43% of a family's annual household income to send one child to an Omega School for one year. If we were to make a similar calculation using the average annual household income in all of Ghana (which is 1217 Cedis), families would have to spend 26% of their household income on education expenditures for one child. Most families in Ghana have more than one child. Low-income households in Ghana cannot afford to pay upwards of 40% of their earnings on educational expenditures for only one child, while other basic necessities such as food, health and shelter must also be met.

In fact, the allegation that Omega Schools are 'low-fee' is highly misplaced. Srivastava (2007a, 2007b) has defined 'low-fee' private schools as those that charge a monthly fee of about one day's earnings of a daily-wage labourer at the primary and junior levels. In Ghana the minimum daily wage is set at 5.24 Cedis, about US$2.45, which is significantly lower than what Omega students pay over a one-month term. Comparing fee levels to income suggests Omega Schools are not 'low-fee', 'budget' or 'affordable' options for the poorest families in Ghana at all. This 'low-fee' private-school model is still far out of reach for the 'last 10%' who still remain out of school in Ghana.

This chapter adds to the research on low-cost private schools and their limitations accommodating the poorest students in low-income countries (Probe, 1999; Watkins, 2004; Rose & Adelabu, 2007; Srivastava & Walford, 2007). It is clear that Omega Schools are not extending access to first-time school users because of the high cost of fees levied. For impoverished families in Ghana, the key factor that prevents access to education is the cost associated with sending children to school (Akyeampong et al, 2012) – a barrier apparently unforeseen by Tooley and Donkoh, who maintained that Omega Schools were geared towards 'those at the bottom of the economic pyramid' (Omega website).

Unsubsidised and fee-paying for-profit providers like Omega 'cannot serve the poor and poorest if they depend on revenue from the communities they serve' (Lewin, 2007, p. 3). Despite Omega's innovative 'pay-as-you-learn' model, and a scholarship fund to support some of the poorest households, it appears at this point that the franchise will have an insignificant impact on extending basic educational services to the 'last 10%' still excluded from school in Ghana. The lowest-income households in Ghana cannot afford to pay 'low-fee' private-school companies up to 40% of their earnings without making dramatic sacrifices that would affect available resources for other basic necessities.

As a concerned mother of an Omega student said: 'Every Cedi I spend on school fees, takes away from the little money I have to feed my family. This is a struggle we face everyday.'

The growth of fee-paying privately held chains of schools like Omega have equity implications that may result in more social differentiation, inequality and polarisation than currently already exists in 'developing' contexts like Ghana (Adea-Mensah, 2000; Lewin, 2007).

Beyond the falsity that Omega schools are 'affordable' for the poorest households in Ghana, another systematic boundary that limits their ability to expand initial access is the location where schools have been established. Omega schools have not been set up in communities where provision is absent, but rather in communities that can more effectively ensure the economic sustainability of the for-profit institution. For example, in the Ga South District in the Greater Accra region where Omega has established six of its schools in close proximity to one another, an official at the District Assembly Education Office explained to me that in 2009 there were 366 private registered schools in the district and by February 2013 that number rose to 598. So if Omega intends to expand the educational franchise in areas where it is now absent, why build clusters of schools in communities where competition between schools is already high? This is as much based on business planning as it is education planning (Figure 1). As the Director of Private Schooling in Ghana explained:

> Unfortunately, the private schools that are coming on board are clustered in urban centres. This is because those low cost or low fee private schools do it as a business enterprise, so they go to communities that can afford to pay. So those children in the villages, in the remote areas – what will be their fate?

The Omega Schools Franchise, and the low-fee private-school sector more generally, are advertised as a way to supplement existing state provision and achieve 'Education For All' goals. However, as Lewin argues:

> Only States can make a reality of the delivery rights to populations, especially those marginalized by poverty. Universal free primary education – the EFA commitment – is essentially a state responsibility. The for-profit private sector has no essential interest delivering free services, and no obligation to provide education to the poor and ultra poor, HIV orphans, excluded girls and those with special needs. (Lewin 2007, p. 2)

Omega's for-profit model is a 'bottom of the pyramid' strategy intended to produce a high volume of services at a low cost, rather than be a method to extend educational services to marginalised groups who otherwise would not have had the right to entry.

The findings presented in this section demonstrate that in its current form Omega's 'low-fee' private schools for the poor are likely to exclude the 'last 10%' who already remain out of school in Ghana, while having little to no significant impact on expanded initial access due to the imposition of *un*-affordable fees and a for-profit business model in the place of an emancipatory education model.

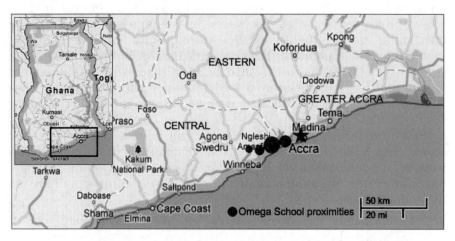

Figure 1. Proximity of Omega Schools in Ghana.

Conclusion

Omega Schools is initiating plans to expand its franchise beyond Ghana and into West African markets including Sierra Leone, Liberia, Nigeria and the Gambia, with plans to 'grow too as many as 340 schools with 200,000 students by 2020' (Donkoh, 2012). On this scale Omega's chain of low-fee private schools will become an immensely profitable venture, since Omega Schools is 'a very low-margin, high-volume business' which can benefit from economies of scale by providing a high volume of services 'at the lowest cost at an unprecedented scale'. As one blog post stated in admiration of Omega's for-profit venture in education: 'Who would ever have thought that money could be made from educating poor African kids [*sic*]?'

Omega Schools represents an 'experiment' into the feasibility and profitability of a large-scale chain of branded private schools serving the more affluent poor in West Africa. This 'experiment' has been largely 'configured by the power of transnational capital' (Gill, 1995) supplied by Pearson – the world's largest multinational education corporation – which has allowed James Tooley and Ken Donkoh to implement their 'McDonaldisation' of education model based on efficiency, standardisation, consumerism and the exploitation of teachers' labour.

The findings presented in this chapter of a 437-student sample conducted across the Omega Schools chain, has shown that these schools are not extending initial access to basic education for first-time school users. This is directly related to the fees levied within the 'pay-as-you-learn' system. This demonstrates that fee-paying private schools like Omega are more an elective for those who can already afford to pay for some type of schooling, rather than being a method to expand access to the poorest. Omega Schools are not a 'low-fee' option for the 'poorest of the poor'.

The findings from this chapter conclude that Omega Schools are not 'affordable' for the 'last 10%' in Ghana since these households would have to spend upwards of 40% of their total annual income to send one child to an Omega school. This level of expenditure would severely compromise their ability to finance other basic necessities such as clean drinking water, food, shelter and health. Omega Schools' fee-paying for-profit venture aimed at serving the 'poorest of the poor' represents a case of for-profiteering, which exists when one 'makes what is considered an unreasonable profit especially on the sale of essential goods during times of emergency'. And while Ken Donkoh proclaims: 'education is the first bridge out of poverty', the ironic and harmful failure is that the Omega bridge levies a high toll for all those who wish to pass, which is more likely to reproduce poverty, than it can be expected to alleviate it.

Acknowledgements

Although some of this chapter is critical of Omega Schools, I am most grateful to Ken Donkoh for allowing me to conduct research in his schools and for agreeing to be interviewed. This research would not have been possible without his help.

Notes

[1] www.omega-schools.com

[2] http://www.affordable-learning.com

[3] www.pearson.com/news/2012/july/new-pearson-investment-fund-to-enhance-education-opportunity-amo.html

Curtis B. Riep

References

Adea-Mensah, I. (2000) *Education in Ghana: a tool for social mobility or social stratification?* J.B. Danqah Memorial Lecture, Ghana Academy of Arts and Sciences, April 2000.

Akyeampong, K., Rolleston, C., Ampiah, J.G. & Lewin, K. (2012) *Access, Transitions and Equity in Education in Ghana: researching practice, problems and policy.* CREATE Pathways to Access Research monograph 72. Brighton: University of Sussex.

Ball, S.J. (2012) *Global Education Inc: new policy networks and the neo-liberal imaginary.* New York: Routledge.

BBC (2012) BBC HARDTalk: Sir Michael Barber, 13 August [Video file]. www.bbc.co.uk/programmes/b01lyz03

BBC (2013) The Bottom Line: the education business, 30 March [Audio file]. www.bbc.co.uk/programmes/b01rgmbh

Bhanji, Z. (2008) Transnational Corporations in Education: filling the governance gap through new social norms and market multilateralism?, *Globalisation, Societies and Education,* 6(1), 55-73.

Donkoh, K. (2012) Pay As You Learn Education, 5 May [Video File]. http://vimeo.com/53508529

Ghana Statistical Service (GSS) (2008) *Ghana Living Standards Survey.* Report of the 5th Round.

Gill, S. (1995) *Power and Resistance in the New World Order.* Basingstoke: Palgrave Macmillan.

Gradl, C., Sivakumaran, S. & Sobhani, S. (2010) *The MDGs: everyone's business.* New York: United Nations Development Programme.

Härmä, J. & Rose, P. (2012) Is Low-Fee Private Primary Schooling Affordable for the Poor? Evidence from Rural India, in S.L. Robertson, K. Mundy, A. Verger & F. Menashy (Eds) *Public Private Partnerships in Education: new actors and modes of governance in a globalizing world*, pp. 243-258. Cheltenham: Edward Elgar.

Lewin, K. (2007) *The Limits to Growth of Non-Government Private Schooling in Sub Saharan Africa.* CREATE Pathways to Access Research Monograph 5. London: Department for International Development (DFID).

Ong, A. (2007) Neoliberalism as a Mobile Technology, *Transactions of the Institute of British Geographers,* 32(1), 3-8.

Prahalad, C.K. (2005) *The Fortune at the Bottom of the Pyramid: eradicating poverty through profits.* Upper Saddle River: Wharton School Publishing.

Prahalad, C.K. & Hart, S. (2002) The Fortune at the Bottom of the Pyramid, *Strategy and Competition,* 6(1), 55-67.

Probe Team (1999) *Public Report on Basic Education in India.* Oxford: Oxford University Press.

Ritzer, G. (1993) *The McDonaldization of Society.* Los Angeles: Pine Forge Press.

Robertson, S.L., Mundy, K., Verger, A. & Menashy, F. (2012) *Public Private Partnerships in Education: new actors and modes of governance in a globalizing world.* Cheltenham: Edward Elgar.

Rose, P. & Adelabu, M. (2007) Private Sector Contributions to Education For All in Nigeria, in P. Srivastava & G. Walford (Eds) *Private Schooling in Less Economically Developed Countries: Asian and African perspectives.* Oxford: Symposium Books.

Srivastava, P. & Walford, G. (2007) *Private Schooling in Less Economically Developed Countries: Asian and African Perspectives.* Oxford: Symposium Books.

Srivastava, P. (2007a) *Neither Voice nor Loyalty: school choice and the low-fee private sector in India.* Research Publications Series, Occasional Paper 134. New York: National Center for the Study of Privatization in Education, Columbia University.

Srivastava, P. (2007b) For Philanthropy or Profit? The Management and Operation of Low-Fee Private Schools in India, in P. Srivastava & G. Walford (Eds) *Private Schooling in Less Economically Developed Countries: Asian and African perspectives*, pp. 153-186. Oxford: Symposium Books.

Tooley, J. (1999) *The Global Education Industry. Lessons from Private Education in Developing Countries*, Hobart Paper 141. London: Institute of Economic Affairs.

Tooley, J. (2004) Private Education and 'Education for All', *Economic Affairs*, 24(4), pp. 4-7.

Tooley, J. (2007) Educating Amartech: private schools for the poor and the new frontier for investors, *Economic Affairs,* 27(2), 37-43.

Tooley, J. (2009) *The Beautiful Tree: a personal journey into how the world's poorest people are educating themselves.* Washington, DC: Cato Institute.

Tooley, J. & Dixon, P. (2003). *Private Schools for the Poor: a case study from India.* Reading: CfBT.

Tooley, J. & Dixon, P. (2005) *Private Education is Good for the Poor: a study of private schools serving the poor in low-income countries.* Washington, DC: Cato Institute.

Tooley, J., Dixon, P. & Amuah, I. (2007) Private and Public Schooling in Ghana: a census and comparative survey, *Review of Education*, 53, 389-415.

Verger, A. (2012) Framing and Selling Global Education Policy: the promotion of public–private partnerships for education in low-income contexts, *Journal of Education Policy,* 27(1), pp. 109-130.

Watkins, K. (2004) Private Education and 'Education For All', or How Not to Construct an Evidence-Based Argument: a reply to Tooley, *Economic Affairs*, 24(4), 8-11.

CHAPTER 14

Interrogating the Private-School 'Promise' of Low-Fee Private Schools

IAN MACPHERSON

The chapters in this book illustrate how privatised education delivery is increasing in many developing countries and is the focus of intense policy debate. They variously demonstrate how this growing provision results from the intersection of differing supply, demand and environmental factors including: the *de facto* increase in the provision of private schools offering comparatively better quality education than state schools, particularly low-fee-charging private schools; the 'ubiquitous desire' (Bhatta & Budathoki, 2013) of parents for private education based on perceptions of better quality and greater accountability; and national spaces shaped by either the formation or absence of policies regulating private education providers and malfunctioning state school systems.

Beyond the examples provided in this volume, similar factors lead to different forms and frequencies of non-state provision that, following Kitaev (1999), comprise all formal schools that are *not* public and may be founded, owned, managed and financed by actors other than the state. This includes for-profit private schools, non-governmental organisation (NGO) schools, faith-based schools and community schools. It also encompasses education public–private partnerships and private tutoring: fee-charging extra classes given outside of normal school hours. Yet while each variant is the product of different configurations of supply, demand and environmental factors and their relative frequencies vary across different geographies, within the global debate, 'privatised education' and 'privatisation' are used as synonyms and proxies to describe these different forms. And whereas this makes generalisations about non-state provision immensely difficult, it is possible to discern what may be described as the 'promise of privatisation', which rests on three key premises: (1) private schools provide real choice for parents including the disadvantaged; (2) private education provision is more effective and more efficient than state education; and (3) competition by private providers increases quality in both the private and state sectors. Nowhere is this promise more discernable than in the growing body of literature on low-fee private schools (LFPS).

In this chapter I analyse the 'promise' of LFPS using recent empirical data from selected developing countries, drawing strongly on the growing library of PERI studies [1], many of which are included as chapter versions in this volume. I suggest that the sanguine rhetoric of LFPS seems rather misplaced in the face of the serious equity questions that are raised by what we know of groups that are excluded from LFPS, but also by what is able, methodologically, to be known about the quality of education in LFPS and the effects of LFPS on quality in state schools. In the final section I assess these equity issues from a social-justice perspective and propose that LFPS entrench an instrumental, human-capital approach to education, which has serious implications for deliberative democracy and the role that education plays in societal development. Its significance lies in the fact that these views seem only to exist on the margins of dominant policy discourse, as against a backdrop of pressing international education targets and neo-liberal reforms supported by international actors, education policies instead favour an increased role for privatised education provision, including LFPS.

The Private-School Promise

Three key premises of the private-school promise include: (1) private schools provide real choice for parents including the disadvantaged; (2) private education provision is more effective and more efficient than state education; and (3) competition by private providers increases quality in both the private and state sectors. By examining each in turn, I argue that the private-school promise does not stand up to scrutiny.

Premise One: private schools provide real choice for parents including the disadvantaged

Some influential research argues that low-fee private schools are affordable to low-income families living in urban and rural areas (see Tooley & Dixon, 2003; Tooley 2005, 2007, 2009; Tooley et al, 2011). Central to the provision of LFPS are the existence of financial resources in the community (however modest) and local state schools (that perform comparatively worse). These factors create competitive local education markets in which parents 'choose' the education service for their child. And because the fees are low, this choice is ostensibly open to the economically disadvantaged.

For the very poor however, choice is often not between private or state school but between schooling and no schooling. Many families rely on children doing seasonal work such as harvesting, working in the informal economy through hawking, or helping with daily chores such as fetching water and looking after siblings. The opportunity cost of having that child in school prevents many poor children – particularly girls – from accessing any school, whether free or fee-paying, a reality that applies to urban and rural areas.

When household budgets do permit choice, economic decisions can be understood as a 'welfare maximisation strategy' (Rolleston & Adefeso-Olateju, 2012) through which the comparison of direct and opportunity costs of schooling options is weighed against not only the returns on other investments they may make but also the future economic benefits to the household in terms of access to further education and, ultimately, the labour market; a family would invest in education if it offered the highest return and delivered a competitive advantage (Rizvi & Engel, 2009). Yet fees comprise only one component of economic considerations; additional costs are incurred though private tutoring as well as books, uniforms and transport. In Jamil and others' 2013 Pakistan sample, private-tutoring costs were only nominally different to private-school fees (US$5.20 and US$6.60 respectively for urban LFPS) and indirect costs increased costs of schooling by 60-80% in addition to fees. Thus total costs for private education in urban areas were around US$10.20 per month, where fees constituted US$6.16, in contrast to total costs of US$4.20 to attend an urban state school. Similarly, Atherton and Aslam (2012) find that while private tutoring was undertaken by both private- and state-school students in their sample in rural Pakistan and India, the 'incidence of private tutoring increases with the ability to pay. Children in the richest income groups in rural Pakistan are almost five times as likely as those in the poorest quintile to be taking private tutoring' (p. 14).

Accordingly, multiple studies affirm that because fees present a barrier for access, private-school attendance increases with wealth. According to the Nepal Living Standards Survey III (CBS, 2011) 60.1% of individuals from the wealthiest income quintile attend private schools and colleges, compared with 6.4% from the poorest quintile. In Pakistan, the World Bank-supported LEAPS study (2007) documents that 'as the wealth of a household increases, so does the probability of enrolling children in private school' (cited in Jamil et al, 2013, p. 24). In India, Norhona and Srivastava assert that in their sample, '61% of average households chose private schools for at least some of their children, and 40% chose them exclusively, compared with respective figures for very poor households at just 17% and 10%' (p. 30) while Chudgar (2012) found that 'children who attend private schools belong to better off households. A greater proportion of their parents are likely to have attended school and these families enjoy a higher SES and are more likely to live in pucca houses' (p. 56). And evidence from Ghana suggests that poor families are sometimes only able to send a child to private school by taking out soft loans against future harvests, or they elect to go without food to cover educational costs (Rolleston & Adefeso-Olateju, 2012). The effect is that fee-paying private schooling not only prices out those unable to pay, relegating those children to state schools if indeed they access schooling at all, but also contributes to household insecurity for those least able to meet the costs.

Welfare maximisation strategies epitomise the human-capital approach that considers education relevant in so far as it 'creates skills and helps to acquire knowledge that serves as an investment in the productivity of the human being as an economic production factor, that is, as a worker' (Roybens, 2003). Indeed, a consequence of monetising access to education is the seeming entrenchment of parents' viewing education as human-capital formation, that is, instrumentally as a means to an economic end. This is critiqued by Roybens for, firstly, the underlying assumption that education is valuable only insofar as it increases productivity, and future wage earnings block out the social, cultural and non-material dimensions of life. Secondly, while it is entirely instrumental towards increased economic activity, not everyone has the same rate of return on education because external restrictions on work are often profoundly social and cultural in nature. Nowhere is this more evident than in the field of gender, which, in turn, has grave implications for girls' education. Gendered divisions of labour are created by social and cultural norms in many developing countries that limit access for women to the labour market, such as in rural India where girls are expected to spend their adult life childrearing and doing domestic work. Citing Dreze and Sen (2002, p. 7), Roybens argues that social expectations create an uncertain value in educating girls, adding that 'the consequence is that money spent on education – if it is conceptualized as an economic investment – is regarded as better spent on boys/men than on girls/women. In conditions of scarcity, this will lower girls' relative chances of being educated.' And evidence supports this: aside from one study from the Lahore School of Economics (LSE) that shows greater female enrolment in private schools relative to boys in their sample [2], an overwhelming pro-male bias in household decision-making for private-school enrolment is evident in research presented in this volume from Pakistan, India, Ghana, Nigeria and Nepal.[3] Interestingly, however, while the LSE study challenges the pro-male bias in private enrolments it supports an instrumental view of education through the fact that parents in the sample considered a valuable consequence of daughters attending LFPS would be their access to jobs as teachers in private schools, echoing Andarabi et al's (2006) suggestion that LFPS in Pakistan tend to rely on the existence of a local girls' secondary school as a source of low-paid labour.

In addition to private-school choice being shaped by the relative wealth of consumers in the local market, social hierarchies seem also to be reflected in private-school enrolment patterns. In Nepal, Bhatta and Budathoki (2013) found that while all social groups were enrolled in private schools in their sample, by far the highest proportion were Brahmin and Chhetri children, the highest social groups in terms of caste, wealth and social status. Enrolment patterns showed lesser proportions of Janajatis (middle social groups) and even lower numbers of Dalits (lowest social group). Similarly, Norhona and Srivasativa (2013) detail how access to 'freeship' places in their Delhi sample under the Right to Education Act in India was secured by members of the community who were relatively better educated, had a steady if modest income and had personal connections with the school or others that could help secure access, leading them to argue that 'in the Bourdieuian sense, these households had higher social capital and actively strategized to ensure freeship access' (pp. 62-63).

Srivatava's (2007, 2008) earlier work showed that disadvantaged parents conceptualised the education sector as socially segmented, meaning 'one where every social group has its place, covering a spectrum where the most advantaged attend elite high-fee schools and the disadvantaged, relegated to the government sector'. Bhatta and Budathoki (2013) echo this view in Nepal by suggesting that public-to-private transfers are creating the 'pauperisation' of public schools, meaning 'places where the poor study' and state that the caste differences in school-enrolment patterns suggests an 'institutionalization of class inequalities in Nepali society' (p. 16). Similarly, Pal (2010) found that in five north Indian states, villages where private schools were present tended to be those that had better infrastructure facilities (piped water, electricity, phone services and roads), were larger in terms of populations, had more educated parents and, critically, lower proportions of low-caste and Muslim populations who were poorer and had fewer assets, and for whom the only schooling options were government schools or madrassas. In their 2013 study, Muralidharan and Sundararaman support this finding indirectly by arguing that Muslim children are the demographic that benefit most from voucher schemes in India.

The proposition that 'private schools provide real choice for parents including the disadvantaged' therefore needs serious qualification. Choice may indeed exist for the relatively affluent and mobilised but this is counterbalanced by the seeming structural exclusion by private schools of the very poor, girls and marginalised groups. In turn, private schools risk entrenching economic divisions, deepening gender discrimination and institutionalising class inequalities.

Premise Two: private education provision is more effective and more efficient than state education

Empirical evidence that private schools are more effective than state schools is heavily contested. Most studies that argue for a relative advantage of low-fee private schools over public schools take comparatively better learning outcomes as a proxy for greater quality (see Kingdon, 1996, 2007; Tooley & Dixon, 2005, 2006; Muralidharan & Kremer, 2006; Aslam, 2009; Pandey et al, 2009; Tooley et al, 2010). Yet 'robust evidence for a quality premium in LFPS is very limited in the context of sub-Saharan Africa' (Rolleston & Adefeso-Olateju, 2012, p. 13) as is the case for South Asia (Atherton & Aslam, 2012; Jamil et al, 2013).

A key challenge is that reliable, representative data on comparative test scores at the primary level does not exist, largely because absent or overly strict regulation and its weak implementation means that many LFPS are unrecognised and/or unregistered. As a result, where empirical studies do posit a private premium, not only does the size of the advantage vary across and between countries as a result of most studies being small-scale and context-specific (Rutkowski & Rutkowski, 2010) but when student backgrounds are controlled (for wealth, socio-economic status and peer group), the size of the raw and uncontrolled attainment-advantage reduces significantly (ASER, 2009, 2010; Wadhwa, 2009). Furthermore, even when regression analyses control for covariates and still indicate a positive private-school advantage, these results can be challenged through other statistical analysis techniques. For instance, Chudgar and Quin's (2012, p. 376) study in India used a nationally representative sample of urban and rural data yet they concluded that 'in [rural and urban] contexts [...] the private school benefit becomes largely, statistically, insignificant after conducting multivariate analysis on data balanced using the propensity score matching technique.' Further still, control of background variables rarely if ever includes control of private tutoring, further distorting judgments on the value added by a private school.

Studies from Ghana, Nigeria, Pakistan, Nepal and India suggest that increased performance in LFPS could be the result of less teacher absenteeism than found in locally competing state schools (Rose, 2009; Jamil et al, 2013; CREB, 2012). Additionally, because school principals are more accountable to parents through the transfer of fees and the reliance on parental reputation of the school in a competitive environment, there is a strong incentive for principals to ensure teachers are performing (Rolleston & Adefeso, 2012). Further, because teachers are poorly paid as result of the low-fee structure, being largely unregulated and entirely unprotected by unions, dismissal is a constant threat, creating a strong incentive for regular attendance by teachers. As a result, teachers in LFPS may be more motivated to teach compared to state-school counterparts even though they lack teaching qualifications, which may compensate for the lack of formal training (Andrabi et al, 2007).

Studies in these countries have also found that pupil–teacher ratios in LFPS tend to be lower than in state schools, creating more contact time with individual students and making learning more effective (Jamil et al, 2013; Bhatta & Budathoki, 2013). Furthermore, there seems to be a strong degree of 'pastoral care' displayed by LFPS teachers and principals in Ghana, Nigeria and Nepal, coming to students' houses when homework is missing or students display difficulties in class.

Several studies also suggest a strong orientation towards performance and exam preparation in many LFPS, evinced through the use of previous exam papers, revision techniques and a wider range of textbooks than those found in local state schools. And in many cases extra classes are provided in the lead-up to exams. Studies in this volume from Cambodia, Ghana, India, Nigeria and Pakistan find that private tutoring – fee-paying extra classes provided outside of normal school hours – to be common practice in both state and private schools. Yet private tutoring is not driven solely by exam preparation but by the poor pay teachers receive, which in the case of LFPS in Pakistan, is often lower than the official minimum wage (Ahmed & Amjad, 2012) and far less than a living wage. The incentive for teachers to supplement their income by charging extra classes to complete the standard curriculum thus exists as a precursor to the provision of additional classes in the lead-up to exams, a pervasiveness that has generated the 'shadow education' moniker (see Bray, 2009).

Yet the literature on the causal impact of private tutoring on student achievement is thin and contested (Atherton & Aslam, 2012) though research does suggest a link between educational expenditure and pupil outcomes (Kingdon, 1996; Aslam, 2009). In light of the fact that other studies suggest the quality of schooling provided by LFPS is often no different from the poor-quality schooling provided by the state sector (Andrabi et al, 2007; Aslam, 2009; Jamil et al, 2013), the link between educational expenditure and learning outcomes suggests a potentially significant private-tutoring effect on learning outcomes.

Atherton & Aslam (2012) use ASER and SchoolTELLS survey tests (for Pakistan and India respectively) in mathematics and reading ability to construct estimated probit models of the link between private tuition and the likelihood of children completing 'higher-level' learning. They demonstrate a significant tuition effect on reading ability, especially for poorer students in state schools, and a less significant effect on maths. They go on to argue that a government-school pupil who takes private tutoring will 'catch up' on average as much as a private-school pupil who also takes tuition over the year (0.46 SD [4] compared to 0.49 SD) and contend that the learning gain for private-school pupils is 75% of a school year.

In similar fashion Jamil and others (2013) supplement 2010 and 2011 ASER results with their own data from Rawalpindi and Peshawar in Pakistan and Delhi and Sona in India to argue that 'private tutoring is prevalent irrespective of whether the student belongs to a government or private school. Nor is it determined by location – in terms of whether the district or whether rural or urban. The lowest percentage of those taking tuition [10.82%] is among public schools students in rural areas and the highest [22.55%] among private school students of urban areas' (p. 20). They go on to suggest that in Peshawar, which demonstrated a private-school advantage in learning outcomes, 'private tutoring or self-selection of intelligent students belonging to educated families might be responsible for the higher performance' (p. 26). This was substantiated in their study by the correlation of higher test scores with increased wealth and 72% of private-school students taking private tutoring classes compared with 61% of state-school pupils.

Thus claims of greater effectiveness and a private premium are not only contested but might be explained by comparative factors including less teacher absenteeism, lower teacher–pupil ratios, greater accountability to parents and students (including an ethic of care), and higher levels of parental education and student ability. Significantly, they are strongly challenged by the potential significance of tutoring effects. As Chudgar (2012, p. 53) notes:

> The primary challenge in understanding private school performance is taking account of the lack of randomness in private school enrolment. Children do not enroll in the local public or private schools randomly. Their schooling decisions are made by their parents. The choice may reflect several factors, including the parent's ability to pay more to educate their child, their access to information about the available choices, and the value they place on education in general. In turn, it is also often likely that those parents who choose (or are able to choose) the private options are better off overall: more educated, well-off and better connected.

Hence the problem of simultaneity – multiple variables acting together on one outcome – makes isolating the private-school effect on learning outcomes immensely difficult, leading some authors to claim that 'the evidence for rising enrollments in private schools is much stronger than that for quality differences between public and private schools' (Rolleston & Adesfeso, 2013, p. 14).

A notable, recent addition to this debate is the India study by Muralidharan & Sundararaman (2013), notable because it appears to be the first randomised control trial of vouchers to attend private schools from a developing country. The report makes several arguments, which have been amplified by the Centre for Global Development (2013), that beg closer attention. One is that 'private schools in [Andhra Pradesh] deliver (slightly) better test score gains than their public counterparts' (p. a1) based on the fact that while comparative scores in Maths and Telegu (the local language) were no better than in competing public schools, they were significantly better in Hindi (O.5 SD greater than students who did not win vouchers and did not attend private schools). Yet the authors make clear that 'government schools do not teach Hindi' (p. 18), raising the question of how a composite, comparative assessment of learning outcomes that includes a statistically significant variable absent from government schools is validated. How might the 'slightly better' results look if this variable were omitted? Another argument is 'the lack of any consistent evidence of heterogeneous effects [on learning gains] along most student characteristics' (p. 20). While parental literacy and households assets were controlled for, there was no control for private tutoring. We know from other studies from India that private tutoring often goes hand-in-hand with private-school attendance, thus how might the learning gains be affected if this were accounted for? Furthermore, any study on learning gains by freeship students takes as its departure point that those eligible are those who are the least affluent and mobilised – the precise reasons they are eligible for vouchers – so we should not expect a strong correlation between student characteristics (those selected) and learning gains for freeship students; those from more educated, affluent households are likely already enrolled in private schools yet we know nothing about their how their test scores compare with freeship students.[5] At the same time, the report clearly spells out that more time on task by teachers who were more present, longer schools days and terms and smaller teacher–pupil ratios in private schools pays dividends on learning outcomes.[6]

Claims of greater efficiency (as opposed to effectiveness) are based on the low unit costs of establishing and running LFPS – a factor driving increased supply – and when fees are comparatively low to other indirect costs, the cost differential to families between LFPS and state schools can be small (Colclough et al, 2003). When coupled with a real or perceived private premium, the low direct costs of fees seem to be a key determinant for households to select private schools because parents perceive value for money, especially when compared with the relatively poor outcomes from local, free, state schools (Rolleston & Adefeso, 2013). Such claims, however, are based on low overheads in private schools and grounded in costs *relative* to state schools.

Research by Pal (2010) in India argues that that in order for private schools to function efficiently, i.e. minimise the cost of production and maximise returns on investment, they need pre-existing and robust public infrastructure. Her analysis shows that private schools are likely to be present not only in areas where public schoolteachers have lower attendance rates, but also where more public infrastructure is available, including access to water, roads, electricity, phones and post offices. Her underlying argument is that access to public infrastructure is likely to lower the production costs of private schools and, subsequently, increase their rate of return. This is supported by the fact that the greatest growth of LFPS has been in urban areas where public infrastructure is greatest: roads, electricity, water and phones.[7] Furthermore, Chudgar (2012, p. 57) argues that 'villages where private schools set up are actually likely to have a stronger government school system present', adding that 'it [is] amply clear that private schools are not merely a response to greater parental demand; they may also be very much a phenomenon that is supported by existing government investments in infrastructure, resources, and public education' (ibid.). This resonates with findings by Andrabi and others (2006), who found that low-fee private schools in Pakistan were more likely to be located in villages with sufficient populations of younger, unmarried women who had a secondary-school education and hence provided a low-paid teacher labour force for employment in low-fee private schools. The essential point is that an educated female labour force was available in villages where the government had invested in girl's secondary education for over 20 years. As Chudgar reflects: 'The emergence of private schools in a given village may be driven not simply by parental demand, but also by the ease and efficiency of supplying private education, *given existing government investments'* (ibid. 58, emphasis added).

Thus the proposition that LFPS are more efficient than public schools needs to be understood within a framework that recognises firstly that LFPS cost efficiency is *relative* to spending on public education where indirect costs to parents are well recognised to be significant and, secondly, the role of public capital on private productivity and the rate of return on private investment. As such, LFPS are not *systematically* cost-effective as their operation relies not only on fee collection (paid by parents and determined by local market conditions and community wealth) but also on pre-existing public infrastructure (paid by the government or community), including poorly performing government schools and the presence of a pool of future teachers in LFPS, which, in the case of Pakistan, tend to be graduates of government secondary schools. Thus we can posit that in the absence of government schools, public infrastructure and community wealth LFPS would not exist because set-up and running costs would not make profit viable. Indeed, evidence from India supports this (see Pal, 2010; Chudgar & Quin, 2012). Further, as regards financial sustainability, because running costs of LFPS are based on fee-collection, not only is the viability of low costs based on low teacher salaries – implying a potential discrimination – but any vagaries in the market will affect the financial sustainability of the model and, ultimately, affordability by parents.

Premise Three: competition by private providers
increases quality in both the private and state sectors

Almost no empirical data exists from developing countries that attests to the Freidmanite hypothesis that competition by private providers increases the quality of education within private schools and that competition between private and public schools increases quality in public schools (Freidman, 1962).

To understand this data deficit its necessary to unpack the hypothesis, which runs along the following lines: the greater the competition among education providers (schools), the lower the prices that consumers (parents) pay compared to what the price would be if there were no competition (monopoly) or to what the price would be if there were little competition (oligopoly); providers need also to accept lower profits, which results is the survival of only the most efficient and effective (Hirschmanite exit of those who cannot compete), which in turn should result in higher-quality schooling and enhanced educational outcomes between the providers.

There is an essential question regarding how the competition effect can be measured. One established approach is the Herfindahl Index, which measures the sum of the squares of per-unit enrolments over total enrolments, where the units are typically schools within a locality. A second measure is the percentage of students in private schools. This can represent competition but may also be influenced by differentiated demand such as religious beliefs or linguistic preferences, or community wealth (see Levin & Belfield, 2002). A third is comparing tests scores between private and public schools as well as other educational outcomes such as education attainments (number of years spent in school) and future graduate earnings.

These measures were used in 25 research projects to assess the competition effect among and between private and public schools in the United States. Over three fifths of the projects showed no correlation between greater competition and increased test scores, the remaining two fifths showed only a modest correlation, and there was no possible suggestion of causality (see Levin & Belfield, 2002 for a summary). Yet the point is not that the competition effect in the United States seems marginal but that such tests require complete information on relative enrolments within a locality (permitting the calculation of Herfindahl Index and relative percentages of enrolments in private and public schools) as well as comparative test scores and attainment data including, ideally, longitudinal data on post-education trajectories including labour-market position and associated earnings. Such information does not exist for LFPS because so many are unregistered and/or unrecognised and because government regulation and its attendant data, when it does exist, is imperfect. Hence the paucity of data on private-school performance negates the possibility of robustly measuring the competition effect of LFPS.

Nonetheless, in an attempt to assess the variation of private-school performance across different villages in India, Chudgar (2012) used raw ASER 2009 data to construct a data-constrained sample of 131,553 children from 6836 villages in 575 districts from 31 states and union territories where children were enrolled in government or private schools in villages where private schools were present. While not formally an attempt to measure the competition effect, Chudgar sought to understand not only whether private-school students (LFPS attendees) performed better than public-school counterparts but what the size of this gap was and what might account for any differences. Her regression analysis suggested that children who attended private school outperformed public-school counterparts on various reading and mathematics tasks, yet the significance of the variance component associated with 'private school' indicated that the private–public gap was unequal across all types of villages. Chudgar argues that contextual factors associated with variations in private-school performance suggested, for children in classes 1 and 2, that an increase in public education (primary, middle and secondary public schools) was associated with a reduction in the private-school advantage. Similarly, for older children in classes 3-5, a strong presence of government services is associated with a smaller private–public gap. Hence (Chudgar, 2012, p. 58) asserts that:

> When we ask if privatisation in education is beneficial, the
> accurate answer is, 'it depends'. It depends on the village in
> which the private school is being established. We find that the
> positive private effect is reduced in villages with a strong
> government presence.

She accepts that strong government-school performance could be a response to private-school competition – though there is no way of knowing this – yet suggests that concerted government investment could mean that government schools were performing well to begin with.

Nepal presents a useful developing-country case because government regulation of private schools is such that data on the School Leaving Certificate (SLC) – taken at the end of *secondary* schooling – for public and private schools exits that allows an albeit limited assessment of competition effect where SLC results are taken as a proxy indicator of quality.

Thapa (2011) uses Ordinary Least Squared (OLS) estimates of the effect of private-school competition on public-school students' SLC performance using data from a nationwide survey of 452 schools and 22,500 students from the SLC batches of 2002, 2003 and 2004. As complete information is lacking he takes the takes the presence of a motorable road within an hour's walking distance from the school as the instrument for private-school competition[8] (the outcome variable being the SLC score of a public-school student). The results of the OLS estimate show that private-school competition is not significant with a coefficient of 0.01 and a standard error of 0.03 (p. 151). Thapa then compares this with an Instrumental Variable (IV) estimate, which shows that the estimate of private-school competition is positive and statistically significant with a coefficient of 0.81 and standard error of 0.38. He argues that:

> [V]ariables other than private school competition show expected signs while explaining their relationship with public school student's performance. For example, variables that are significant with positive relationships are: peers, expected division, annual family expenditure, number of SLC graduates in the family, language spoken at home (if Nepali), school having a library, school having a science lab and a computer lab, number of school days at school, and percent of girls in higher secondary grades. (Thapa, 2011, p. 155)

Thus a range of variables have statistically significant correlations with SLC results of public-school students, leading Thapa to conclude that 'private school competition does have a positive impact, though not large, on the public student's performance in the case of Nepal' (p. 156).[9] Naturally we cannot transfer the results of Thapa's study to LFPS in Nepal, although the methodological challenges are notable as is the limited size of the competition effect when considered alongside other variables positively affecting learning outcomes.

These examples raise several points. First is that the paucity of reliable, representative data to conduct analysis of competition effects negates the possibility of robust analysis according to established measures. The lack of evidence on the competition effect in developing countries could therefore be the result of technical and methodological difficulties of measurement rather than lack of an effect per se. But how feasible is this given the above analysis on quality? Even if we acknowledge a premium on learning outcomes from locally competing private primary schools, it was argued above that background **AND?** the problem of simultaneity make it almost impossible to isolate and therefore attribute improved test scores to a private-school effect.

Second, understanding the competition effect is further complicated because in many contexts the demand for private-school enrolments increases when public-school performance *declines*, introducing a negative relationship between public-school quality and private-school enrolment. Research on private secondary education in Pakistan and Cameroon suggests that where public supply is lacking, James's theory of excess demand holds (Alderman et al, 2001; Boyle,

1996). Government supply of secondary schools in these studies was limited – but, critically, of acceptable quality – and private secondary schools appeared to be a lower-quality alternative for students who could access the limited public supply. Extending this line of thinking and drawing on research from Madagascar, India and Colombia, Lincove (2007) argues that 'in countries with a more well-developed public supply, private schools address differentiated demand ... These markets provide higher quality education for parents who are willing and able to pay for better quality than is offered in public schools' (p. 3). Hence in contexts where public supply can accommodate all students and is of an acceptable quality, private schools either provide higher-quality education – by being competitive – or respond to differentiated demand. The corollary is that when public-school supply is low, or where quality is low, 'private schools fill the gap but with no competitive incentive to improve quality' (p. 3).

A crucial distinction exists between the limited government supply of good-quality schools and the adequate supply of poor-quality schools. As noted, the supply of LFPS in many developing countries is correlated to the supply and quality of public schools: evidence of public-to-private transfers in Nepal suggests that where provision of public schools is adequate but of poor quality, parents transfer children from public to private schools (Bhatta & Budathoki, 2013). Similarly, Pal and Chudgar's analysis in India suggests that private-school quality is related to public-school performance, both negatively (teacher absenteeism creates a demand-pull for private education by parents) and positively (the private–public gap is attenuated where government schools performed well). These examples illustrate how localised environmental factors shape the supply and demand of LFPS that respond to and shape the context in which they operate. It is therefore possible to counter-argue that competition by public schools in these instances shape the quality of the private schools; evidence of a reverse effect appears limited.

Some studies do document public schools adopting the use of English medium in response to private-school competition, yet the effect on quality is questionable. Teachers in Nepal reported that they 'had to do this to continue the existence of the public school' (Bhatta & Budathoki, 2013, p. 12) yet they equally reported great difficulties in teaching in English given their own limited fluency. Studies on adopted English medium in LFPS in India, Ghana and Nigeria suggest similar flaws and challenge the suggestion that this effect raised quality; rather, the opposite seemed to hold.

Hence the Freidmanite proposition of competition leading to increasing quality in public and other private schools is far from straightforward. Not only does lack of data present serious methodological constraints, but competition is not solely uni-directional but multi-directional, and the supply and quality of public education affects the relative quality of competing LFPSs. There seems to be no evidence that private-school competition increases the quality of public schooling; evidence of public-to-private transfers and the adoption of English language unmatched with the ability to teach it suggests the opposite may be true. Furthermore, recall that evidence of private premiums from developing countries are limited to small-scale comparative samples between selected private schools and selected state schools, often drawing on *perceptions* of quality rather than systematic analysis of test scores. The only commentary on a possible competition effect is between the private and public schools in a sample, where the low bar set by the public school provides the point beyond which the private school needs to reach to be 'better' quality. Research does not suggest that this results in a grade-acceptable standard of quality. Nor do we know the extent to which private-school competition increases the quality in other private schools – as per the hypothesis – as absent data prevents robust testing. The best (and only) available research on this seems to be the non-parametric testing by Muralidharan and Sundararaman (2013, p. 21) who suggest that 'voucher winners do significantly better when there are four or more schools within a half kilometer distance from their homes or when there are six or more schools within a one kilometer radius' yet concede that 'while suggestive, these [results] are not very robust, and the rural setting may not be the best one to study the effects of competition.'

The introduction to this volume outlines how the dynamics of globalisation are deepening the influence of a particular set of ideas that stop short of prescribing policy yet have been remarkably influential in creating the discursive framework within which a particular conception of globalisation is promoted. The private-school promise and its underlying propositions and hypotheses exemplify this discursive framework, yet this section has that argued that the veracity of the private-school promise is highly questionable. The final section of this chapter examines some of the social-justice implications of LFPS.

Social Justice and the Private-School Promise

As argued at start of this volume, social justice concerns the dynamics of how different institutions (including the state and the market) and socio-cultural and politico-economic processes structure the (re)distribution of resources, rights and values across, between and within societies with reference to democratic societal development. Education (in the Deweyian sense) and social justice are therefore intrinsically linked in the development of open, democratic societies because the effects of education (as a system and as discrete forms of provision) on justice (as parity of participation) has consequences for deliberative democracy, while the manner in which social injustice (economic maldistribution and cultural misrecognition) affect education access and quality has implications for deliberative democracy.

The very poor are structurally excluded from accessing LFPS, hence they can be understood as suffering the injustice of economic maldistribution, i.e. not possessing the economic means to pay direct and indirect costs of schooling, while opportunity costs often make the choice one between schooling or no schooling, whether fee-free or fee-charging. Yet while this group outwardly occupies the economic end of Fraser's spectrum of disadvantage (see introduction), I suggest there are associated cultural-valuational dimensions too. Recalling the notion of education as a positional good, we can understand the enrolment of a student in a private school as conferring not only ostensively better educational opportunity but also status and recognition on both the student and the household in terms of social and cultural capital dividends. Within the universe of potential enrolees, attendance at LFPS becomes an insignia of upward mobility with clear cultural-valuational currency. Equally, the relegation of the very poor to badly performing state schools suggests a misrecognition of their moral worth that further limits (if not precludes) their equal participation in society through lessened educational opportunity attainable through state education. The essential point here is that the market-based distribution of educational opportunity confers both status and recognition on those who are able to compete and, conversely, de-values and demeans those who are not.

The previous section also illustrated that economic and cultural expectations of women create an uncertain value of educating girls. For Fraser, gender is a paradigmatic bivalent collectivity because its political-economy dimension is a key structuring principle in the division of labour that assigns women to lower-paid work, often in various forms of casual labour in the informal economy. The pro-male bias in private-school enrolment patterns reflects the limited employment opportunities for women – which are central to the instrumental calculation of household choice – while cultural norms deepen the reproductive and domestic roles for women. The uncertain value of girls' education can be understood then as an effect of the hybrid disadvantage of economic maldistribution (poor access to the labour market) and cultural misrecognition (norms and values that shape roles and perceptions of women), and the choice over girls' schooling an educational consequence of bivalent disadvantage, evidenced by generally lower female enrolment rates in LFPS and correspondingly higher rates in public schools in the examples in this volume.

Ethnicity is another paradigmatic bivalent collectivity for Fraser that structures the labour market. Kabeer (2000) extends this analysis to argue that caste in the Indian context is a bivalent collectivity rooted in economic disadvantage, religiously sanctioned segregation and the ordering of professions with the lowest castes associated with the most stigmatised occupations. Research cited above from Nepal and India indicates that enrolment patterns in LFPS reflected social hierarchies wherein Brahmin and Chhetri caste children were disproportionately represented in LFPS in Nepal, while LFPS were more prevalent in Indian villages that had lower proportions of low-caste and Muslim populations; freeship access to higher-paying private schools were availed of by those that had higher social capital in the Bourdieusian sense. In these examples, the bivalent collectivities of ethnicity (Fraser, 1995) and caste (Kabeer, 2000) can be understood to privilege access of those groups with higher economic distribution and greater cultural recognition while equally hindering access of lower social groups to LFPS (and freeship access to higher-fee private schools in India).

Viewed through the lens of Fraser, the structural exclusion of the very poor, girls and marginalised groups is therefore unjust on the basis of both economic maldistribution and cultural misrecognition. The corollary is an unintended but nonetheless palpable social closure by private schools for the relatively less disadvantaged and the pauperisation of public schools, to where excluded groups seem increasingly to be relegated. Such an analysis begs the question of why such patterns seem to be emerging and what societal consequences may result if they persist or intensify.

As discussed, monetising access to comparatively better-quality education leads households to deploy welfare-maximisation strategies, which frame education as a means to increased economic productivity and the responsibility of parents as securing a competitive advantage for their children. This mirrors what Lemke (2002) describes as the purpose of neo-liberalism: to 'unite a responsible and moral individual and an economic-rational individual. It aspires to construct responsible subjects whose moral quality is based on the fact that they rationally assess the costs and benefits of a certain act as opposed to other alternative acts' (p. 59).[10] On the one hand this narrows the role of education to the degree that, as Miller elegantly states: 'It is the economy that has needs. Educational systems are expected to satisfy those needs through the production of workers. The economy becomes a human subject; people become objects that support the economy's wellbeing' (2006, pp. 252-253). On the other hand, as Hursh (2009) argues, because individual choice is in the private realm of families' own interest, 'neo-liberalism not only changes social structures but also changes the relationship between the individual and society' (p. 155), that is, 'they can choose without engaging others regarding the consequences of the choice beyond their own family' (p. 161). One effect is to recast education not as a public or societal good grounded in democratic principles of justice and equal opportunity, but as an individualised, atomised and personalised private good that benefits the individual and/or household: any societal effect is by virtue of the aggregation of individual private pursuit, the predominant one in policy discussions being poverty alleviation and national growth. Naturally these ends need to be pursued, yet monetising access, the *raison d'etre* of LFPSs, aggravates inequality through the structural exclusion of certain groups, entrenching a neo-liberal vision of society at the cost of a humanitarian view of society wherein human capital is prioritised over human development. Indeed, as Muralidharan and Sundararaman (2013, p. 25) state: 'It may be possible to substantially increase human capital formation in developing countries like India by making more use of private provision in the delivery of education.' Yet as Hursh (2009, p. 162) pointedly asserts: 'For neoliberals, social justice requires that individuals are given access to markets, if they fail to achieve educational and economic success, then individuals only have themselves to blame.'

Thus while exclusion from LFPS may be coherent within the neo-liberal framework, it is problematic from the Deweyian perspective because the stratification of education systems along economic and cultural-valuational terms (social closure of private schools for the less disadvantaged and pauperisation of public schools for the more disadvantaged) compromises the extent to which education (as a system and as forms of provision) can build on the respect for every person's equal moral worth and engage in the task of human, rather than solely economic, development. As such, LFPS not only constrain social justice *in* education (privileging access for some over others) but social justice *through* education (aggregative democracy through individual, private pursuit). The stakes are high for this growing 'ontological individualism' (Roybens, 2006) and Lipman (2004, pp. 171-172) argues that a consequence of policymakers embracing a neo-liberal discourse is the 'shift [of] responsibility for social inequality by the state onto parents students, schools, communities and teachers'. Furthermore, affirmative action such as vouchers and freeship places in India, which aim to correct inequitable outcomes of social arrangements without disturbing the underlying frameworks that generate them, are problematic because not only do they fail to overcome the redistribution–recognition dilemma discussed in the introduction, but because they maintain a priority on access through making private schools 'free at the point of delivery', avoiding the serious concerns over quality and what is learned in LFPS, and perpetuate the private-school promise. Transformative action, historically associated with socialism and as proposed by Fraser (2008) is unlikely and undesirable in an increasingly globalised, neo-liberal world, yet the social-connection model of responsibility proposed by Young (2006), who argues for the increased responsibility of those in positions of greater influence, provides an important framework to ensure that the mantra of evidence-based policy is adhered to and is inclusive and informed. This is imperative in the agenda setting and formulation of the post-2015 goals.

Notes

[1] Privatisation in Education Research Initiative (PERI). Published research is available at www.periglobal.org

[2] See Ahmed and Amjad (2012) and this volume.

[3] In Nepal, numerous households have transferred their children from public to low-fee private schools, demonstrating a pro-male bias through a growing proportion of girls attending public schools and a growing proportion of boys attending private schools (Bhatta & Budathoki, 2013).

[4] Standard Deviation.

[5] The report also suggests that student characteristics (sic) were not significant in the application for vouchers. This challenges the findings of Norhona and Srivastava (2013) who found that it was the more aspirational, connected and mobile families that applied for and availed themselves of freeship places in Delhi: i.e. those that had more social capital. Muralidharan and Sundararaman's finding may therefore resonate with an emerging study at the Department of Education at Oxford University that suggests the facilitation of parents by NGOs in the application of freeship places in Rajasthan distorts, even compensates, for an unmediated process in which lower-caste and poorer parents are less likely to apply for freeship places (personal communication).

[6] Private schools were also more likely than public schools to have drinking water, functional toilets (as well as separate toilets for girls), functional electricity, and to have a computer, with the differences being quite stark on some of these measures. Not only that, but private schools tended to be larger than public schools. This rather remarkable assessment raises questions about how 'low-fee' these schools in fact were: Rs2334.03 (US$35) per month (see Muralidharan &Sundararaman, 2013, Table 3, p. 33) is significantly more than an average monthly fee of US$6 for low-fee private schools in rural India.

[7] Pal (2010) argues that a natural corollary of this proposition is that remote villages, deprived of public infrastructure facilities, will be deprived of access to private schools.

[8] The study uses the presence of a motorable road within an hour's walking distance from the sample school as an instrument for the number of private schools in the neighbourhood. This accords with studies by Pal (2010) and Chudgar (2012) that suggest private schools are more prevalent in villages that have greater public infrastructure such as roads and piped water. Thapa's paper thus exploits the fact that private schools in Nepal usually do not choose to build in areas where they cannot attract students because of financial constraints. Therefore, the idea behind this instrument is that having a motorable road provides a high chance of

having more private schools in that locality, but it does not have any direct relation to the students' test scores. In other words, the claim is that presence of a motorable road is correlated with private-school competition, but not correlated with the SLC score of the public-school student.

[9] It is worth noting that his analysis suggests the competition effect was modest between 2002-04, yet the latest SLC 2013 results suggest an even more limited effect. The latest SLC results (June 2013) have been so poor that the Nepali government has, for the first time, chosen not to publish them in national media; the pass rate has dropped from 68.47% in 2008 to 41.57% in 2013, a decline of 26% (Republica, 2013). Further, 78% of the 2013 examinees were from public community schools and 24% from private schools, yet 80% of private students passed compared to only 30% of public students (ibid.). While this clearly indicates a serious problem with public-sector education quality, and a stronger performance by private schools, these results would indicate that private-school competition seems not to have had a positive effect on public schools.

[10] Cited in Hursh (2009, p. 155).

References

Ahmed, H. & Amjad, S. (2012) *Determinants of School Choice: evidence from rural Punjab, Pakistan.* Lahore: Center for Research in Economics and Business, Lahore School of Economics.

Alderman, H., Orazem, P.F. & Paterno, E.M. (2001) School Quality, School Cost, and the Public/Private School Choices of Low-Income Households in Pakistan, *Journal of Human Resources*, 36(2), 304-326.

Andrabi, T., Das, J. & Khwaja, A. (2006) *A Dime a Day: the possibilities and limits of private schooling in Pakistan.* World Bank Policy Working Paper 4066. Washington DC: World Bank.

Andrabi, T., Das, J., Khwaja, A. et al (2007) *Insights to Inform the Education Policy Debate*, 20 February. www.leapsproject.org/assets/publications/LEAPS_Report_FINAL.pdf

ASER (2009) *Annual Status of Education Report.* Pratham, India. http://img.asercentre.org/docs/Publications/ASER%20Reports/ASER_2009/Aser2009ReportFull.pdf (accessed 14 September 2013).

ASER (2010) Annual Status of Education Report. Pratham, India. http://img.asercentre.org/docs/Publications/ASER%20Reports/ASER_2010/ASERReport2010.pdf (accessed 14 September 2013).

Aslam, M. (2009) The Relative Effectiveness of Government and Private Schools in Pakistan: are girls worse off?, *Education Economics*, 17(3), pp. 329-354.

Atherton, P. & Aslam, M. (2012) The 'Shadow' Education Sector in India and Pakistan: the determinants, benefits and equity effects of private tutoring. PERI Working Paper. London: Privatisation in Education Research Initiative.

Bhatta, P. & Budathoki, S. (2013) *Understanding Private Educationscape(s) in Nepal*. PERI Working Paper. London: Privatisation in Education Research Initiative.

Boyle, P.M. (1996) Parents, Private Schools, and the Politics of an Emerging Civil Society in Cameroon, *Journal of Modern African Studies*, 34(4), 609-622.

Bray, M. (2009) *Confronting the Shadow Education System: what government policies for what private tutoring?*. Paris: UNESCO-IIEP.

Central Bureau of Statistics (CBS) (2011) *Nepal Living Standards Survey 2010/11: statistical report volume 1*. Kathmandu: CBS Secretariat, National Planning Commission, Government of Nepal.

Centre for Global Development (2013) 7 Questions about Low Fee Private Schools in India That We Can Finally Answer. http://international.cgdev.org/blog/7-questions-about-low-cost-private-schools-india-we-can-finally-answer (accessed 17 October 2013).

Centre for Research in Economics and Business (CREB) (2012) *Determinants of School Choice: evidence from rural Punjab, Pakistan. PERI Working Paper*. London: Privatisation in Education Research Initiative.

Chudgar, A. (2012) Variation in Private School Performance: the importance of village context, *Economic and Political Weekly*, 47(11), 52-59.

Chudgar, A. & Quin, E. (2012) Relationship between Private Schooling and Achievement: results from rural and urban India, *Economics of Education Review*, 31, pp. 376-390.

Colclough, C., Al Samarrai, S., Rose, P. & Tembon, M. (2003). *Achieving Schooling for All in Africa*. Aldershot: Ashgate.

Dreze, J. & Sen, A. (2002) *India: development and participation*. Oxford: Oxford University Press.

Fraser, N. (1995) From Redistribution to Recognition? Dilemmas of Justice in a 'Post-Socialist' Age, *New Left Review*, 212 (July–August), 68-93.

Fraser, N. (2008) *Scales of Justice: reimagining political space in a globalizing world*. Cambridge: Polity Press.

Friedman, M. (1962) *Capitalism and Freedom*. Chicago: University of Chicago Press.

Hursh, D. (2009) Beyond the Justice of the Market: combatting neoliberal educational discourse and promoting deliberative democracy and economic equality, in W. Ayers, T. Quinn & D. Stovall (Eds) *Handbook of Social Justice in Education*. London: Routledge.

Jamil, B., Javaid, K. & Rangaraju, B. (2013) *Investigating Dimensions of the Privatisation of Public Education in South Asia: case studies from Pakistan and India*. PERI Working Paper. London: Privatisation in Education Research Initiative.

Kabeer, N. (2000) Social Exclusion, Poverty and Discrimination: towards an analytical framework, *IDS Bulletin*, 31(4), pp. 83-97.

Kingdon, G. (1996) The Quality and Efficiency of Private and Public Education: a case-study of urban India, *Oxford Bulletin of Economics and Statistics*, 58(1), 57-82.

299

Kingdon, G. (2007) *The Progress of School Education in India.* London: Economic and Social Research Council.

Kitaev, I. (1999) *Private Education in Sub Saharan Africa: a re-examination of theories and concepts related to its development and finance.* Paris: UNESCO.

Learning and Educational Achievements in Punjab Schools (LEAPS) (2007) *Insights to Inform the Education Policy Debate,* 20 February. www.leapsproject.org/assets/publications/LEAPS_Report_FINAL.pdf

Lemke, T. (2002) Foucault, Governmentality and Critique. *Rethinking Marxism,* 14(3), 49-64.

Levin, H. & Belfield, C. (2002) *The Effects of Competition on Educational Outcomes: a review of US evidence.* National Center for the Study of Privatization in Education. New York: Columbia University.

Lincove, J.A. (2007) *Do Private Markets Improve the quality or Quantity of Primary schooling in Sub-Saharan Africa?* Austin: LBJ School of Public Affairs, University of Texas at Austin.

Lipman, P. (2004) *High Stakes Education: inequality, globalization, and urban school Reform.* New York: RoutledgeFalmer.

Miller, V. (2006) Pointing toward Benevolence in Education: indicators in the subjunctive mood, in S. Inayatullah, M. Bussey & I. Milojevi (Eds) *Neohumanist Educational Futures: liberating the pedagogical intellect.* Taiwan: Tamkang University Press.

Muralidharan, K. & Kremer, M. (2006) *Public and Private Schools in Rural India.* 22 March. http://citeseerx.ist.psu.edu/viewdoc/download?doi=10.1.1.168.3057&rep=rep1&type=pdf

Muralidharan, K. & Sundararaman, S. (2013) *The Aggregate Effect of School Choice: evidence from a two stage experiment in India.* http://ipl.econ.duke.edu/bread/papers/1013conf/muralidharan.pdf (accessed 23 October 2013).

Norhona, C. & Srivastava, P. (2013) *India's Right to Education Act: household experiences and private school responses.* PERI Working Paper. London: Privatisation in Education Research Initiative.

Pal, S. (2010) Public Infrastructure, Location of Private Schools and Primary School Attainment in an Emerging Economy, *Economics of Education Review,* 29, 783-794.

Pandey, P., Goyal, S. & Sundararaman, V. (2009) Community Participation in Public Schools: impact of information campaigns in three Indian states. Policy Research Working Paper Series number 4776. Washington DC: World Bank.

Republica (2013) *41.57% Make it Through SLC.* http://myrepublica.com/portal/index.php?action=news_details&news_id=56075 (accessed 13 June 2013).

Rizvi, F. & Engel, L. (2009) Neoliberal Globalisation, Educational Policy and the Struggle for Social Justice, in W. Ayers, T. Quinn & D. Stovall (Eds) *Handbook of Social Justice in Education*. London: Routledge.

Rolleson, C. & Adefeso-Olateju, M. (2012) *De Facto Privatistion of Basic Education in Africa: a market response to government failure? A Comparative Study of the Cases of Ghana and Nigeria*. PERI Working Paper. London: Privatisation in Education Research Initiative.

Rose, P. (2009) NGO Provision of Basic Education: alternative or complementary service delivery to support access to the excluded?, *Compare*, 39(2), 219-233.

Roybens, I. (2003) Is Nancy Fraser's Critique of Theories of Distributive Justice Justified?, *Constellations*, 10(4), 538-554.

Roybens, I. (2006) Three Models of Education: rights, capabilities and human capital, *Theory and Research in Education*, 4(1), 69-84.

Rutkowski, L. & Rutkowski, D. (2010) International Determinants of Private School Attendance. Paper presented at the 2010 American Educational Research Association conference, Denver, USA.

Srivastava, P. (2007) For Philanthropy or Profit? The Management and Operation of Low-Fee Private Shools in India?, in P. Srivastava & G. Walford (Eds) *Private Schooling in Less Economically Developed Countries: Asian and African perspectives*, pp. 153-186. Oxford: Symposium Books

Srivastava, P. (2008) School Choice in India: disadvantaged groups and low-fee private schools, in M. Forsey, S. Davies & G. Walford (Eds) *The Globalization of School Choice?* pp. 185-208. Oxford: Symposium Books.

Thapa, A. (2011) Does Private School Competition Improve Public School Performance? The Case of Nepal. PhD Thesis, Columbia University, New York.

Tooley, J. (2005) Private Schools for the Poor, *Education Next*, 5(4), 22-32.

Tooley, J. (2007) Could For-Profit Private Education Benefit the Poor? Some A Priori Considerations arising from Case Study Research in India, *Journal of Education Policy*, 22(3), 321-342.

Tooley, J. (2009) *The Beautiful Tree: a personal journey into how the world's poorest people are educating themselves*. Delhi: Penguin.

Tooley, J., Bao, Y., Dixon, P. & Merrifield, J. (2011) School Choice and Academic Performance: some evidence from developing countries, *Journal of School Choice*, 5(1), 1-39.

Tooley, J. & Dixon, P. (2003) Providing Education to the World's Poor: a case study of the private sector in India, in B. Davies & J. West-Burnham (Eds) *The Handbook of Educational Leadership and Management*, pp. 342-354. London: Pearson.

Tooley, J. & Dixon, P. (2005) *Private Schools Serving the Poor: a study from Delhi, India*. New Delhi: Centre for Civil Society.

Tooley, J. & Dixon, P. (2006) The Failures of State Schooling in Developing Countries and the People's Response, in M. Miles, K.R. Homes & M.A. O'Grady (Eds) *Index of Economic Freedom: the link between economic opportunity and prosperity,* pp. 27-37. Washington, DC: The Heritage Foundation and Wall Street Journal.

Tooley, J., Dixon, P., Shamsan, Y. & Schagen, I. (2010) The Relative Quality and Cost-Effectiveness of Private and Public Schools for Low-income Families: a case study from developing countries, *School Effectiveness and School Improvement,* 20(4), 1-28.

Wadhwa, W. (2009) Are Private Schools really Performing Better than Government Schools? In ASER *Annual Status of Education Report.* Pratham, India.
http://img.asercentre.org/docs/Publications/ASER%20Reports/ASER_2009/Aser2009ReportFull.pdf (accessed 14 September 2013).

Young, I.M. (2006) Responsibility and Global Justice: a social connection model, *Social Philosophy and Policy Foundation,* 23(1), 102-130.

Notes on Contributors

Modupe Adefeso-Olateju is Director of The Education Partnership Centre (TEP Centre), an education partnership consultancy specialising in the design, implementation and evaluation of multi-sectoral partnerships in education in sub-Saharan Africa. She has six years of research experience in private-sector participation in education. As an education-policy specialist, she leads on a range of donor-funded education-sector support programmes where she provides technical assistance in the spheres of strategy, monitoring and evaluation, and programme management. Serving as a member of the Federal Minister of Education's Technical Task Team, she also contributed to the development of the 2011–15 strategic education-development plan for Nigeria. Modupe holds a PhD in Education and International Development from the Institute of Education, University of London, where her research assessed the effectiveness of public and private schools in Nigeria.

Hamna Ahmed is a senior research and teaching fellow at the Centre for Research in Economics and Business, Lahore School of Economics (Pakistan). She has a Master's in Economics from Warwick University (UK) and has been affiliated with the Lahore School since 2008. On the macro side, Hamna is interested in issues relating to trade and export competitiveness. On the micro side she is interested in issues such as firm and innovation, education and child labour. She is currently working on community-led organisations across Pakistan in collaboration with the Pakistan Poverty Alleviation Fund (PPAF) and researchers from Oxford University, UK.

Momina Afridi is a PhD candidate at the Ontario Institute of Studies in Education, University of Toronto, Canada. Her research interests include global governance institutions, education policy and public–private partnerships in education. In the past Momina has worked with various non-profit organisations in Pakistan and Canada on development programming related to youth and gender. Momina holds a Master's in Development Studies from York University, Toronto, Canada.

Sahar Amjad is a Teaching Fellow in the Department of Economics at the Lahore University of Management Sciences, Pakistan. Her research centres on the debate between private versus public education in

Pakistan, with a focus on the determinants of school choice and the role of shadow education. Previously she held a position as a Teaching and Research Fellow at the Centre for Research in Economics and Business at the Lahore School of Economics. Sahar holds an MPhil from the University of Cambridge (UK) and a BSc from the Lahore University of Management Sciences.

Duong Thi Viet Anh is Deputy Director of the Centre for Development and Integration. She was the National Education Coordinator of ActionAid Vietnam and is currently steering member of the Vietnam Coalition of Education for All (VCEFA) and focal person in Vietnam for the Asia South Pacific Association for Basic Adult (ASPBEA). Anh earned her Bachelor's in International Relations from Hanoi Dong Do University (Vietnam) and her Master's in Business Administration from Wales University at the Management Development Institute of Singapore. Her research interests are in education and ethnic minorities in Vietnam.

Monazza Aslam is an Education Economist with more than 10 years of experience working on education, labour markets and gender issues in developing countries. A Rhodes Scholar from Pakistan (Wolfson, 2000), Monazza completed her DPhil in Economics at the University of Oxford, United Kingdom followed by a post-doctoral position at the Centre for the Study of African Economies, University of Oxford. Her work has featured in several peer-reviewed journals and she has been invited to present her findings at prestigious events and conferences. Currently a Visiting Researcher at the Institute of Education, University of London (UK) and Senior Research Fellow at the Idara-Taleem-o-Agahi (ITA, Pakistan), she has significant experience advising organisations such as the World Bank and the Department of International Development.

Paul Atherton is a reformed economist working on education issues in developing countries. He is currently working for the Education Policy Team in the UK's Department for International Development. Prior to this he was a Lecturer in the Economics of Education at the Institute of Education in London. His work has featured in several peer-reviewed journals and he has been invited to present at numerous international events. All views expressed are his own, and do not reflect the views of the UK government.

Pramod Bhatta, PhD, is the General Secretary of Martin Chautari (MC), a research institution in Kathmandu, Nepal. At MC, he has conducted research on various aspects of Nepal's education system and also trained young researchers from various marginalised groups. He teaches sociology of education, public policy and research methods to graduate and post-graduate students at the Central Department of Sociology and

Anthropology, Tribhuvan University (Nepal). He is also involved in the government of Nepal's on-going School Sector Reform Program as a consultant through the Asian Development Bank. He has edited several books and published research articles in the areas of foreign aid, decentralisation and inequalities in education.

William C. Brehm is a PhD candidate at the University of Hong Kong. He graduated with a Bachelor's degree in International Relations from Lehigh University (Bethlehem, PA, USA) in 2008, and completed his Master's degree in comparative and international education from the same institution in 2010. His dissertation research focuses on the political economy of education in Cambodia. From 2010 until 2012, Brehm lived in Siem Reap, Cambodia, and worked as the Director of Research for This Life Cambodia (TLC), an Australian non-governmental organisation.

Masooma Habib is an Associate Professor in the Economics Department and Senior Fellow at the Center for Research in Economics and Business, Lahore School of Economics. She has worked at the World Bank (Washington, D.C.) on education and gender, conducted research related to education reforms in the United States at the George Washington University, and worked as an economist at an engineering firm in Lahore. Masooma has a Doctorate in Education Policy and Administration from George Washington University and a Master's in Economics from McGill University, Canada. Her research interests include contract teacher reform, teacher incentives, private and public schooling and economics of education.

Ian Macpherson has over 10 years' experience in international education and development. He has conducted and managed research in education in over 25 countries, as well as managed education programmes in Africa, South Asia and Latin America. In addition to a core concern with social justice and human-rights issues in education, he is particularly interested in the international and transnational dynamics of advocacy in and around education and the role of civil-society organisations in education-policy reform. Ian is Deputy Director of the Open Society Foundation's Education Support Programme and has directed the Privatisation in Education Research Initiative (PERI) since its inception in 2010. Ian holds a DPhil in Education Studies from St Peter's College, Oxford University (UK); an MSc in Educational Research Methodology from St Anne's College, Oxford University; an MSc in Development Studies from the School of Oriental and African Studies, London University (UK); and an MA (Hons) in Mental Philosophy from Edinburgh University (UK).

Francine Menashy is an Assistant Professor in the Department of Leadership in Education at the University of Massachusetts Boston (USA). Her research centres on aid to education and private-sector engagement, with a focus on the policies and operations of international financial institutions. Previously she held a position as a Post-Doctoral Research Fellow at the Comparative, International and Development Education Centre at the University of Toronto, Canada. Her research has been funded by such sources as the Ontario Ministry of Economic Development and Innovation, the Social Sciences and Humanities Research Council of Canada and the Open Society Foundation. She has published extensively on the topics of public–private partnerships, international education policies and educational theory. In the past she has worked with an NGO in Laos, and as a teacher in Canada. Francine holds a PhD from the University of Toronto/OISE, an EdM from the Harvard Graduate School of Education (USA) and a BA from McGill University (Canada).

Karen Mundy is Professor and Canada Research Chair at the Ontario Institute for Studies in Education, University of Toronto, Canada. Her award-winning research has focused on the politics of international education assistance in the developing world, educational reform in Africa, the role of civil-society advocacy in educational systems and global citizenship education in North American schools. Her recent research, published in more than two dozen journal articles and chapters and in her five coedited volumes, is concentrated on the evolution of global efforts to ensure 'education for all'; the role of the World Bank in education; and civil-society activism in Africa. Mundy has carried out sponsored research for such organisations as UNICEF, UNESCO, the Hewlett Foundation, the World Bank, the MasterCard Foundation, the Canadian International Development Agency, the Open Society Foundations, UNESCO and USAID. She is also the founder and co-chair of the Canadian Global Campaign for Education, a coalition of NGOs, teachers' unions and universities committed to advancing education for all.

Claire Noronha is a Director of Collaborative Research and Dissemination (CORD) and has over 15 years of experience conducting field studies in education in India. She was a member of the PROBE team which conducted the research and analysis for the landmark Public Report on Basic Education (PROBE) (Oxford University Press, 1999). With CORD she has been researching issues related to private schools for the poor for over a decade in several studies ranging from a field study of private schools in three northern states in 1999, to the more recent qualitative research on private schools with RECOUP from 2005–10. Claire was Principal Investigator for the RECOUP research in India that focused on improving education outcomes for disadvantaged young people. The issues investigated through qualitative methodology ranged from health, fertility and skills development to disability and citizenship.

Curtis Riep is currently a Senior Policy Analyst at the United Way in Calgary, Alberta, Canada. In this position he is active in local and provincial policy and research related to poverty-reduction initiatives. Curtis holds a BA in International Relations from the University of Calgary, Canada, and an MEd in Education Policy from the University of Bristol (UK). Upon completion of his Master's degree in 2012, Curtis was a research consultant with the Open Society Foundation. This commissioned research focused on the transnational corporate activity of the edu-business, Pearson Education and how it is shaping educational privatisations worldwide. His research interests include the privatisation of education and its implications for social (in)equity.

Susan Robertson is a Professor of Sociology of Education in the Graduate School of Education, University of Bristol (UK). She is founding Director of the Centre for Globalisation, Education and Societies (GES) at the University of Bristol as well as founding co-editor (with Roger Dale) of the journal *Globalisation, Societies and Education*. Her research has been focused on the study of education and broader social, economic and political forces by analysing the complexities of globalising and regionalising projects, strategies and materialisations, particularly around the complexities of the privatising of education. She has chaired the Open Societies Steering Group on the Privatising of Education Initiative (PERI) since 2010.

Caine Rolleston is a Lecturer in Education and International Development at the Institute of Education, University of London. He is also a researcher for Young Lives at the University of Oxford (UK). He previously worked as a researcher for CREATE (Consortium for Research on Educational Access, Transitions and Equity) at the University of Sussex (UK), and has experience in education research in countries including Ghana, Sri Lanka, India, Vietnam and Ethiopia focusing on access, educational effectiveness and the economic benefits of education. He received his PhD from the Institute of Education, University of London (UK).

Chona S. Sandoval has extensive experience in indigenous education provision and policy advocacy. She was a former principal of the indigenous elementary school of the Apu Palamguwan Cultural Education Center (APC) in Bendum, Northern Mindanao. She is a Research Fellow of E-Net Philippines and currently a lecturer at the

Ateneo de Manila University. She holds an MA in Industrial/ Organizational Psychology from the same university.

Mandan Gopal Shrestha is the Founder and President of Friends of Sankhu (FOS), a national-level NGO, as well as an Associate Professor and Researcher at the Tribhuvan University (Nepal). He is currently pursuing a PhD.

Iveta Silova, PhD, is an Associate Professor and Program Director of Comparative and International Education in the College of Education, Lehigh University (Pennsylvania, USA). Her research and publications cover a range of issues critical to understanding post-socialist education-transformation processes, including the professional development of teachers and teacher educators, gender-equity trends in Eastern Europe, Central Europe and Central Asia, and minority/multicultural education policies in the former Soviet Union, as well as the scope, nature and implications of private tutoring in a cross-national perspective. She serves as the co-editor (with Noah W. Sobe) of *European Education: issues and studies* (a peer-reviewed journal published by M.E. Sharpe).

Christine Sommers spent a year and a half in Bangladesh researching rural primary education as a Fulbright Fellow through the US Department of State and as a grantee for the Open Society Foundations' Privatisation in Education Research Initiative (PERI). Christy has worked as a teacher, teacher trainer, researcher and international development consultant in West Africa, South Asia and Washington. Her research interests include South Asia, Education for All, basic and primary education, education privatisation and madrassa education. Christy holds a MA in International Education and Development from the University of Sussex (UK) and BA in Political Science and International Studies from Northwestern University (USA).

Cecilia 'Thea' V. Soriano was a founding Board member of the Civil Society Network for Education Reforms (E-Net Philippines), which was formed in 2000. In 2006, she worked as National Coordinator of this coalition until 2012. She studied a Master in Public Management major in Development and Security from the Development Academy of the Philippines. She is currently the Programmes and Operations Coordinator of the Asia Pacific Association for Basic and Adult Education (ASPBAE).

Prachi Srivastava is Associate Professor at the School of International Development and Global Studies, University of Ottawa, Canada. She holds a doctorate from the University of Oxford (UK). She has published on issues of education and international development, and is among the first researchers to undertake original empirical work on low-fee private schooling in India, where she has conducted research for over a decade. She has published more than two dozen contributions in the areas of private non-state actors in education and development; education in India; education governance and reform in developing and conflict-affected countries; and international education-policy discourse. In addition to the PERI study reported in this volume, she recently completed a review of the private sector in India over the first decade of Sarva Shiksha Abhiyan for DFID (with Claire Noronha and Shailaja Fennell). She is Principal Investigator on a major grant funded by the Social Sciences and Humanities Research Council of Canada (SSHRC) to continue work on non-state actors and the right to education in India. Her latest book is *Low-fee Private Schooling: aggravating equity or mitigating disadvantage?* (Symposium Books, 2013).

Govinda Subedi, PhD, is the Principal of the Tribhuvan University Kathmandu, Nepal. He is engaged in several academic and non-academic researches in both the national and international arenas.

Mukti Suvedi is a Visiting Lecturer at the Tribhuvan University in Nepal and the University of Warsaw in Poland. He has abundant research experience, including 12 years of experience working in international development and humanitarian support.

Ta Van Tuan is currently Vietnam Country Director of the Australian Foundation for the Peoples of Asia and the Pacific (AFAP). Tuan is providing overall leadership, strategic direction, organisational and programme management for the AFAP in Vietnam. Tuan graduated from Ha Noi University (Vietnam) and holds a Master's Degree in Social Development from Ateneo de Manila University in the Philippines. He has more than 14 years of working with international organisations and civil-society organisations (CSOs) in Vietnam on such development issues as public services and social policies. Tuan used to work for ActionAid International, Plan International, the EU and Asian Development Bank (ADB)-funded projects in Vietnam. Tuan's research interests include governance, public service and social accountability. His work has been published in Asian Development Bank research publications and the *International Journal on Culture, Health & Sexuality*.

Geoffrey Walford is Emeritus Professor of Education Policy and Emeritus Fellow of Green Templeton College at the University of Oxford (UK). He has degrees from Oxford, Kent, London and the Open University, and is author of more than 150 academic articles and book chapters. His books include: *Life in Public Schools* (Methuen, 1986); *Privatization and*

Privilege in Education (Routledge, 1990); *City Technology College* (Open University Press, 1991, with Henry Miller); Choice *and Equity in Education* (Cassell, 1994); *Doing Qualitative Educational Research* (Continuum, 2001); *Private Schooling: tradition and diversity* (Continuum, 2005); *Markets and Equity in Education* (Continuum, 2006); and *Private Schooling in Less Economically Developed Countries* (Symposium, editor, 2007 with Prachi Srivastava). He was Editor of the *Oxford Review of Education* from 2004 to 2010, and has been a Deputy Editor of *Ethnography and Education* since it started in 2006. His research foci are the relationships between central-government policy and local processes of implementation, private schools, choice of schools, religiously based schools and qualitative research methodology. He has been a member of the Steering Committee of the Open Society Foundations' Privatization in Education Research Initiative (PERI) since 2010.